Walk With Me

Editors
Charlotte Bonduel, Luc Derycke

Photographers
Wonge Bergmann (p.133), Roy Bijhouwer (p. 142-143), Griet Blomme (p. 93),
Pascal Cornet (p. 98), Carl De Keyzer (p. 46-59), Honoré δ'O (p. 38-39, cover),
Paul Gees (pp. 24-28), Anja Ghesquière and Darry Hellebuyck (pp. 75, 76, 79, 81, 83),
Jean Godecharles (pp. 94-98), Martine Kint (p. 14), Boris Saverys (pp. 77, 78, 80,
82, 106), Luc Schaltin (p. 140)

Cover design
Impromptu installation by Honoré δ'O on a visit to Constructies Espeel during the production of the motor for *Waailicht* [Waving light], a rotating lamppost on the Heidel-
berg roundabout in Zedelgem.

Design
Luc Derycke, Jeroen Wille, Studio Luc Derycke, Ghent

Printing
Erasmus-Euroset, Wetteren

With thanks to
The employees of Constructies Espeel
The collaborating artists with Constructies Espeel

© Uitgeverij Lannoo nv, Tielt, 2009
ISBN 978-90-209-8111-7
D/2009/287
NUR 640/658

Walk With Me

On artists,
the Constructies Espeel
company and their journey together

Charlotte Bonduel & Luc Derycke (eds.)

Lannoo

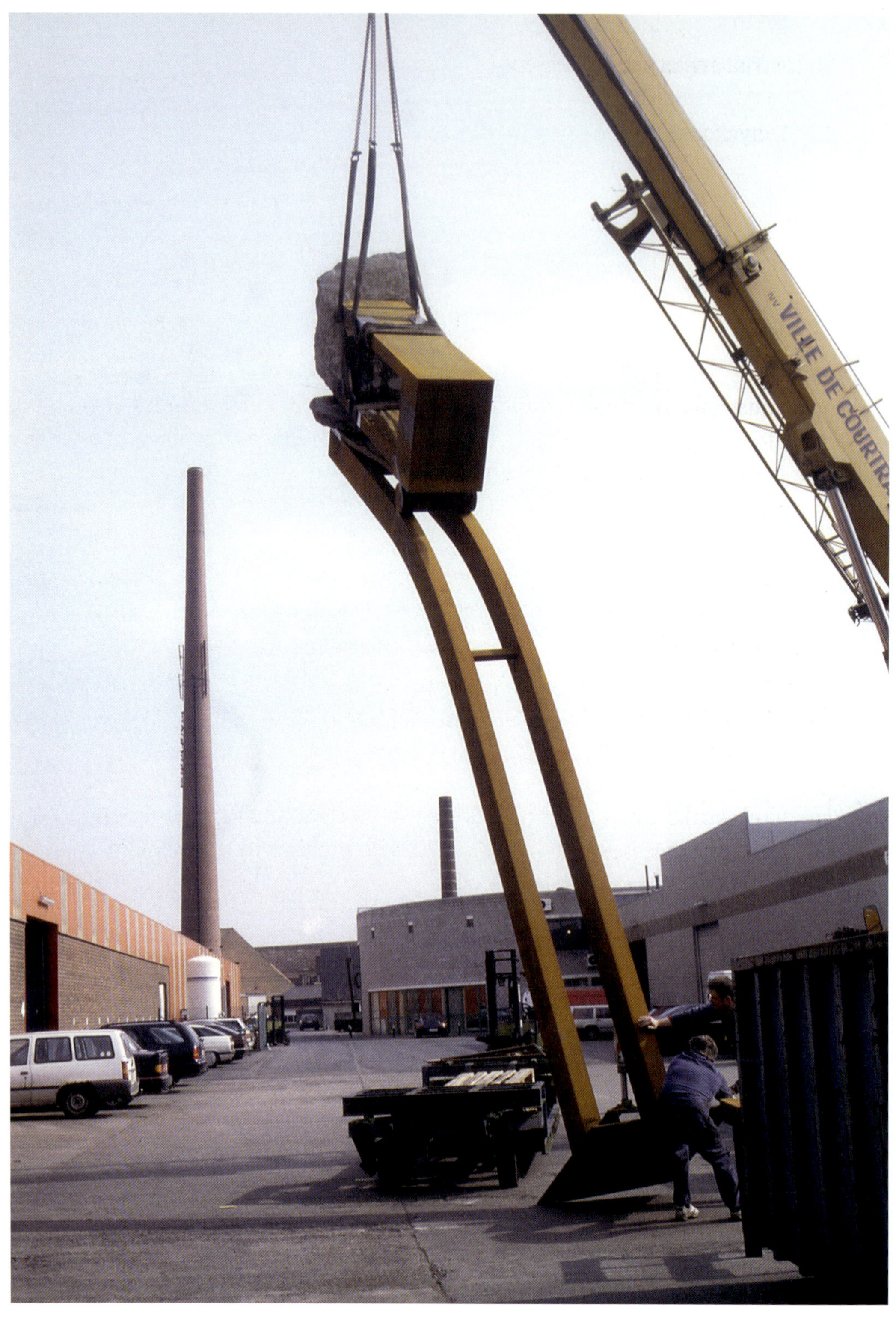

fig. 1

4

fig. 1   Paul Gees, Trial run of the erection of *De Reiziger* [The Traveller], 1999, with its final location on the *Stationsplein* [Station square] in Turnhout.

Industrial art, artistic industry

Luc Derycke

An industrial enterprise is a rational and competitive environment. It is a world of engineers and planners, where nothing is left to chance. Anyone who has ever had to deal with a manufacturing error during a purchase will appreciate this.

Industrial companies are often linked (p. xx) to a complex supply chain in which products are assembled by another firm. In our globalised society, that firm may be located on the other side of the world, which makes the potential cost of irregularities or mistakes extremely high. And it is not always just an economic loss; flaws in transport or equipment, or collapsing buildings, can cost lives, too.

Industry works on the principles of rational analysis, planning and conformity. Processes must be planned with precision and reliability if they are to yield precise and reliable results. The economy demands that all elements of organisation be financially measurable: an industrialist must always know the cost of a product, so that he/she can compare it with the market value and determine the effects of any changes on the cost price. For this reason, industrial processes are divided into small, measurable components. This applies to machines and people alike. The perfect example of this is the assembly line developed by Henry Ford for his auto industry.

Insofar as the *output* of industry consists of material objects which, within a given series or 'model', are all identical and intended for a specific use – such as a construction crane with a given height, span and lift capable of being disassembled and transported within a given volume – the

Fordist production process appears to be the only workable rule, and as such, continues to govern the lion's share of industrial production.

However, since the 1970s, production processes have shifted to what the Italian thinker Paolo Virno called 'post-Fordism', marked by the passage from tangible to intangible labour and from the production of tangible to intangible goods. The notion of 'symbolic value' has crept into industrial production, to the extent that in many sectors of industry, it is no longer sufficient to deliver a technically reliable, ready-to-use product. Rather, the commercial success of a product has become increasingly dependant on its 'added value'. Competition has shifted from the material quality necessary for a product's use – which has become a basic condition – to the symbolic value for consumption. This kind of competition is conducted by way of advertising and marketing strategies as well as by constant adaptation and 'retooling' of models on to which the industrial production chains are grafted. Models for various series are being churned out faster than ever, as industry tries to give the impression that their production does not simply consist of reliable and user-friendly series, but of a steady stream of 'innovative' and original models.

According to Virno and others, this shift has affected the industrial workplace. Despite the fact that a large part of 'Fordist' labour has been relocated to low-wage countries, the production logic is increasingly seen from the perspective of intangible values. Workers do not only produce useful items; they are part of a process that produces *meaning*. And workers are expected to relate to and identify with this *meaning*.

Therefore, a worker involved in manufacturing Jaguars should feel different from one who works on an assembly line producing tractors, even though the material output of their individual contribution may be more or less the same. In addition to manufacturing tangible products, a worker is simultaneously part of his/her company's intangible culture. In order to put his/her technical knowledge and skill to good use and help to create that 'added value' that makes the company successful, a worker must have communication skills, flexibility and inventiveness.

The value of a worker's labour will increasingly be judged on the basis of the unique nature of his/her contribution, which demands potential that goes beyond the rationally organised production process. In order to tap into this potential, both employer and employee must be involved in ongoing negotiations. The prerequisite for such negotiations is 'active' potential on the part of the worker: he/she must be fit, mentally available and 'inspired'. An employer cannot expect potential from wage slaves. A worker who produces intangible goods must be in a position to convey added value by way of communication, informal exchanges and inspired initiatives.

In his speech at the Fontys University of Applied Sciences in Tilburg, entitled 'The Murmur of the Artistic Masses', the art sociologist Pascal Gielen formulated the fascinating hypothesis that the early modern art world could have been the laboratory for the post-Fordism of today. Intangible work, with its characteristics of physical and mental mobility, a potent labour force, biopolitics, communication and opportunism, is recognisable in early modern artistic practice. This is evident primarily in the way in which attention shifts from the artefact to the *space* between artefact and perception. The way in which this space is occupied by language and the way in which artists have developed from skilled craftsmen into virtuoso *performers* of ideas, reflects the practices found on the intangible shop floors of today. Duchamp's ready-mades and Warhol's 'Brillo Boxes' could not have become important works of art without the presence of language and linguistic virtuosity in the interplay of meanings.

We can deduce that a potential outcome of Pascal Gielen's hypothesis is that all members of post-Fordist society would, as intangible workers, participate in an artistic and economic practice, and that the age-old dichotomy between art and society has *de facto* disappeared. A glimpse of this outcome is perhaps what we have witnessed in the Constructies Espeel company over the past few decades.

A worker, who was encouraged by his/her company's culture to make suggestions at a planning meeting of his production line, which, if implemented, would improve the workflow as well as make the work more enjoyable, would be unlikely to link the success of these proposals to the experiences of early modern art, but rather to the unfailing efforts of the trade unions to create a more humane working environment. The employer would attribute the benefits of his worker's suggestions to the success of his/her human resources strategy.

If the ancient dichotomy between art and society has in fact disappeared, and the logic of the art world has made its way to the centre of our economic society, it has long since been shaped by new, post-Fordist concepts. Creativity, innovation, dynamism, informality and emotion are all terms that are fully integrated into economic systems. But rarely will someone – except perhaps on a single company-sponsored artistic team-building day – personally concern him/herself with an artistic logic. Art is the result of what artists do, and most people still tend to romanticise the artistic process. One might assume that the intangible worker, however conscientiously he/she strives for the pseudo-rational goal of market share and corporate profit, considers him/herself to be part of the 'hard' sector, and art as part of the 'soft' sector. Art, in the absence of any direct usefulness, appears to be speculative, and connected to no other social meaning than its own existence. This is why its logic appears to anyone outside the art world as incapable of serving a goal, even though, paradoxically, these same people *do* use its logic while at the same time deny doing so.

People often ignore the fact that the artistic enterprise and the role of its artists constitutes just as rational and competitive an environment as that of industry. They fail to understand that in the artistic world nothing can be left to chance either and that processes must be organised in a precise and reliable manner in order to ensure the outcome of specific and effective results. Economic reality dictates that all parts of the process be financially measurable.

Artists usually produce their work on their own. But on occasion they may call upon the skills of others that may only be available in an industrial setting.

Constructies Espeel is an industrial company. Its products are not consumer goods, so strictly speaking it could continue to follow traditional Fordist principles. Its output consists of reliable solutions for transport within companies and for assembly elements at industrial plants. However, the background and vision of Constructies Espeel's CEO, Michel Espeel, imbued as he was with the social struggles of the 1960s and 1970s, led him to introduce certain post-Fordist cultural elements. In effect, the company culture was what Virno has called 'a communism of capital', with the most horizontal organisational structure possible and an emphasis on humane principles. The resulting flexibility has made the company highly competitive on the project market, and it has therefore enjoyed steady growth to this day.

Artists have become clients in the midst of its industries. Constructies Espeel has brought a great many projects with artists to successful conclusions, and its expertise and production potential as an industrial company has been able seamlessly to link up with an artistic practice. To this end, it has been necessary for Constructies Espeel to appropriate the logic of art and to respect the various consequences of that art. Yet it has at all times managed to keep its *sangfroid* and to continue to demand respect for its own industrial logic. As a result, the company has not been able to adopt every kind of artistic practice, in the same way that it may not always be able to offer a particular solution to one of its industrial partners.

Strangely, despite what has been said above, Constructies Espeel's trajectory appears to have been exceptional. Perhaps because it did not come about as a company strategy but as the consequence of supply and demand within a particular artistic practice that deems it essential to create large-scale works in which metal can be one of the materials used. Partly due to the initiatives of Julie Vandenbroucke, Michel Espeel's wife, Constructies Espeel has allowed artists to play an important role in its company culture, but without ever becoming an arts company or a critical institution. Constructies Espeel cannot do without art and art cannot do without Constructies Espeel. Unlike a bronze foundry or an arts press, it is not an arts supply business, rather an industry for industry. And yet it was willing and able to help make the journey from a design to a finished work of art. It did this for artists rather than for the sake of art, and thereby recognised artists as industries that pro-

9

duce works of art. The reverse is also true. The collaboration required artists to have some insight into the intangible potential of an industrial firm. In this regard, artists have great confidence in Michel Espeel and recognised him as a person with an artistic consciousness, albeit focused entirely on a metal company. Sometimes, to their surprise, they discovered a similar artistic consciousness among several Constructies Espeel employees. And anyone who has an artistic consciousness is part of the art world.

In the final analysis, Espeel is the story of a journey undertaken by people, by human beings. A road movie – why not? The story itself begins in the next section.

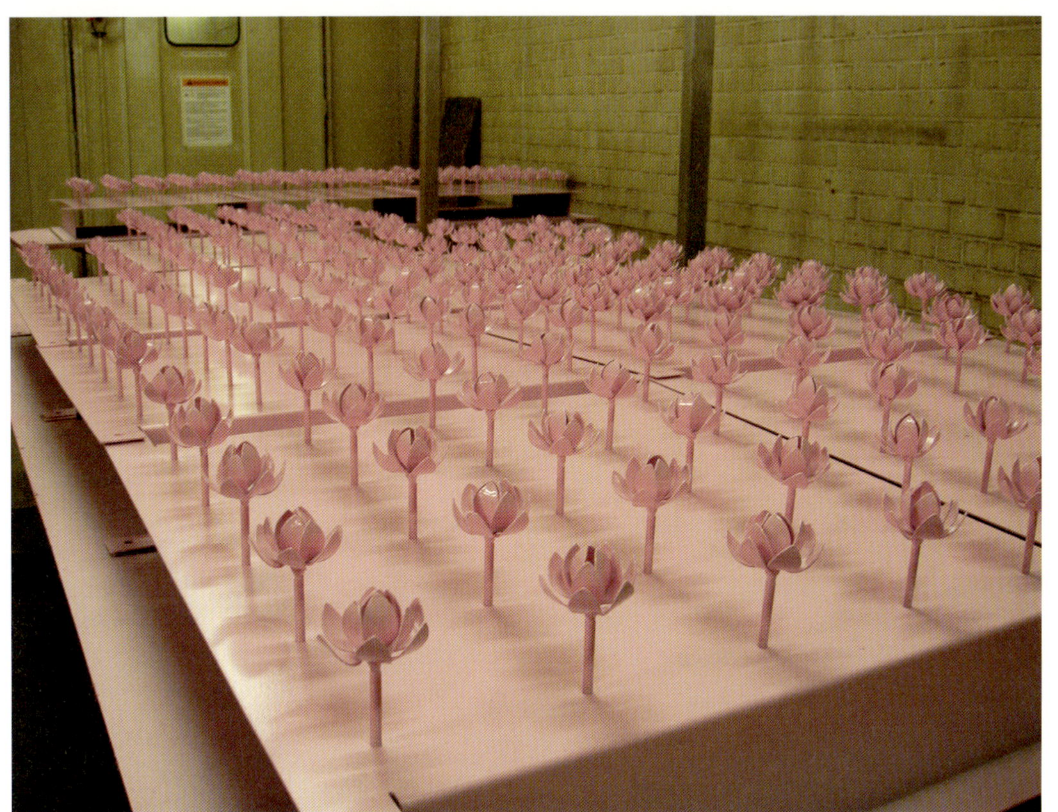

fig. 2

fig. 2   Hans Op de Beeck & Wim Maes, *Bloesem* [Blossom], 2006. The spraying.

fig. 3   Drawing from the guestbook of Julie and Michel Espeel, of the journey made by the architects of 51N4E during the celebration of Espeel's 50th anniversary, in 2004

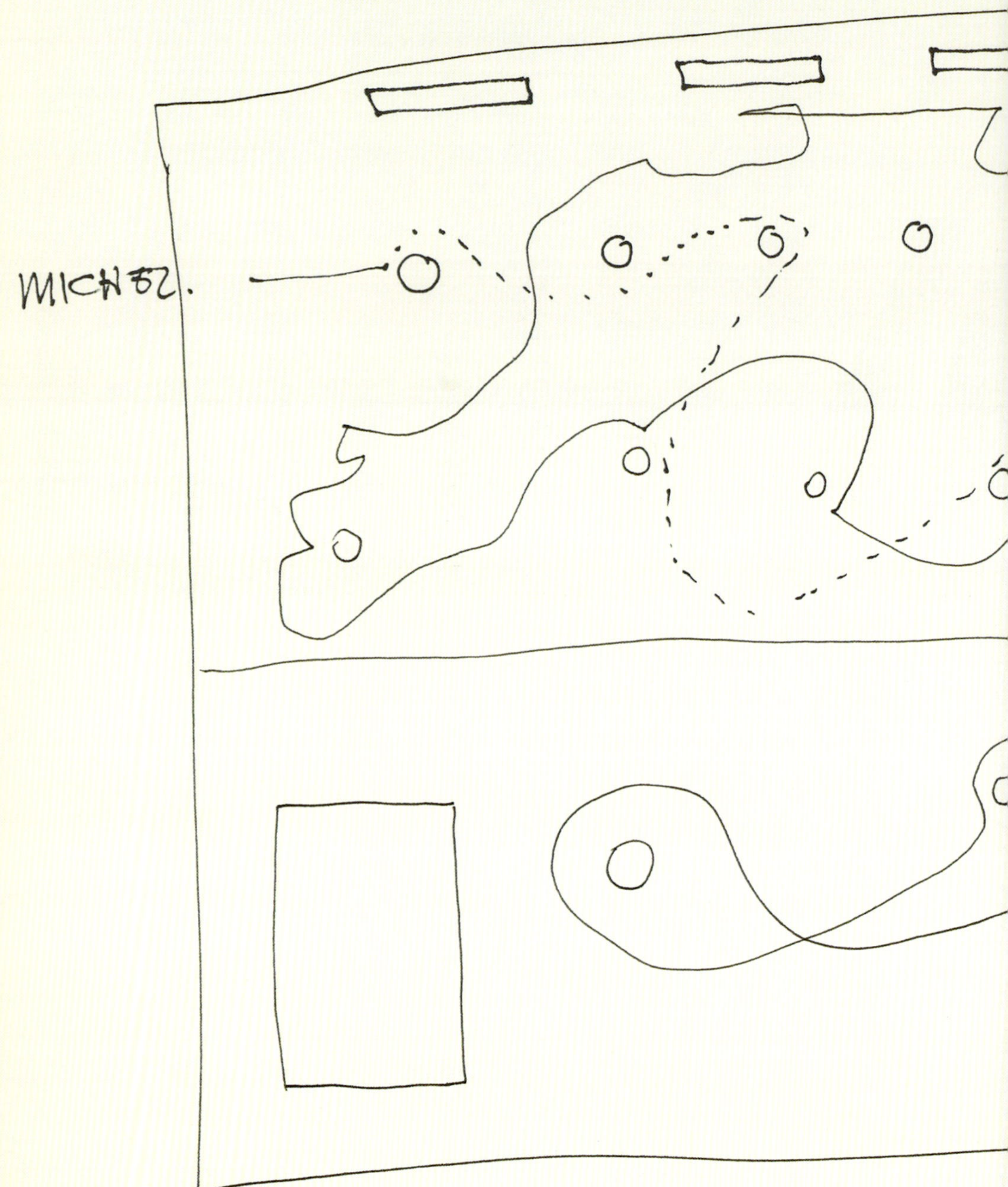
MICH 82.

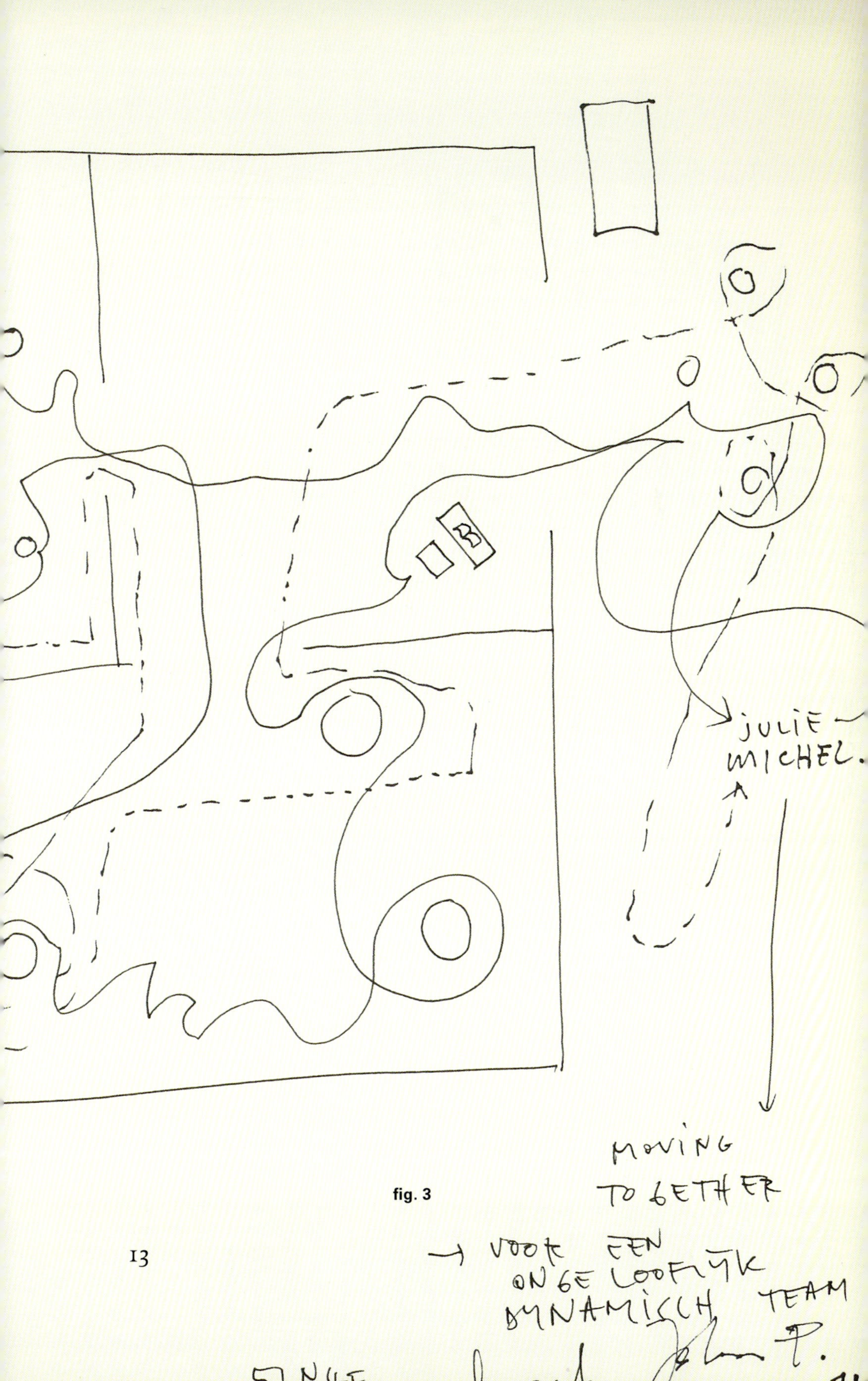

JULIE
MICHEL.
MOVING
TOGETHER
VOOR EEN
ONGELOOFLYK
DYNAMISCH TEAM

fig. 3

13

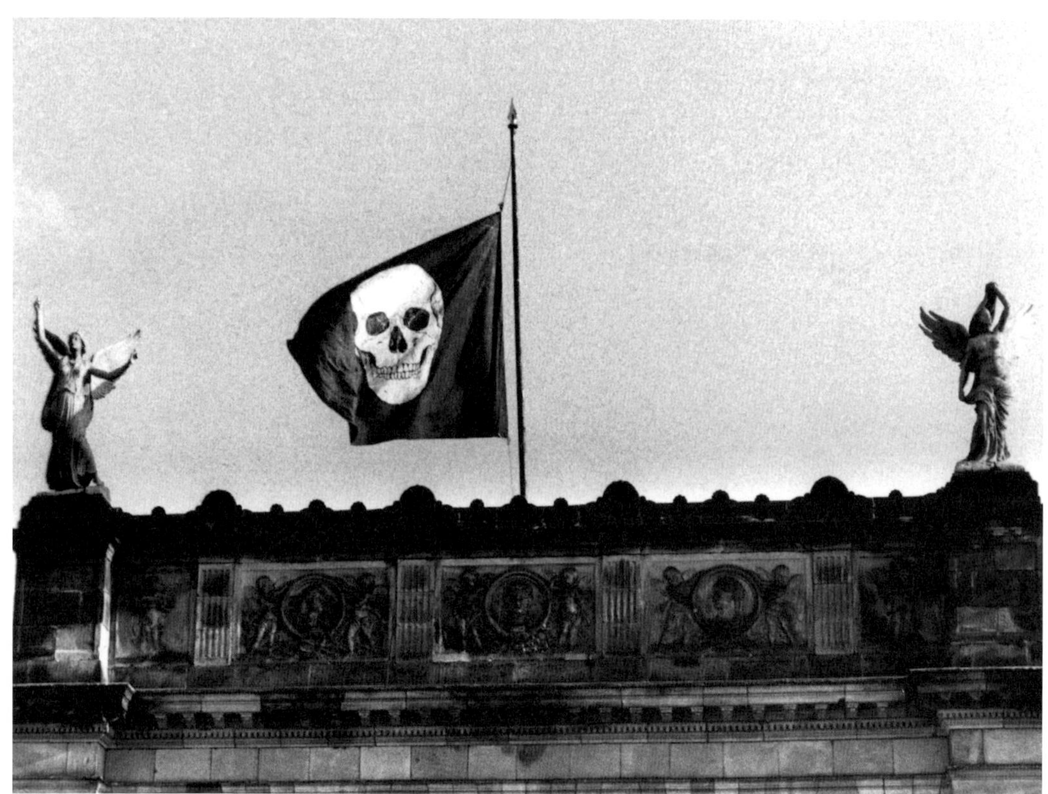

fig. 4

14

fig. 4   Leo Copers, *Vlag* [Flag], 1979.
Leo Copers' flag was raised for a few
minutes on 20 March 1979 at 4 p.m.
above the Ghent Museum of Fine Arts
on the occasion of the exhibition on
Contemporary Art in Belgium, *Inzicht
Overzicht/Overzicht Inzicht* [Insight
Oversight/Oversight Insight]. An
appropriate symbol for the state of
detachment that is the object of Julie's
passion for contemporary art. Photo:
Martine Kint.

Walk With Me

Charlotte Bonduel

Welcome, then, to this *road movie*. The protagonist of the story is the Constructies Espeel company in Rumbeke. Constructies Espeel has been involved in collaborative projects with artists for the last twenty years. Let us trace the imaginary trail that has been blazed for the journey that we shall recount here.

The contemporary road movie is a descendant of the historical genre of epic poetry, such as Homer's *Odyssey* and Virgil's *Aeneid*, a heroic poem about the deeds of Aeneas. What these ancient tales and their twenty-first century variant have in common is that they both celebrate the development and achievements of a protagonist. He goes through a process. The same is true of the entrepreneur, the artists and the employees in this story; at some point they encounter each other and themselves. After twenty years of collaboration, no one has remained quite the same.

Now that Michel Espeel has handed over Constructies Espeel company to a new proprietor, a part of the firm's journey is commemorated in the form of a selection from among the various collaborations it engaged in over the years and of the artworks that were created in the process. To relate this in book form may give the impression that this was a premeditated path. In reality, this is far from the case. In retrospect, the facts seem only to reveal mutual relationships. Espeel's collaboration with artists began and unfolded spontaneously. Sometimes the path led to a dead end, was abandoned or was intuitively postponed. For the most part, there was no clear destination, but there was an ever shifting company of fellow travellers and a predilection for remaining constantly in motion.

A road movie is usually episodic in structure. In each episode, the protagonist faces a challenge but his success is not always assured. The Espeel story follows this tried and tested structure. The journey begins modestly. Espeel Senior opens his business. Julie and Michel meet, and follow their natural inclinations (**Part I**). Michel takes charge of the metal company. Under Julie's guidance, the first artists arrive at the factory where Michel manages the business in a spirit of openness. These are the early years (**Part II**). With the company in full swing, the gates open to a number of major artistic events. Julie then sets out into the world to bridge the gulf separating art and economy. With the non-profit association Arteconomy vzw, she builds bridges across which these two mutually alienated worlds can meet (**Part III**). Three new travel accounts are recorded in Espeel's log book (**Part IV**), after which the road movie closes with an invitation: "Walk with me."

Perhaps you, too, would like to join this journey? A part of the trail has already been blazed. The book in your hands attests to this. But the journey is far from over. With this book, we lay out a path through the thicket for a journey that is well worth following. If the path remains untrodden, it will turn to weeds and remain but a faint memory. But if we can persuade you to follow in our footsteps, then the landscape may change for ever, giving rise to a wider road along which the competent ministers can travel.

Part I

The Constructies Espeel company is established, Michel joins the firm, Julie and Michel marry and Julie develops her passion for art.

Ernest Espeel's trolleys

Ernest Espeel, Michel's father, was a blacksmith by trade and opened his business in 1954. When the flax industry moved to Russia on account of the low wages there, he joined a workshop in the Moorseelsesteenweg in Rumbeke and produced trolleys for use in the furniture industry. His design met with success and found a growing market. This set the tone: metal and internal transport became the leitmotifs throughout the various transformations that Constructies Espeel would undergo.

The firm was a 'sole proprietorship', although Mrs Espeel and the children also lent a hand. The first expansion took place as early as

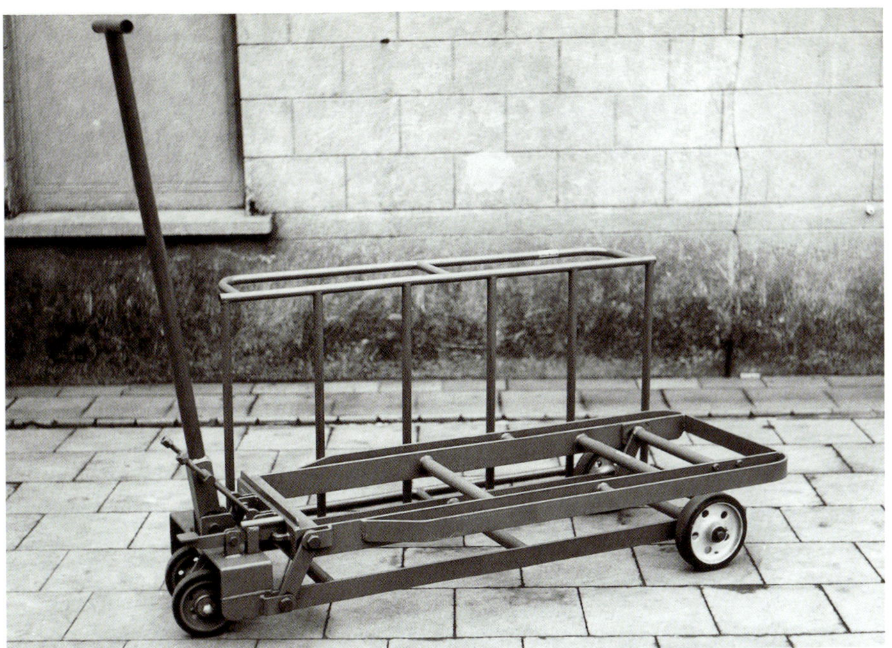

fig. 5

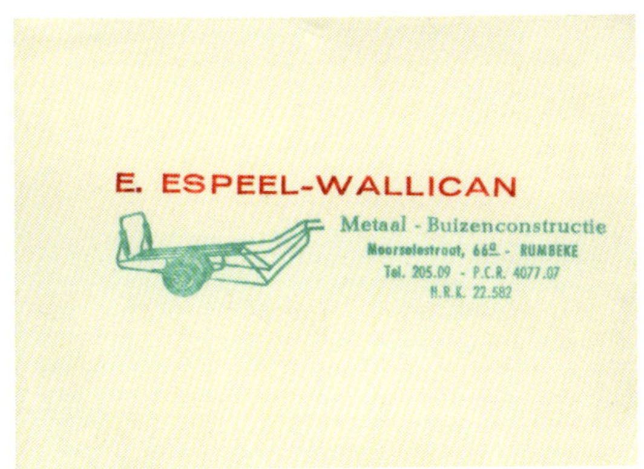

fig. 6

fig. 5   Ernest Espeel's trolley. Internal transport and metal are the starting points for the company's production.
fig. 6   The original logo of the Espeel-Wallican company.

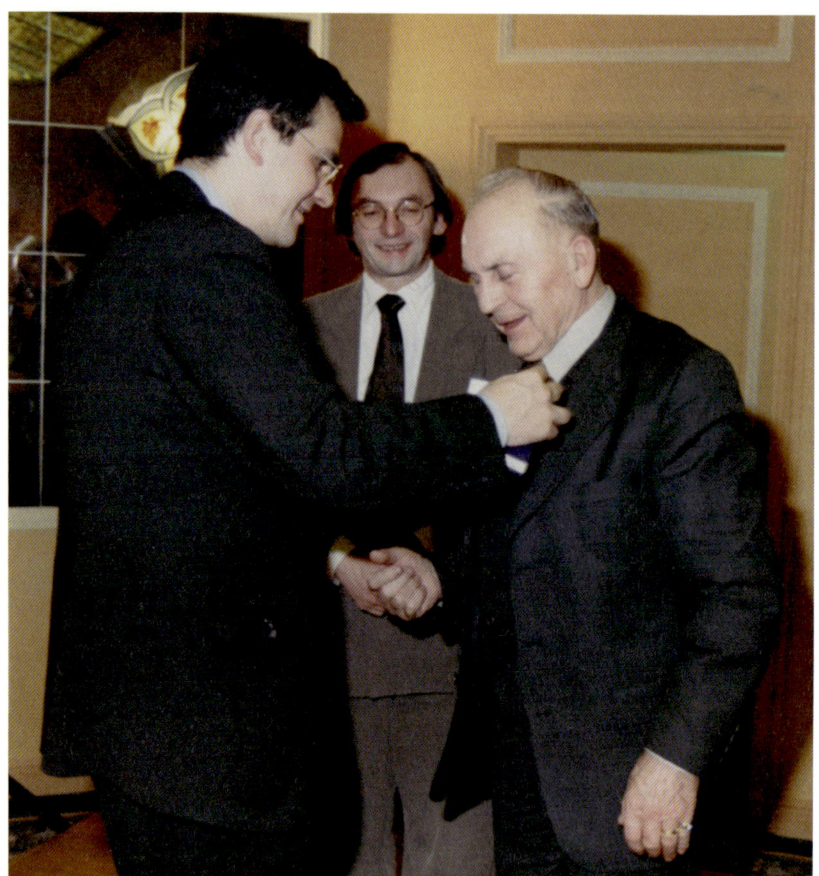

fig. 7

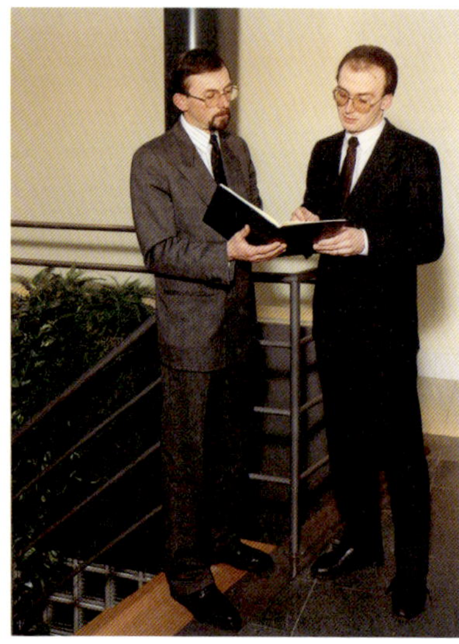

fig. 8

18

fig. 7   Ernest Espeel is elevated to
the rank of Knight in the Order of
Leopold by Mr Kris Peeters, Managing
Director of Unizo, 1997.

fig. 8   Brothers Michel and Luc Espeel
on the 35th anniversary of the company,
on 29 September 1989.

1960. Nine years later, Michel officially joined the company, and a limited partnership was established between father and son. The young *soixanthuitard* who attended the Minor Seminary of Roeselare now donned overalls as an independent entrepreneur among the workers. Through his experience on the shop floor, he acquired a feeling for metal and began to discover the meaning of leadership. A further expansion of the firm would follow.

In 1974, the trolleys were no longer enough to withstand the threats of the oil crisis. Constructies Espeel began to collaborate with the Vyncke Energietechniek company in Harelbeke, and built supply systems for their boilers. Thus, the principle of co-production came to be a well-established part of Constructies Espeel's business. In subsequent years, the company increased its deliveries to other firms and was equipped for that purpose. The number of Espeel employees grew rapidly. In 1982, Michel's brother Luc joined the business, which was transformed into a limited company and moved to a former brickyard, also on the Moorseelsesteenweg. The plant's smokestack remained in place and the Espeel name stood high above the flatlands of Rumbeke (West Flanders). By the end of 2007, the company employed 70 workers and had a turnover of 11 million euros.

The Espeel-Vandenbroucke couple

Michel Espeel and Julie Vandenbroucke were born in the same year and met in elementary school. Julie and Michel met their match in each other – they competed for first and second place in their class.

Julie comes from a working-class family. Her father worked in a brickyard and her mother ran a small farm. When Julie was learning to type, Mr Espeel offered her a typewriter on which she could practise by typing invoices on Wednesday afternoons. In the meantime, Michel had gone on to secondary school, but the former rivals ran into each other again at the Constructies Espeel company. The rivalries of the past reappeared. They became partners, and were married in 1972. During the 1980s, Julie worked in the social sector and for family services in Kortrijk. The couple made their social commitment a shared priority. They had lived through hard times, enough to know what that feels like and not to be obsessed with possessions. Rather, they sought to share their own well-being.

Julie's passion

Although she had never had a formal introduction to the arts, the teen-age Julie filled the walls of her room with prints from the popular art magazine *Openbaar Kunstbezit*. Posters of Picasso and Giacometti hung alongside *The Beatles*. She kept a scrapbook of clippings about artists from the Sunday paper (*Zondagsvriend*). After she married, Julie yielded to the temptation to buy four etchings by Alfons Blomme for their freshly painted house. This was a youthful and spontaneous sign of a sensitivity that she would increasingly follow and explore. The arrival of Emiel Veranneman in Kruishoutem marked a significant moment in her life. This world-class furniture designer, the nephew of the Belgian painter Constant Permeke, returned from Brussels to his native region in order to open a gallery, and brought the Brussels art scene in his wake. Julie attended the opening, discovered the work of international artists and gained access to a world that fascinated her. But the combination of a large family and a demanding job forced her to postpone any pursuit of her interest. It was not until the end of the 1980s that Julie renewed her training in art. Michel's interest in art was aroused by Julie's enthusiasm and he sometimes accompanied her to exhibitions and openings. They occasionally purchased a work of art and gradually built up a collection.

Julie invested her father's legacy in two sculptures by the artist José Vermeersch. These terracotta statues connected her life in the brickyard to the artistic world in which she found herself. When among artists, Julie gave free rein to her predilection for the absurd and in that world she found her wings. She did not become a collector of artworks. Possessing the works was only of moderate interest to her. Rather, she instinctively became one with the works and they became part of who she was.

A Great gulf

On what might be considered the eve of the journey, the cards that lay before the Espeel couple were as follows: Michel was head of Constructies Espeel company and although he was a committed citizen, the company was his world and Julie respected his territory. She herself had no ambitions in relation to the firm. Neither would she become the

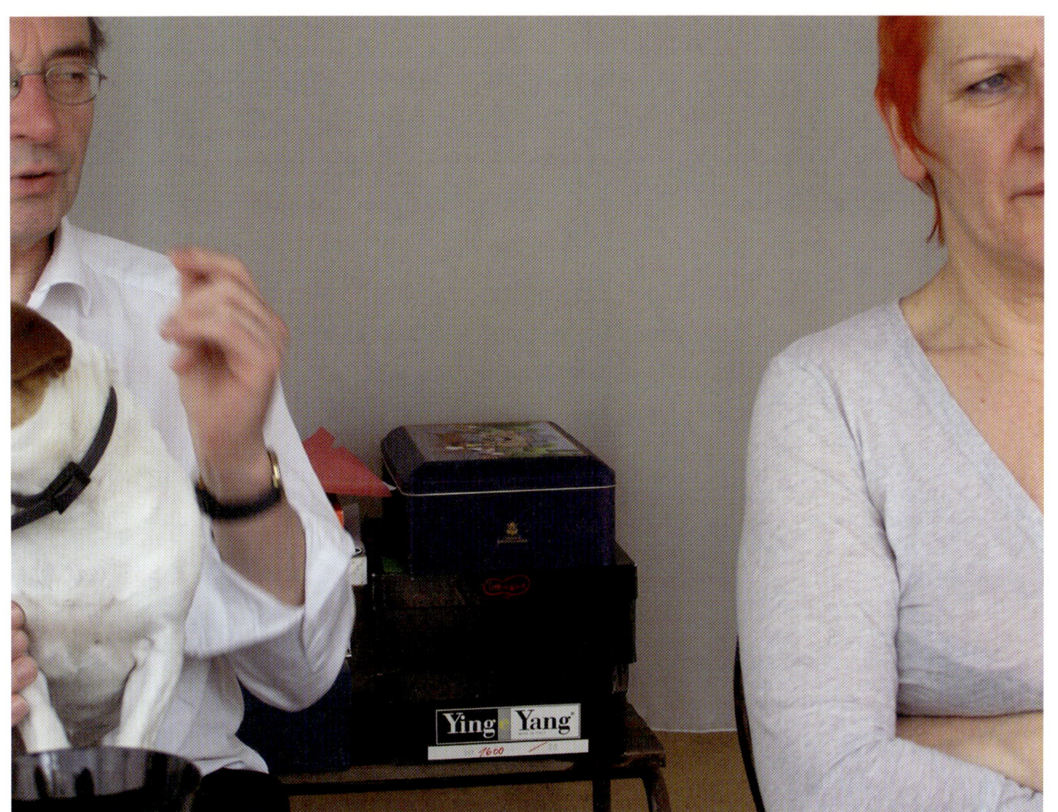

fig. 9

fig. 9   Michel Espeel and Julie
Vandenbroucke in 2008.

'boss's wife'. Her world encompassed the world of art. But when two fires burn alongside each other, once in a while a spark will leap from one to the other. It is in the light of this gulf between Julie and Michel, between their respective biotopes, between art and economy, that we should read what follows. Unaware of it themselves, their quest for genuine common ground is what drives the journey forward.

Part II

Julie and Michel meet Paul Gees, the artistic presence at the company proliferates and Michel builds his business with vision.

Paul Gees

Some time in 1989, Julie and Michel visited a gallery in Aalst, where the artist Paul Gees was also present. Paul is a sculptor. His work is suffused with physical tension among three materials: wood, metal and stone. But executing his designs on a large scale posed a common problem: Paul had neither the space nor the technical means for creating sculptures of that size in his studio. He spoke of this difficulty to Julie as a friend, whereupon Julie introduced him to Michel. Michel spontaneously invited Paul to his factory: "Then we'll see what we can do."

Paul's request fell on fertile soil with Michel. It was second nature for him to offer to help. He had been a volunteer for many years with the ambulance and fire department, and as CEO his door was always open at seven in the morning for anyone seeking advice on private matters. When Michel travelled to Tanzania with a programme to help entrepreneurs from the South, he met a simple blacksmith in Arusha. The evening after the visit, Michel realized that with a few simple tools readily available in the West, the blacksmith could work much faster and more safely. The next day he decided to revisit him and see what could be done.

Michel made no distinction between Paul Gees' request and his desire to help the blacksmith in Arusha, as long as the spark caught fire. Everyone felt a certain affinity with Michel during their first encounter with him. It made no difference whether it was a great artist or an ambitious amateur, the personality was more important to Michel than name

22

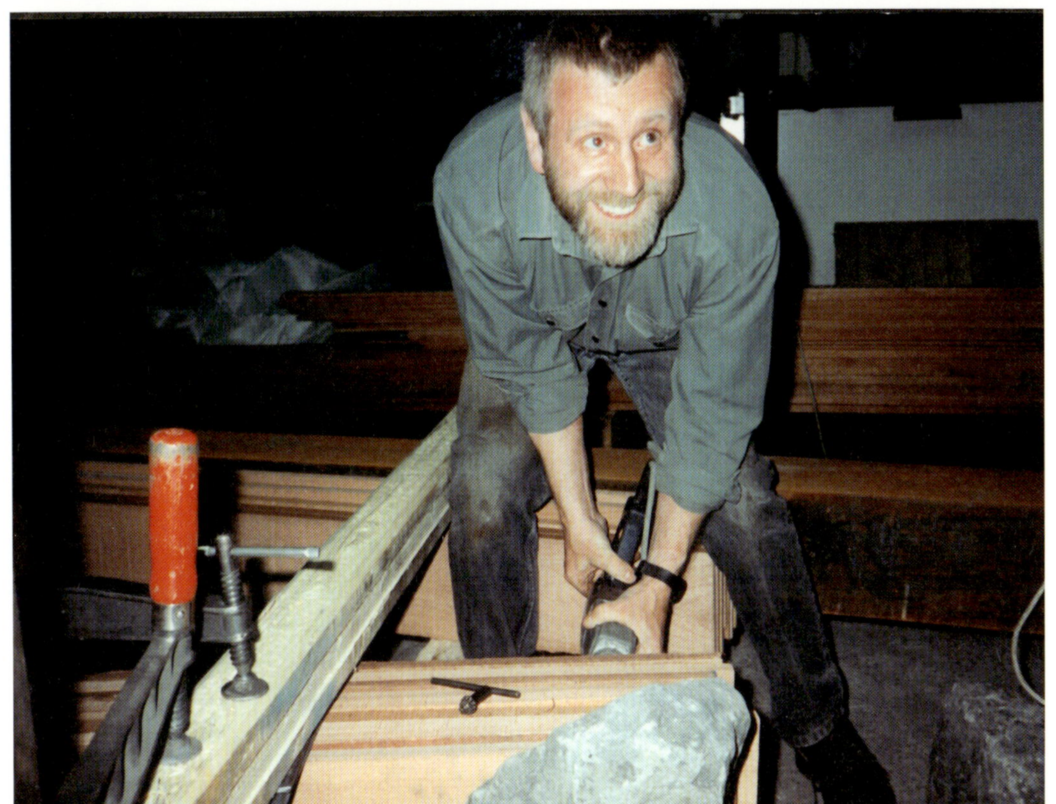

fig. 10

23

fig. 10   Paul Gees during the assembly
of an artwork, 1989.

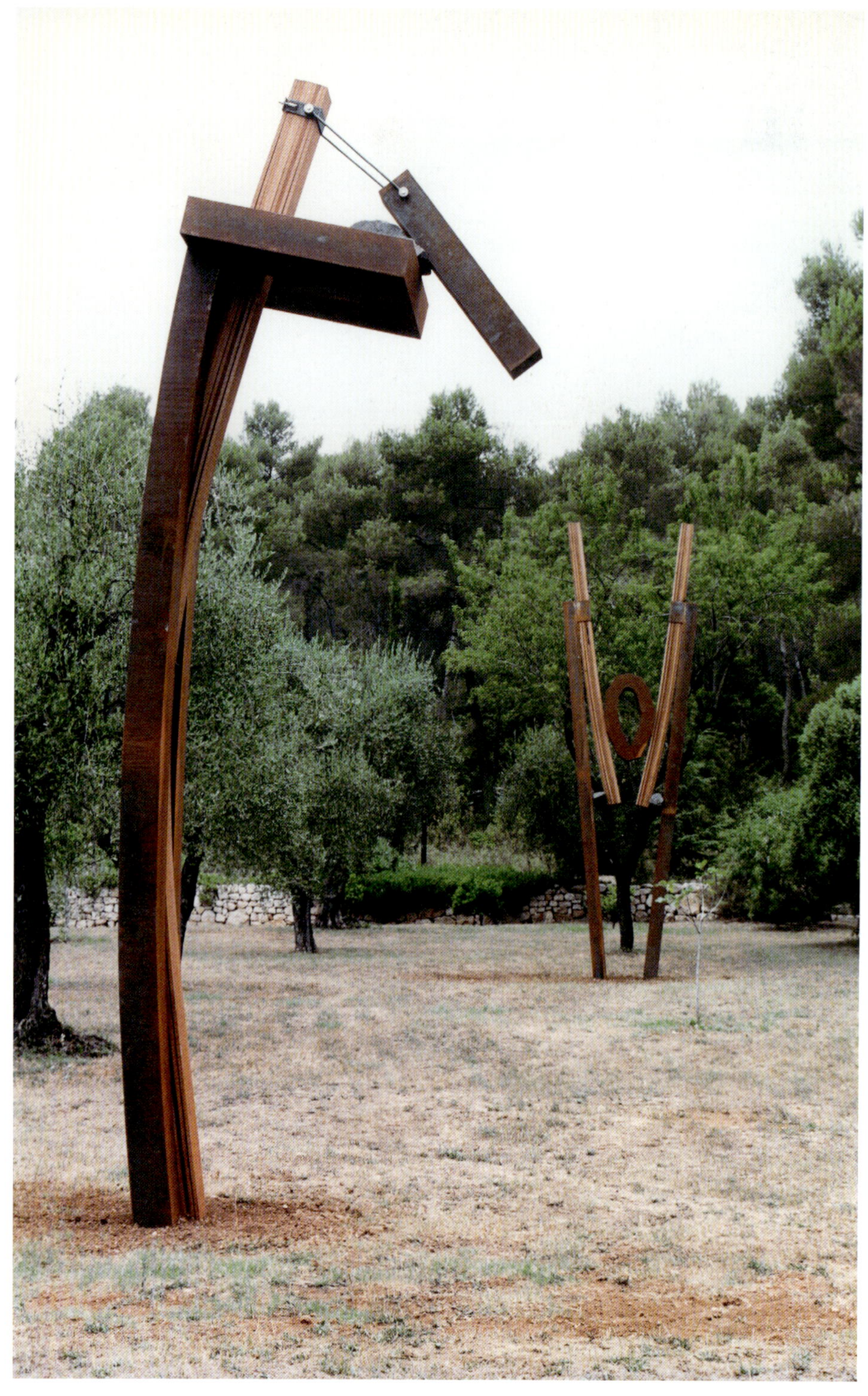

fig. 11

fig. 11   Paul Gees, *Dakhuis* [Roof house], 1994. Private estate of François Lippens, Roquefort-les-Pins. Photo: Paul Gees.

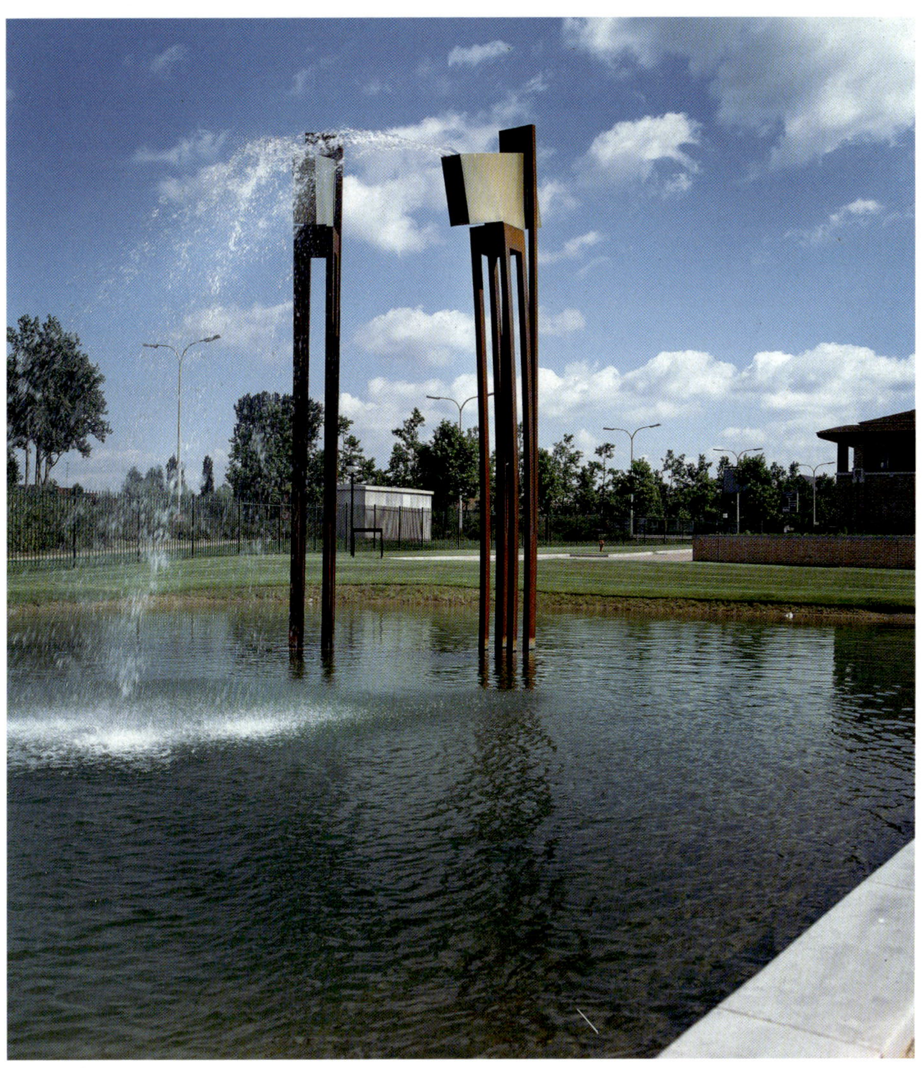

fig. 12

25

fig. 12   Paul Gees, *Dialoog* [Dialogue],
1994. Provinciehuis [Provincial administrative centre], Hasselt. Photo: Paul Gees.

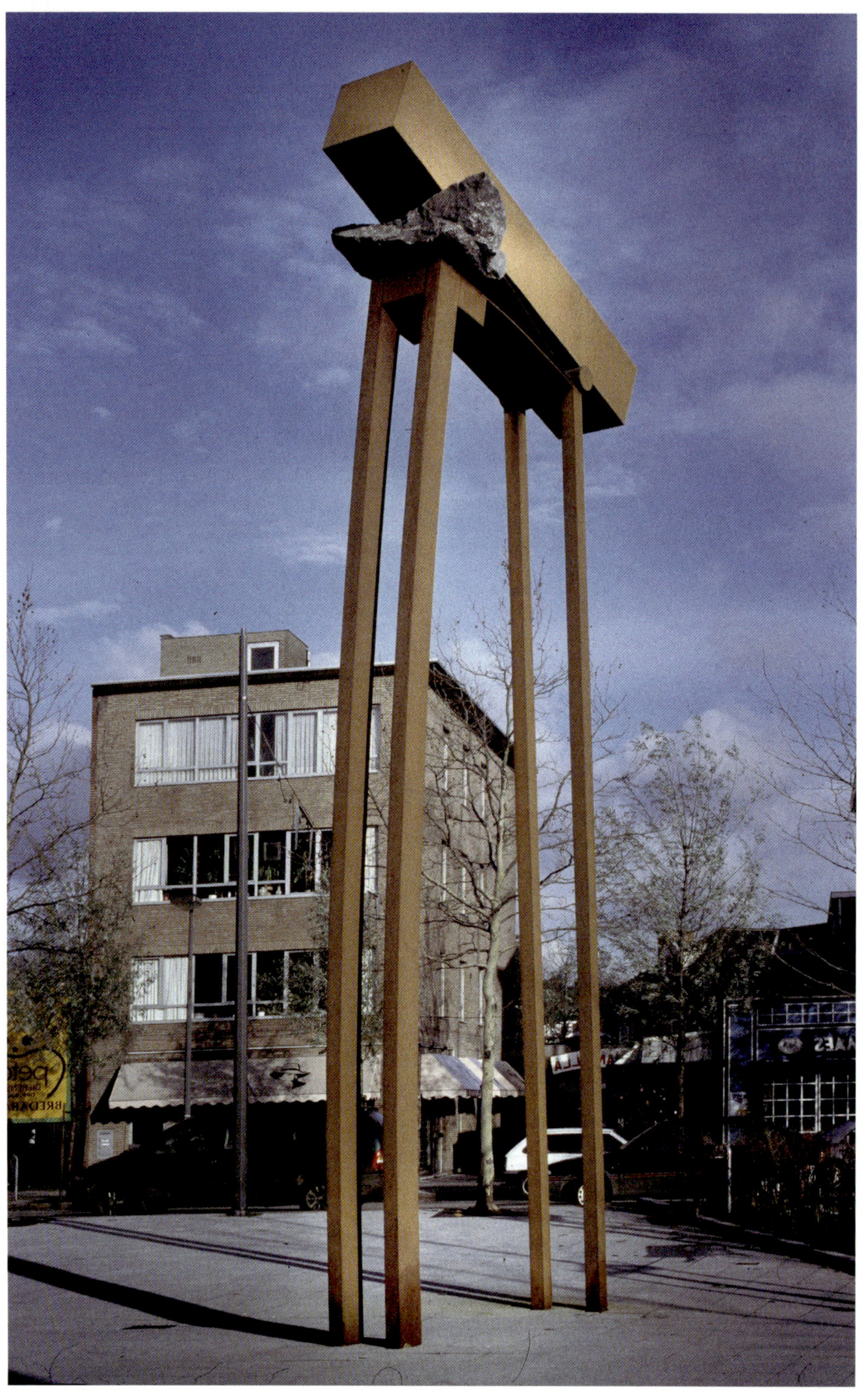

fig. 13

26

fig. 13   Paul Gees, *Dakstoel* **[Roof chair], 1997. Brasschaat. Photo: Paul Gees.**

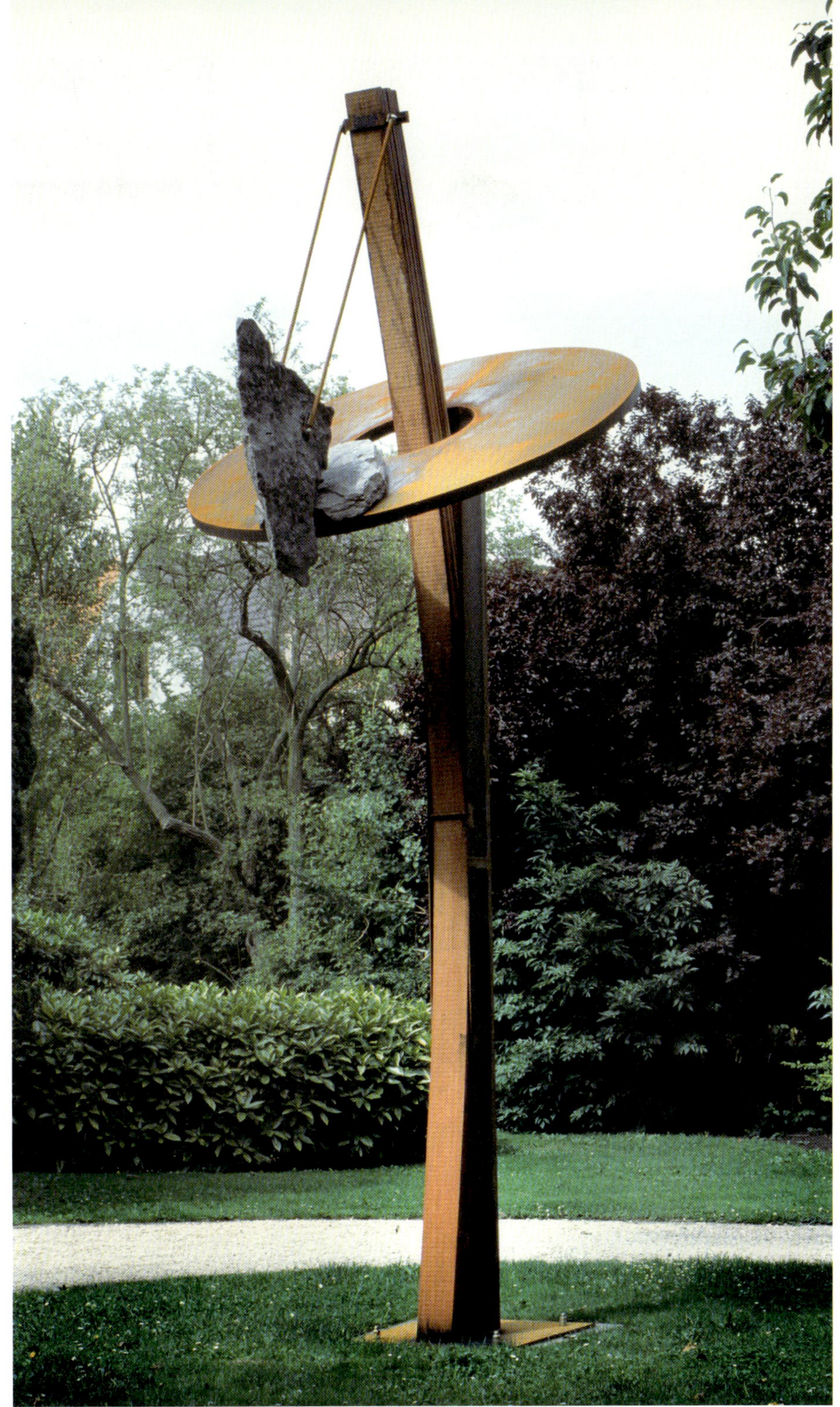

fig. 14

27

fig. 14   Paul Gees, *Vertically Pierced*,
1994. City of Lokeren. Photo: Paul Gees.

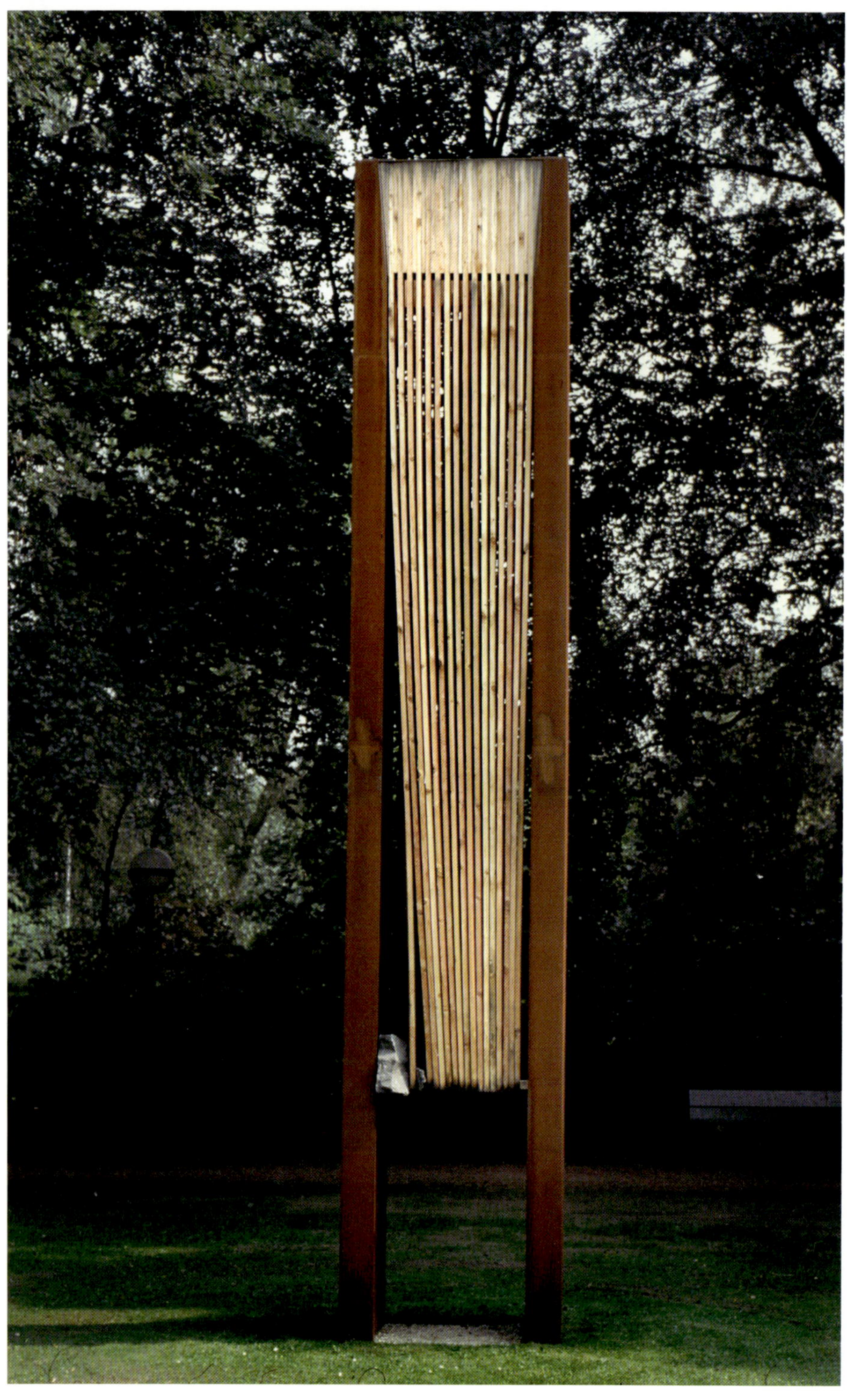

fig. 15

28

fig. 15   Paul Gees, *Een huis voor de stilte* [A house for silence], 1997. Private collection, Sint-Eloois-Winkel. Photo: Paul Gees.

or fame. What counted above all was that the artist himself was willing to get involved in the company. He or she had to be prepared to get along with the employees and work with them on an equal footing.

At first, artists came to Constructies Espeel because of their acquaintance with Julie. Without realising it, in those years she made a kind of pre-selection in the early years of the company. She had a feel for who would and wouldn't click with the company. And as the reputation of Constructies Espeel spread, and (un)known artists turned up, this became *the* criterion for collaboration. The artist and the company must click in every respect.

Metal

The metal 'factor' served as an ice-breaker in this process, because it was the sole common denominator in the art works that the firm helped to create. If it were not, the output would be as varied as the artists were numerous.

Once an artist has the support of Constructies Espeel, he or she is given a workshop in which to create. Material and machines are made available as well as the necessary staff. Artists do not always have the skill and knowledge to handle metal. Sometimes they just have an idea. In this case, it is the job of the workers on the shop floor to work out the technical aspects.

The musings of the artist pose a challenge to the craftsman. The latter has to place himself into the thought-world of the artist and respond to his wishes with flexibility and technical know-how. In this way, the technician's skills and expertise take on an unusual quality. He can no longer take his competencies for granted, and as a result, he grows in self-awareness. Whereas the results of the craftsman's work would normally remain anonymous, it now crystallises into a unique object, singular and durable, with which he feels a personal connection. The special status and attention the object receives is now reflected in his work. "When I drive past a work of art, I will always stop and say: 'Look, we made that', even if I myself had nothing to do with it."[1] Even the employees not directly involved in these projects identify with the firm to which they belong. They take pride in seeing the strengths of the firm displayed so visibly.

From an administrative point of view, the artists are treated as regular customers. Some are difficult to work with and others are a pleasure. Even though artists are involved, the usual economic regulations are not set aside. Constructies Espeel makes projects possible but does not serve as their sponsor. A tailor-made agreement is drawn up for each project, but nothing is given away for free.

A period of rampant growth

Paul Gees and Michel reached an agreement and completed their first project. Eventually, this art work ended up on Michel's desk, but normally art works were not conspicuously displayed. Although media attention to Constructies Espeel grew over time, the collaboration with artists was never a publicity stunt. Art is not an advertisement. Once, a bank manager visited Constructies Espeel and exclaimed in surprise: "Is this a factory that works with artists? I don't see any art works!"

The anecdote emphasises how marginal the collaboration with artists really was for the company, especially in the early stages. From 1989 to 1997, art proliferated rapidly. Collaborative projects came and went, without anyone really taking much notice. Imperceptibly, however, a considerable distance had already been travelled with the likes of Paul Gees, Leo Copers, Martine Platteau – who learned to weld at Constructies Espeel – Hans De Pelsmaecker, Honoré δ'O, Tjok Dessauvage and Tine Vindevogel. This period would later be referred to as the period of 'wild growth'. Paul Gees's request took root in Michel's soil and, because his wife was fond of ornamental plants, the young shoot was allowed to stay. For the boss's word is law. No one trimmed the plant. The presence of these artists did much to set Constructies Espeel in motion, but it was some time before people recognised that an ornamental plant also bears fruit.

Michel's vision

The collaboration with artists was never set down in a strategic business plan. It worked its way in from the outside, but came to be firmly implanted in the company's culture. Julie's passion made its way into the company only because Michel's vision of entrepreneurship had paved the way. For not every entrepreneur would allow artists into his

30

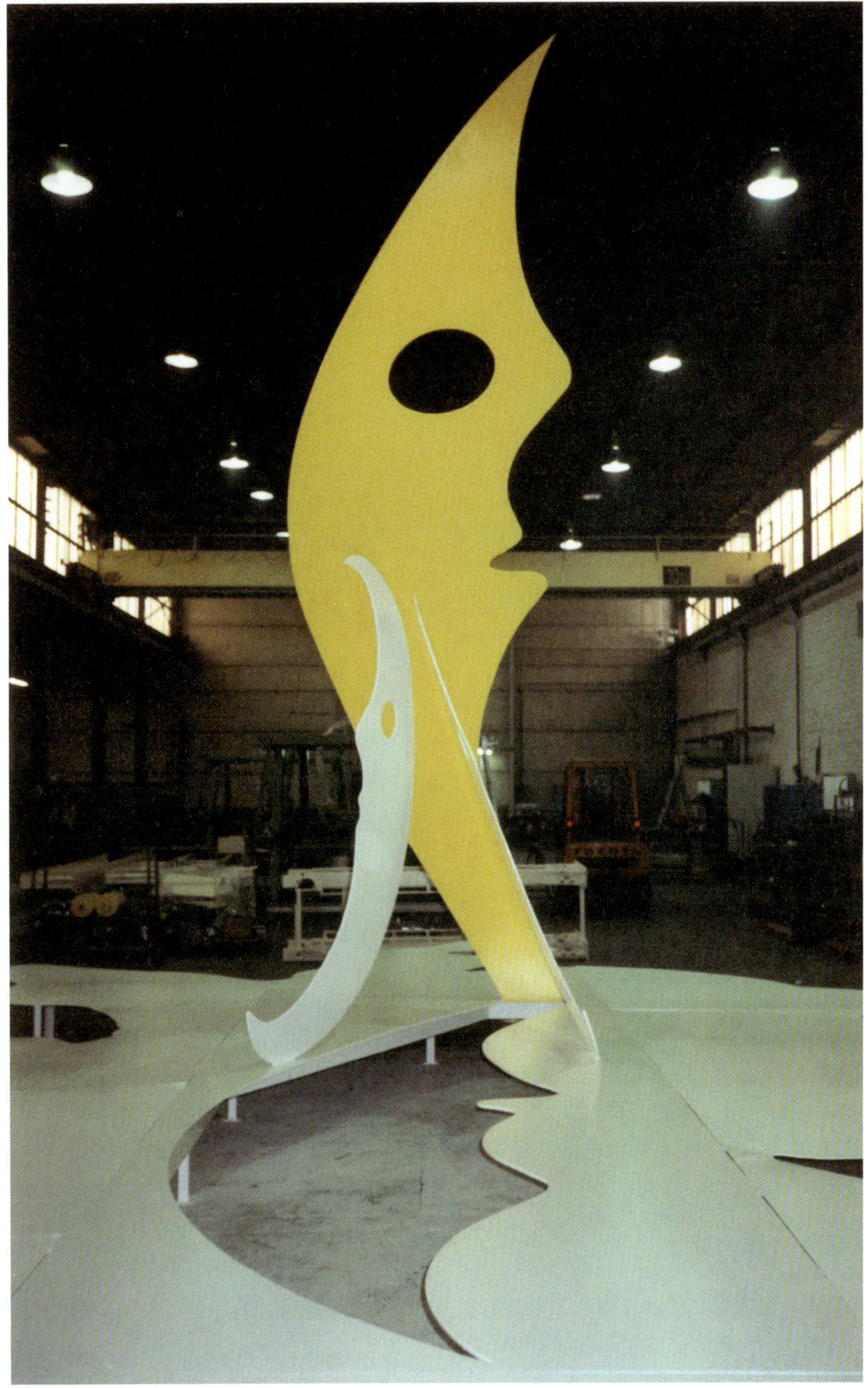

fig. 16

31

fig. 16   Test set-up at Constructies
Espeel, Tjok Dessauvage & Philippe
Bouttens, *Maanfontein* [Moon fountain],
1994.

Maanfontein mikpunt van vandalenstreken

door **Patrick GHYSELEN**

Kortrijk

De Maanfontein in de vijver van het park Plein is definitief bezweken onder de aanvallen van vandalisme. Eerst zorgde het aanhoudende vriesweer bij de fontein voor een prachtige ijskolom, die het skulptuur de nodige steun gaf. Tegelijkertijd vormde zich bovenaan een zware ijsklomp. Vandalen hakten de ondersteunende stalagmiet weg van onder de maanpunt, waardoor het ijzeren skulptuur volledig plooide onder de ijsklomp. Het is niet de eerste aanslag op dit kunstwerk. Drie keramische drijvende potten in de vijver van Dessauvage, die het kunstwerk ontwierp samen met Kortrijkzaan Philippe Bouttens, moesten het ook al ontgelden. Het kunstwerk werd door het duo opgedragen aan de multikulturele verdraagzaamheid.

De dienst patrimonium van de stad overlegt vandaag met de kunstenaars, hoe het skulptuur terug kan worden rechtgetrokken. In deze tijd van het jaar is dit geen evident werkje. De Maanfontein ligt verankerd in de vijver. Er komt wellicht een kraan aan te pas om de geplooide maansikkel terug recht te krijgen.

Willy Roets van de dienst kultuur: „Kontraktueel stond bepaald dat het kunstwerk weerbestendig moest zijn. Maar wat heet weerbestendig? Vorig jaar lieten we de fontein tijdens het vriesweer spuiten uit veiligheidsoverwegingen, omdat de vijver niet zou dichtvriezen. De reden ligt voor de hand. Wanneer de vijver dichtvriest, kunnen vandalen zomaar bij het kunstwerk geraken.''

Dit jaar waren de vriestemperaturen een stuk lager. De ijsgoden haalden het op de waterkracht van de fontein. Of het bij dergelijke temperaturen opportuun bleef om de fontein te laten aanliggen, blijft een open vraag. Kunstenaar-ontwerper Tjok Dessauvage: „Er vormde zich een ijsstalagmiet, onder de fontein, die de ijsklomp bovenop de maansikkel enigszins ondersteunde. Vandalen sloegen die ijskolom doelbewust weg, waardoor de maan ging plooien.''

„Dit was niet de eerste vandalenstreek tegen de Maanfontein'', vervolgt Dessauvage. „Ik heb de stad aangeraden, de fontein 's nachts te verlichten. Nu is het een donkere plek, die vrij spel laat aan vandalen. Maar men ging hier niet op in. Op de zorg vanwege de stad voor dit monument, valt toch wel iets aan te merken. Zo vormden zich tijdens de voorbije warme zomer, algen in de vijver. Die werden door de krachtige vijverpomp aangezogen en kwamen op het skulptuur terecht. Ik heb het monument toen op eigen initiatief volledig gekuist.''

Vreemd

Het aanhoudend vandalisme tegen het kunstwerk vindt Dessauvage „zeer eigenaardig. Op het plein voor het Centre Pompidou in Parijs staan gelijkaardige zaken al tien jaar onaangeroerd'', zegt Dessauvage. Hij vervangt straks de kapotgegooide keramische schalen door betonnen elementen, die niet meer stuk gaan.

Twee jaar geleden is de fontein geïnstalleerd in de vijver van het park Plein ter gelegenheid van vijftig jaar Radio 2 West-Vlaanderen. De wedstrijdjury die het ontwerp uitkoos, sprak in haar verslag over „de monumentale struktuur met diverse verrassingselementen, die nergens anders voorkomen, als het meest exklusieve kunstwerk voor die plaats.''

Voor het kunstwerk trok Kortrijk 1 miljoen frank uit. „Het projekt spreekt aan door de keuze van kleur, materiaal en verrassingselementen. De grillige vormen, het koloriet en de niet-konventionele materialen spelen goed in op de omgeving. Het geheel leeft in harmonie met de bezoekers van het park, die vooral kinderen zijn. De drijvende kompositie is monumentaal en toch poëtisch. Ook de multikulturele kontekst, met de zeven werelddelen is kreatief'', vond de jury toen.

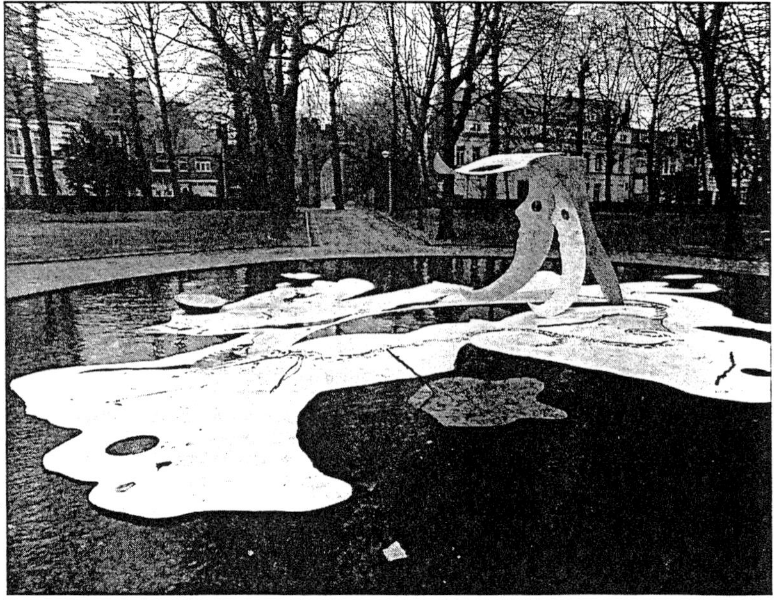

De Maanfontein bezweek niet alleen onder de weerselementen, maar vooral onder niet aflatend vandalisme.
(Foto Patrick Holderbeke)

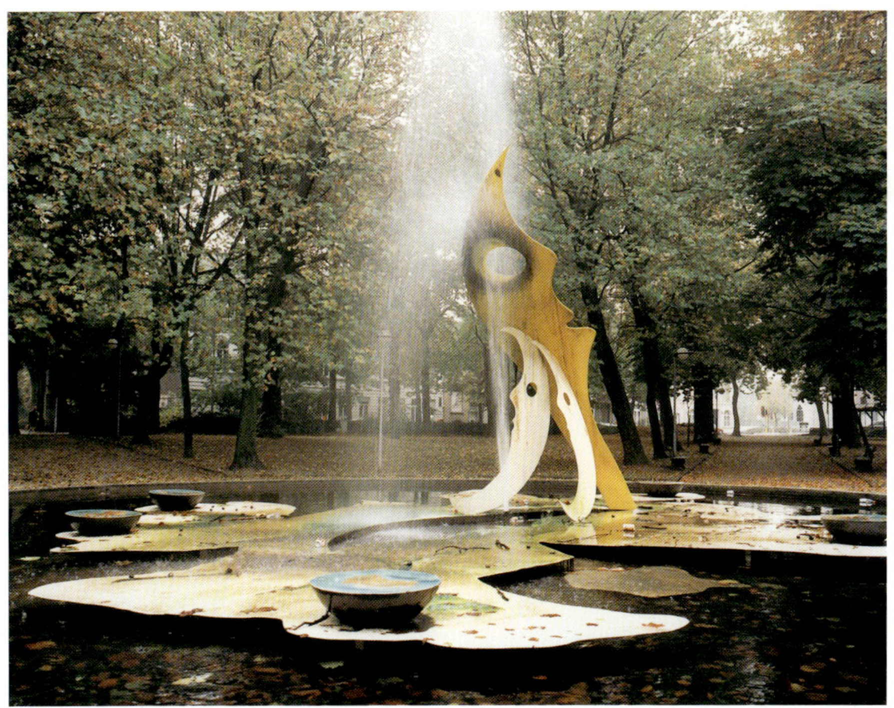

fig. 17

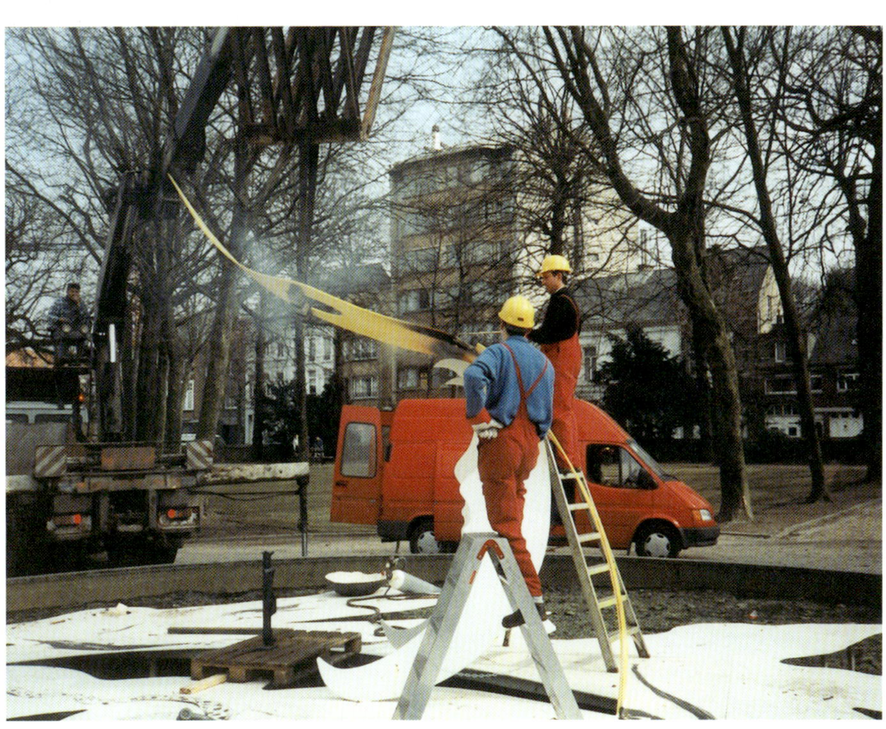

fig. 18

33

fig. 17   Tjok Dessauvage & Philippe
Bouttens, *Maanfontein* [Moon fountain],
1994.
fig. 18   Tjok Dessauvage & Philippe
Bouttens, *Maanfontein* [Moon fountain],
1994, being dismantled.

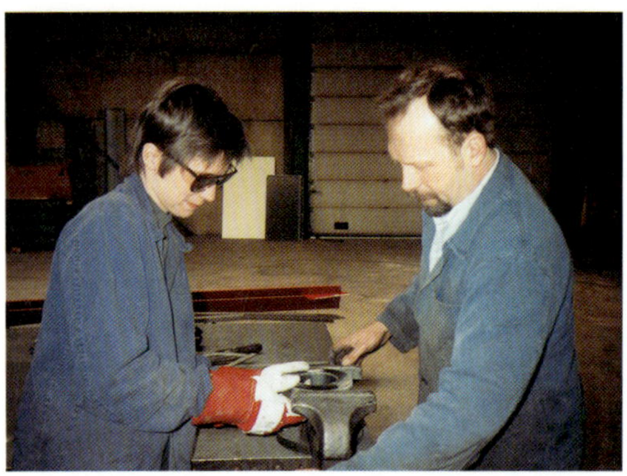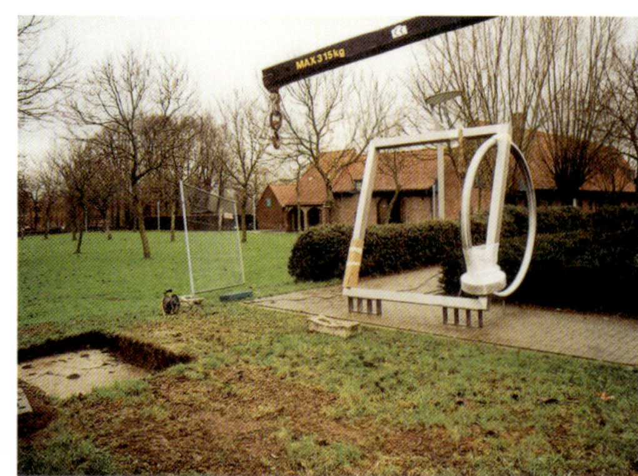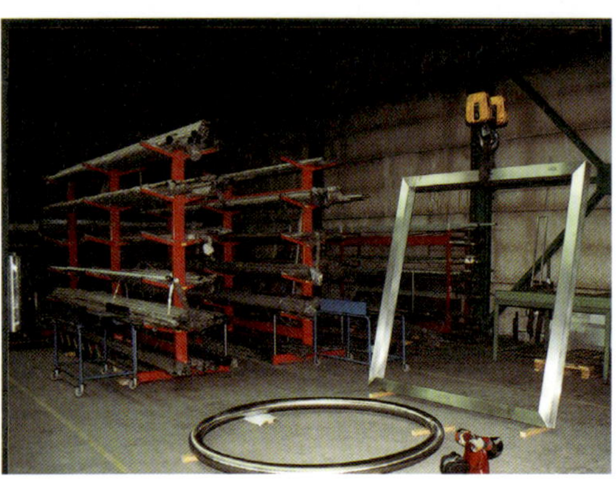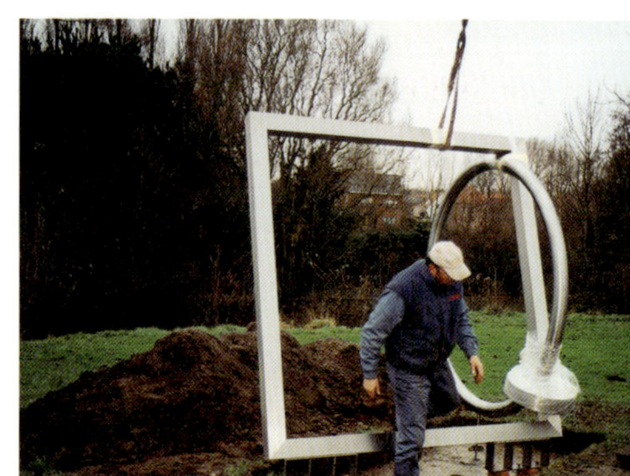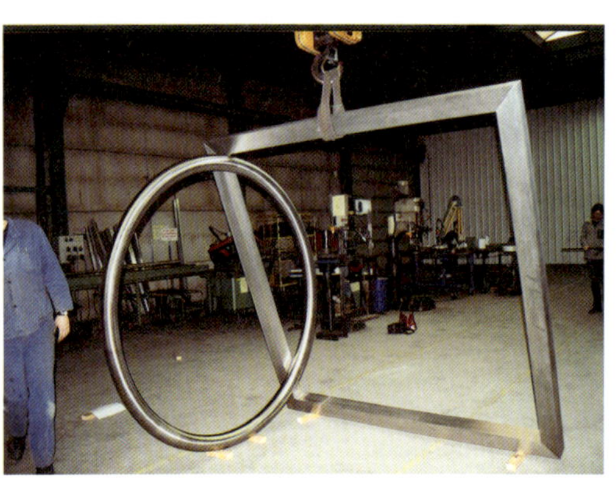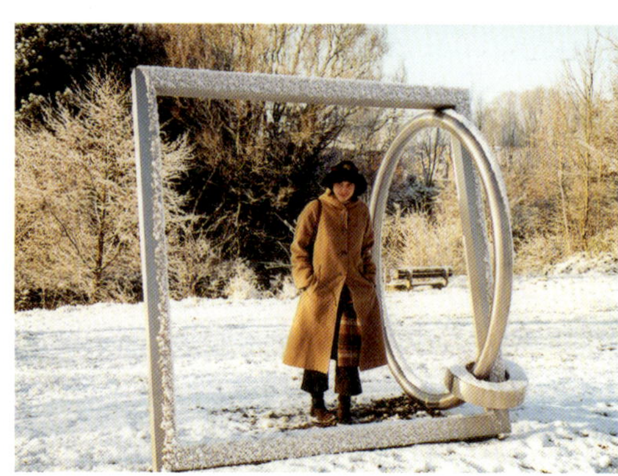

fig. 19

34

Tine Vindevogel is a jewellery designer who sometimes expands the scale of her designs. In 1999, she won the *Prize for Young Talent* (Henry van de Velde prize) awarded by the Flemish Institute for Independent Entrepreneurs (VIZO).

fig. 19   Creation the sculptural installation *Cirkel-Vierkant* [Circle-Square], 2002. Marke.

company. Entrepreneurship is a risky business. It is a never-ending struggle against uncertainty. The last thing one wants is a freewheeling artist who will rock the boat.

"A good entrepreneur stands at the midpoint between people and Figures," says Michel. "How can he motivate his staff and yet at the same time keep an eye on the financial situation? There are four 'C's' that must be respected."

A company needs a Concept which must be followed with flexibility, yet consistency. In order to implement the concept, you need Co-ordination. Coordination in turn demands Control. But there is also something known as a company Culture. The entrepreneur very clearly shapes the culture of his firm. What kind of leadership style does he pursue with his employees?

At Constructies Espeel, the approach is result-oriented. A task must be completed within a certain deadline. How the workers achieve this is up to them. There is an atmosphere of trust. Informal moments are important as they promote open communication. Cooperation is the rule, not only internally but also with the firms with which Constructies Espeel co-produces. These guidelines have been translated by Michel into a flat organisational structure, where the chain of communication to the top is short and clear. There is structure, but not too much. Employees have a free hand to fill in the blanks themselves.

Michel is a business leader. He stands at the head of an organisation, a part of society that links us and surrounds us. In this capacity, a firm has a task that transcends its purely economic nature. The outside world does not distract from work, but gives it meaning. Thus, Michel has involved his company in projects in the Third World and has collaborated with schools and the art world.

Give and you shall receive

For Julie and Michel, working with artists is a source of pleasure and personal fulfilment. But while Constructies Espeel sometimes achieves technological *tours de force*, they felt just as strongly about the rotating pedestal that the company produced for the statue of St Francis turning on its axis in the cloister garden of San Francesco della Vigna, which Honoré δ'O happily exhibited at the 1995 Venice Biennale.

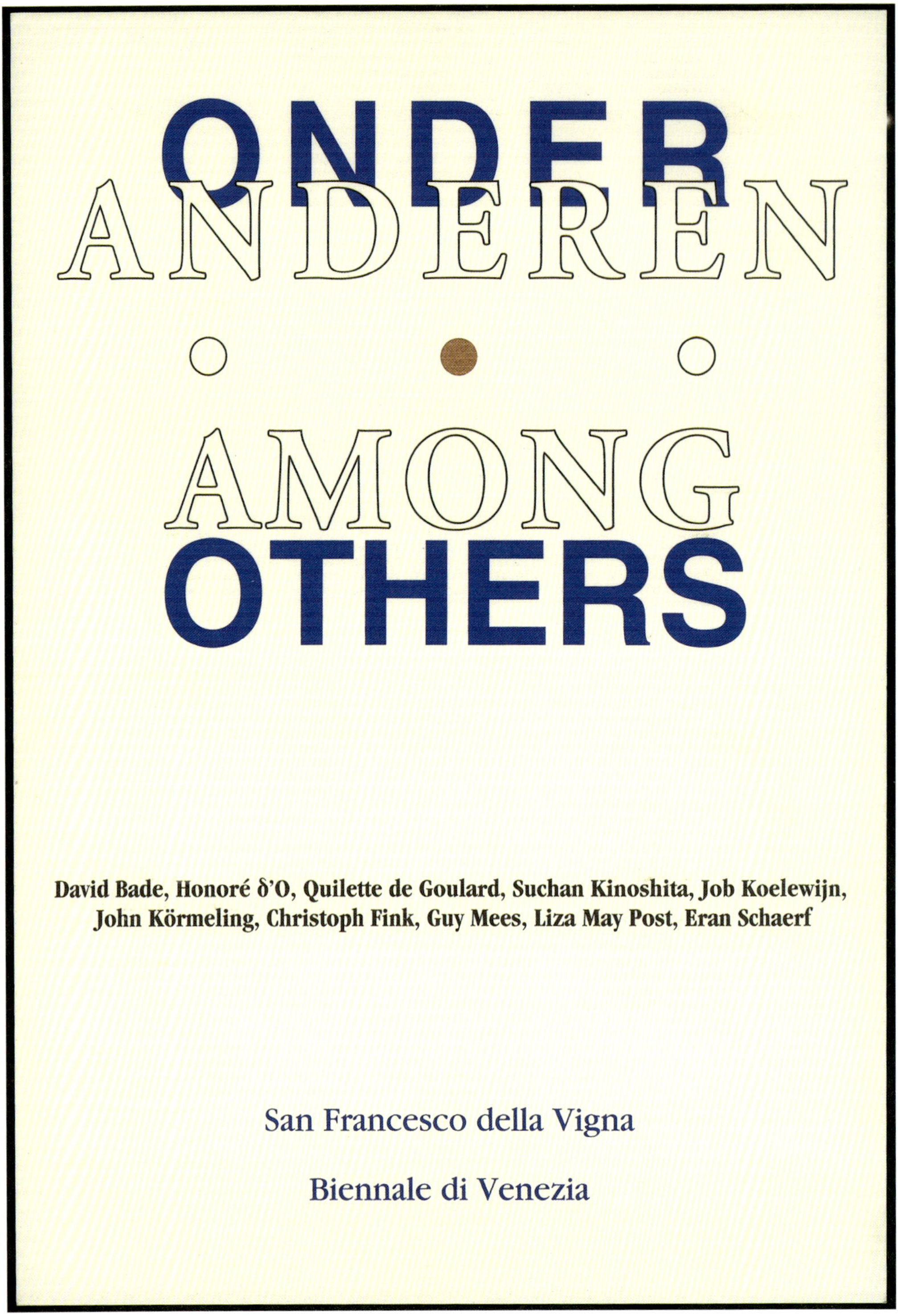

ONDER ANDEREN

AMONG OTHERS

David Bade, Honoré δ'O, Quilette de Goulard, Suchan Kinoshita, Job Koelewijn, John Körmeling, Christoph Fink, Guy Mees, Liza May Post, Eran Schaerf

San Francesco della Vigna

Biennale di Venezia

fig. 20

fig. 20 *Onder Anderen/Among Others*, a group exhibit in the Franciscan convent of *San Francisco della Vigna* (Venice) during the Venice Biennale, 1995. Curator, Bart De Baere.

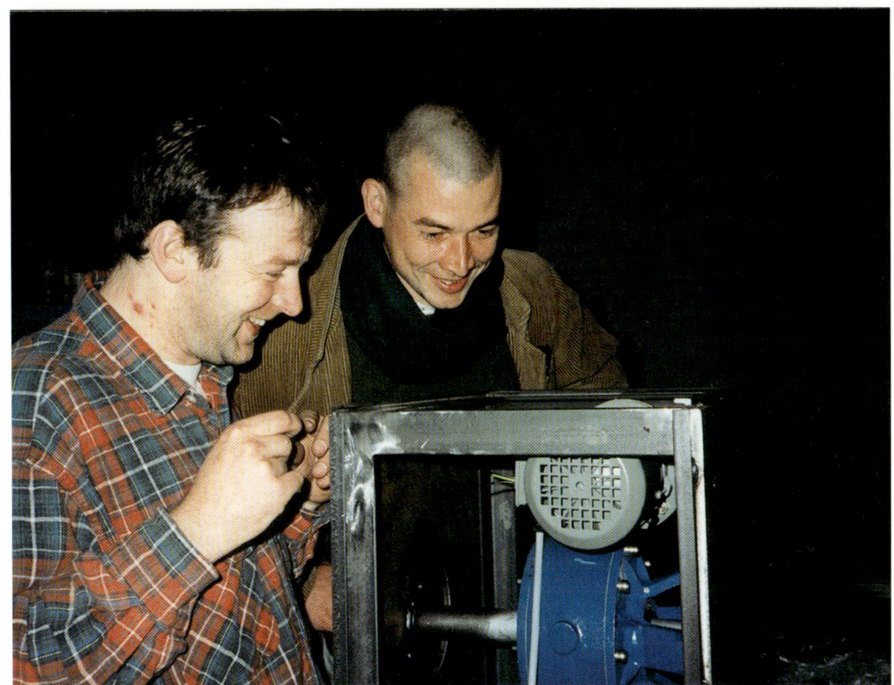

fig. 21

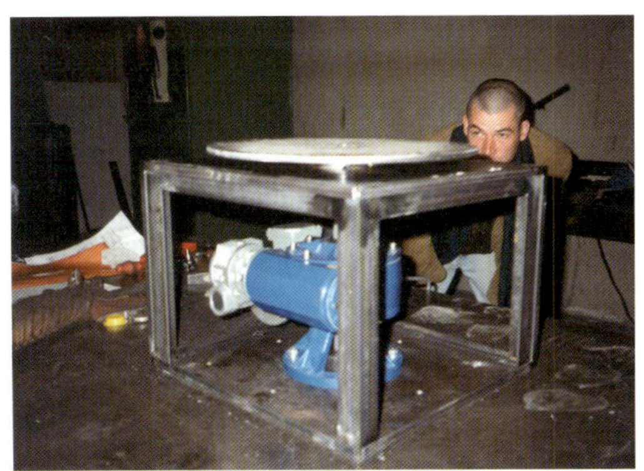

fig. 22

figs. 21, 22, 25   A few weeks before *Among Others* opened, Honoré δ'O called on Michel. He was fascinated by an idea: in the inner courtyard of the convent there was a statue of St Francis. For the duration of the exhibit, he wanted to create a diversion, and have the statue rotate on its axis so that it could take in the whole 360° of the garden. Persuading the friars was no problem, but how could this be done from a technical point of view? An employee at Constructies Espeel put together the motor, and Honoré went off to Venice with a large "cookie box" under his arm. At the convent, the motor was mounted on the pedestal and St Francis was set in motion.

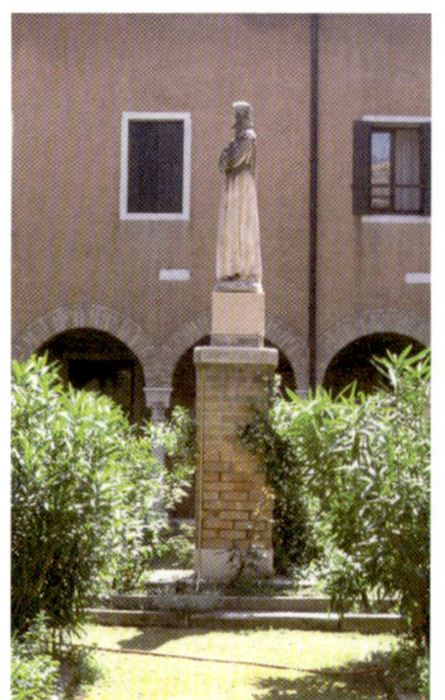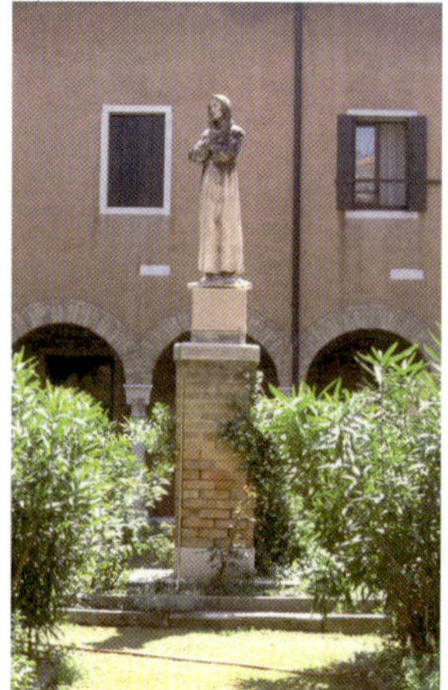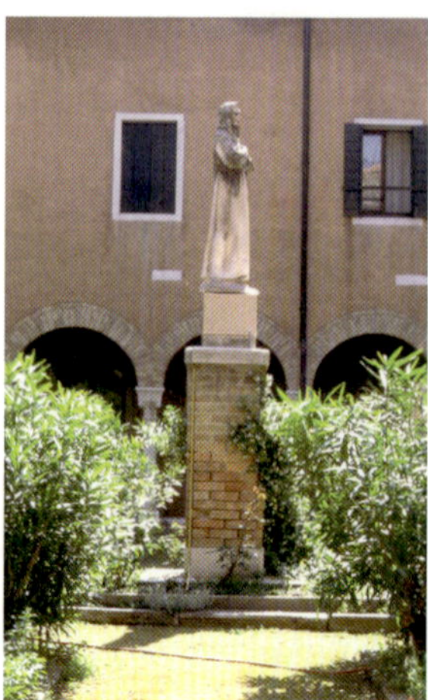

fig. 24

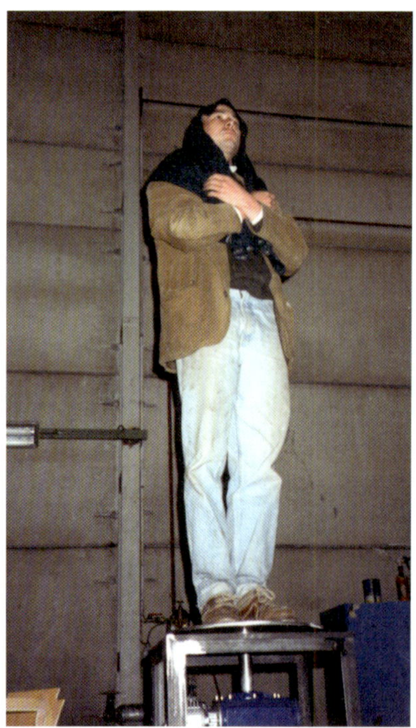

fig. 25

38

fig. 24   Honoré δ'O, *St Francis*, Among
Others, 1995. Photo: Honoré δ'O.
fig. 26   Honoré δ'O, *St Francis*, Among
Others, 1995. Photo: Honoré δ'O.

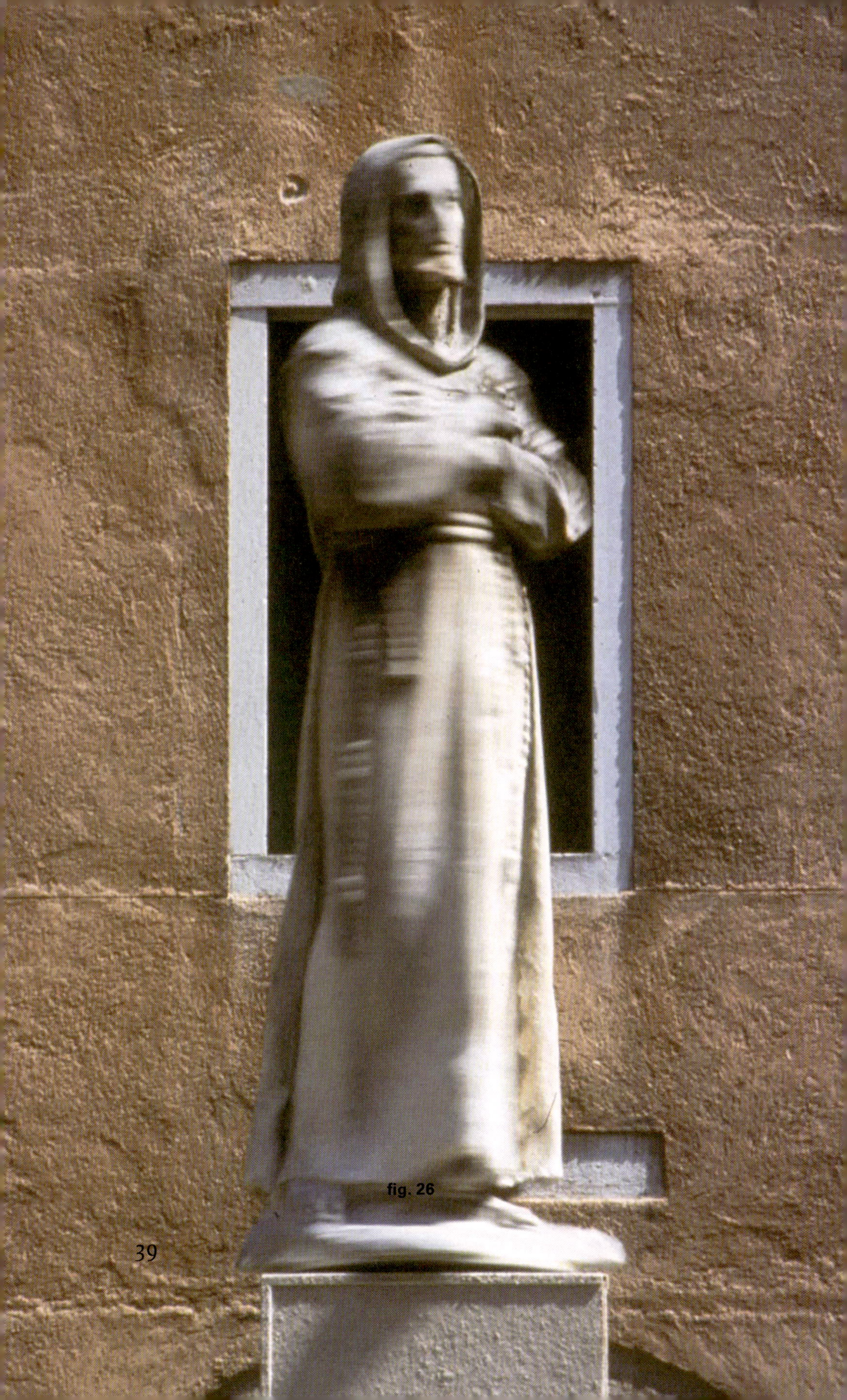

fig. 26

39

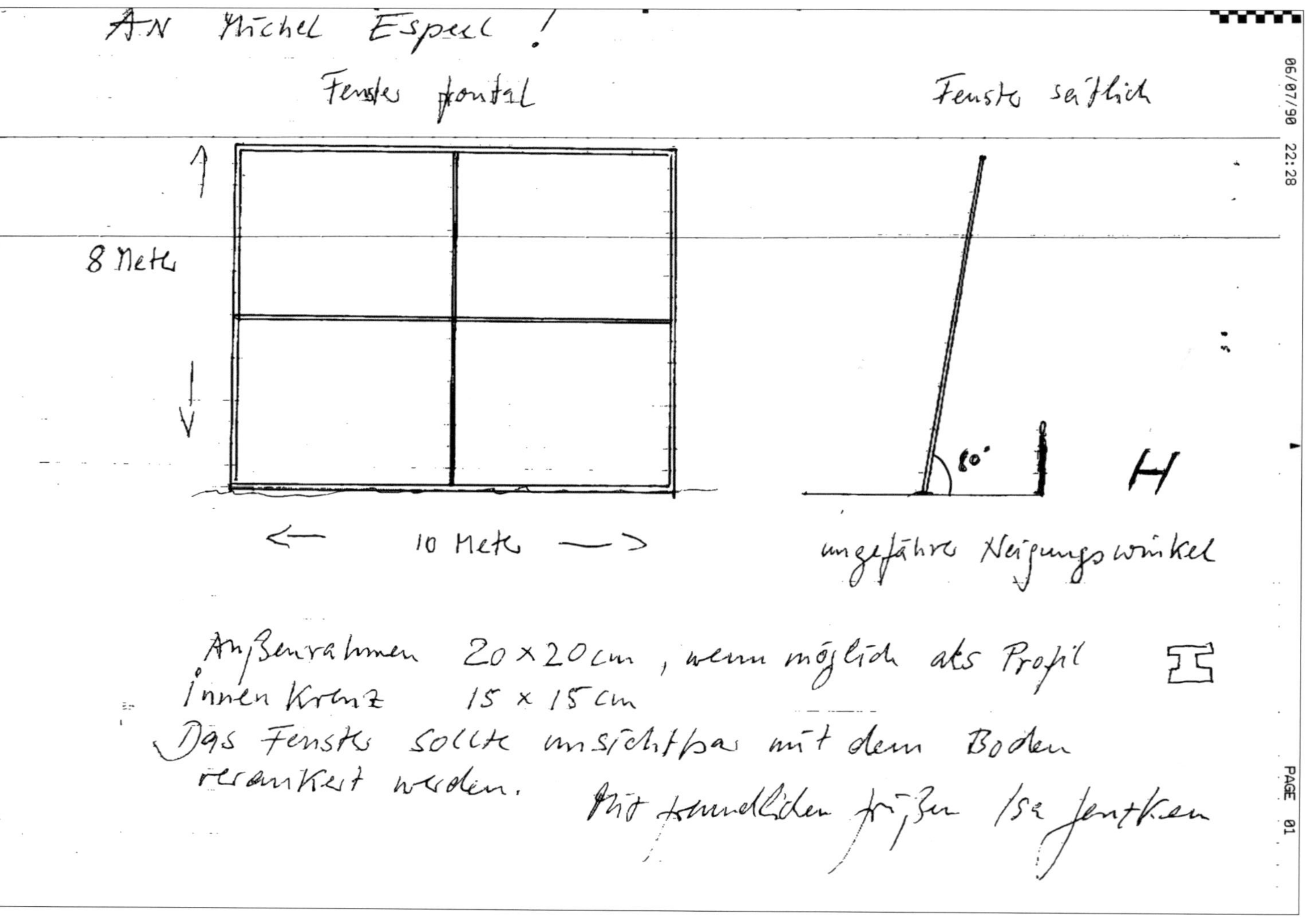

fig. 27

40

fig. 27   Design for *Das Fenster* [The Window] by Isa Genzken, 1996. Based solely on this design, the employees of Constructies Espeel created this 4-ton stainless steel window.

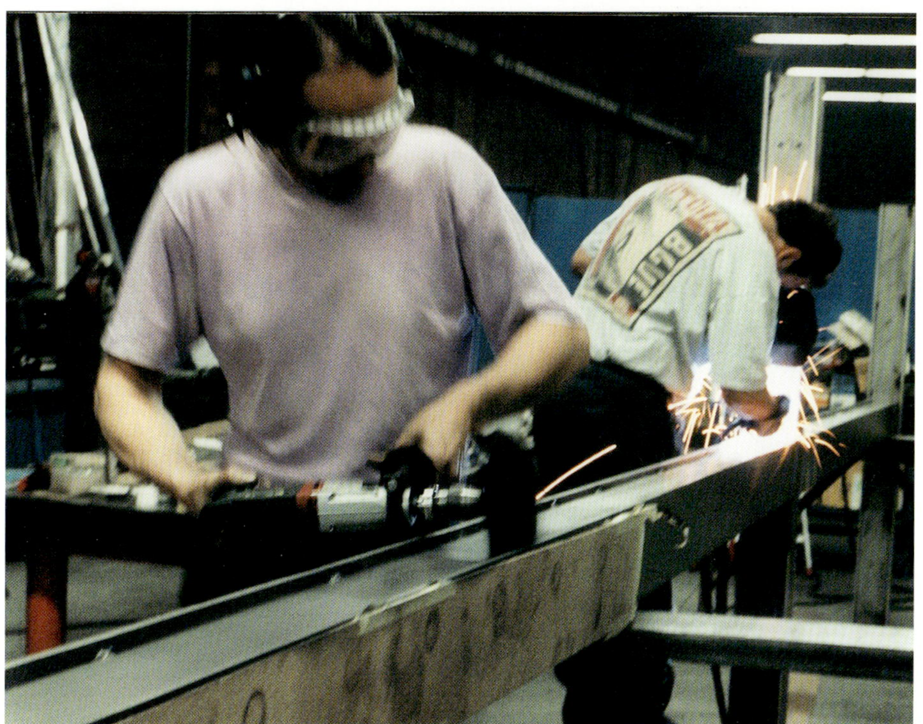

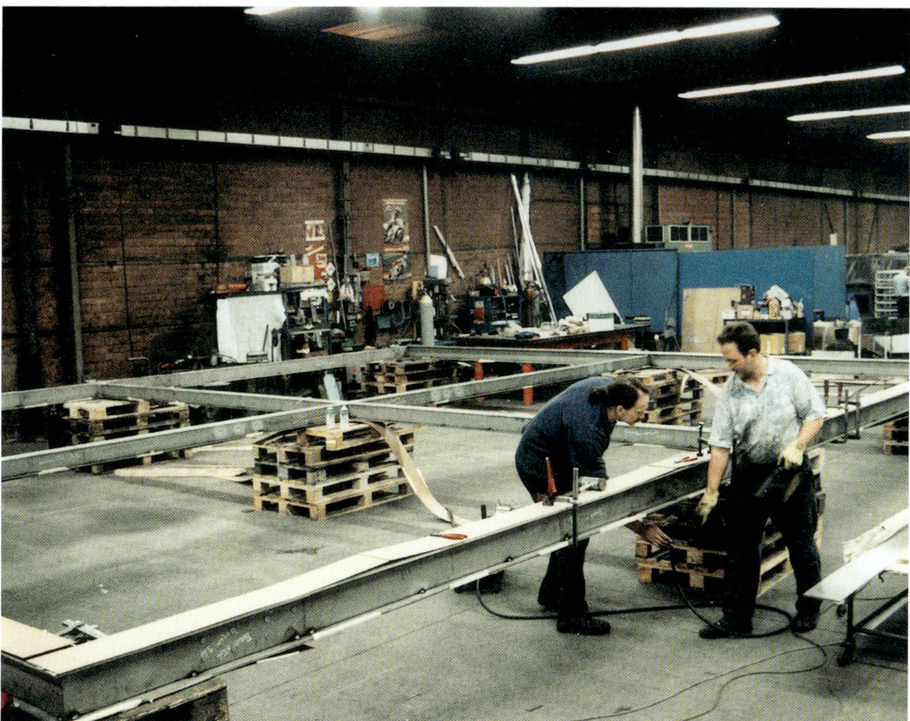

fig. 28

fig. 28   Isa Genzken, creation of *Das Fenster*, 1996.

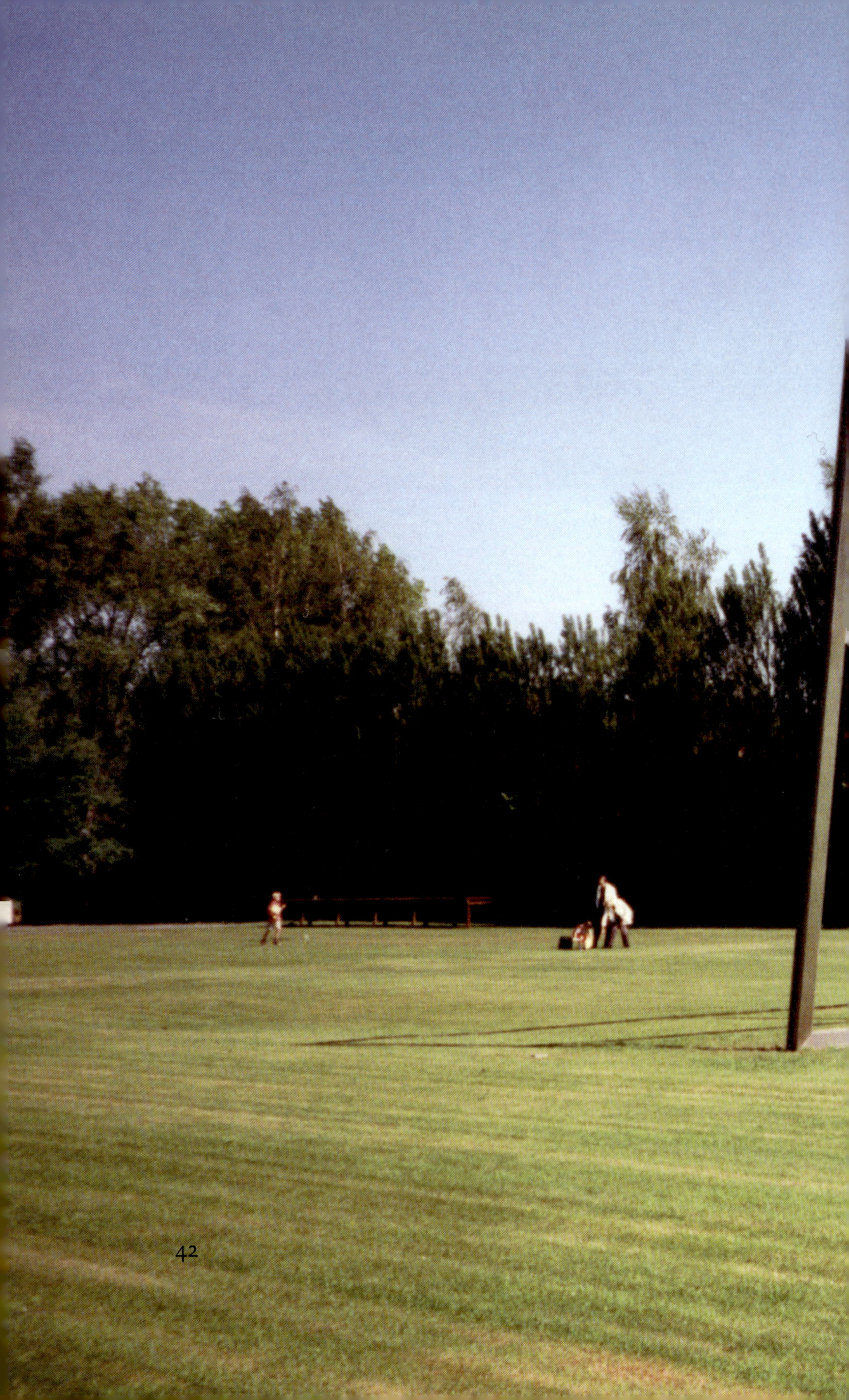

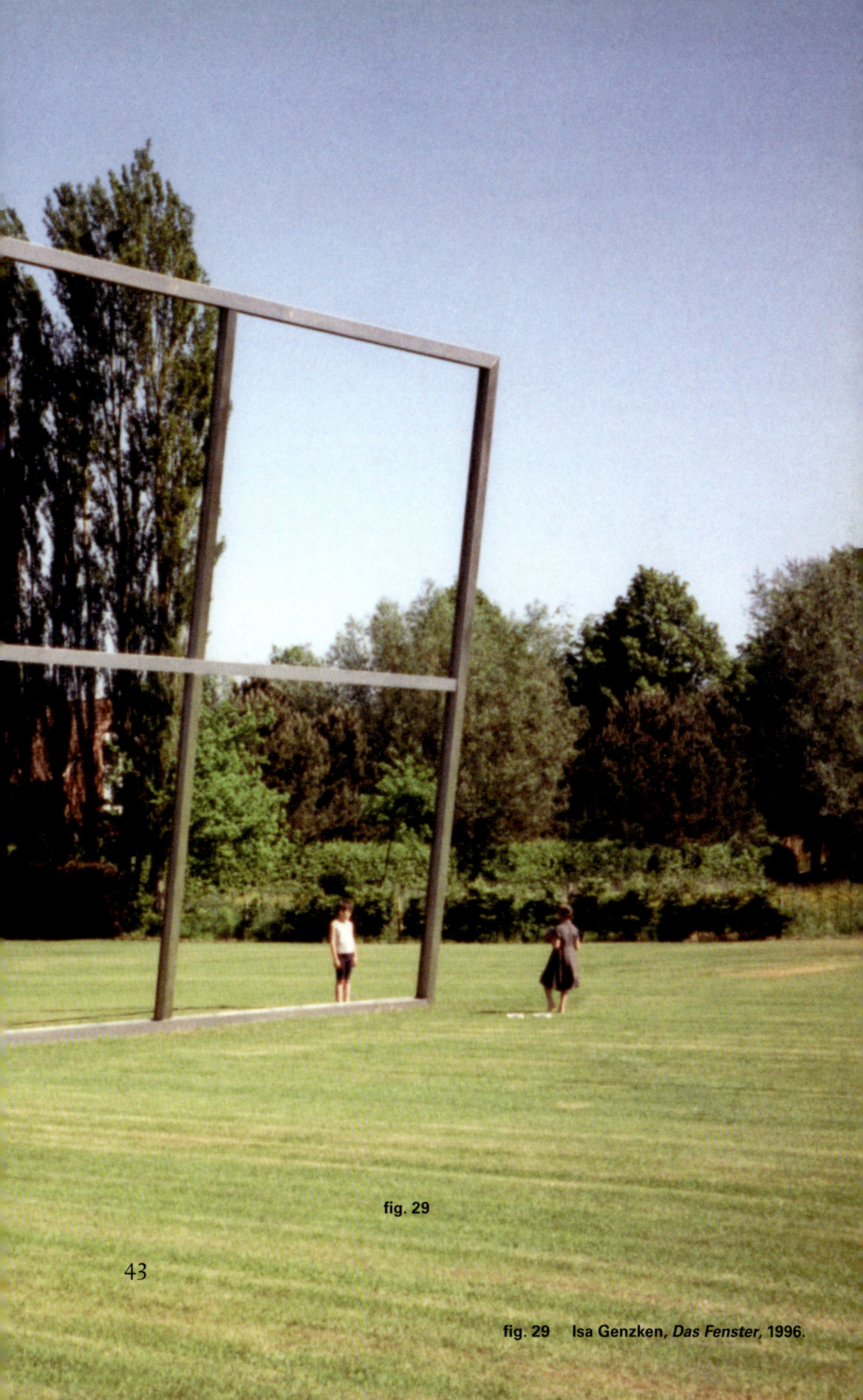

fig. 29

43

fig. 29   Isa Genzken, *Das Fenster*, 1996.

What would perhaps be considered as child's play for an engineer, but fascinated Julie and Michel, were the symbolic changes that a simple motor could set in motion.

A new stage in the travel story was soon to come about. Besides the spontaneous collaboration with artists, Julie decided to organise a series of artistic events at the company. Whenever a journey finds a destination, the pace picks up rapidly.

Part III

Begins with Noodingang [emergency entrance], Heavy Metal and Touch Me, then leads the birth of Arteconomy and ends with a celebration.

From art to Julie, Julie to Michel, Michel to Constructies Espeel and from Constructies Espeel to Julie. This is the point we have reached. Julie was motivated by what was going on at the company: Constructies Espeel was doing something for artists. Why not go a step further? Allow artists to do something for Constructies Espeel? Let us invite the art world explicitly into the company to do its thing. Between 1998 and 2001, three steps were taken towards this goal.

First step: *Noodingang* [Emergency Entrance]
(16 January – 22 February 1998)[2]

Among the visual artists who had worked with Constructies Espeel, the Magnum photographer, Carl De Keyzer, made a series of portraits at the company. One day, these photos were to be exhibited at the De Spil cultural centre in Roeselare. Along with them were some artworks in metal that had been produced at Constructies Espeel. The idea was to set these up in the exhibition rooms at De Spil, but the artists declared that the site was 'unliveable' and no one found the areas attractive. Honoré δ'O declared: "We can't stay in this place," and went in search of an 'emergency entrance'. He proposed that the rooms in question be evacuated and exhibited completely empty, and that the building itself be treated as a site. The arts caravan used this emergency plan, and took refuge in the foyer of De Spil. A green neon light by Honoré δ'O, a visual

44

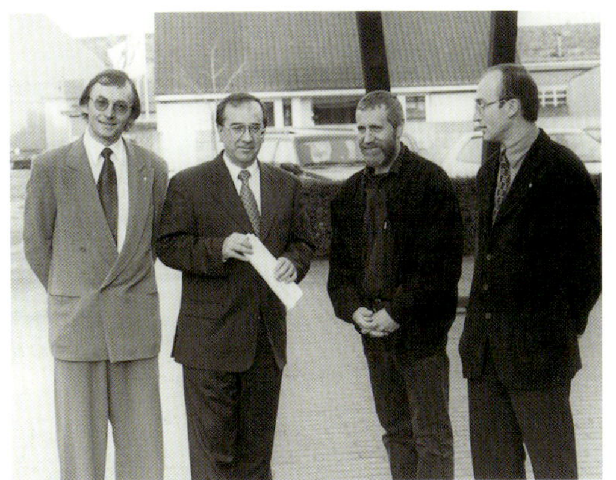

fig. 30

fig. 30   Minister Luc Martens visits Constructies Espeel in 1996. The company's collaboration with artists is made public for the first time. During the meeting, the idea arises of organising an exhibition in the Roeselare cultural centre De Spil, displaying new work created by artists at Espeel. In the run-up to Noodingang (1998), photographer Carl De Keyzer was commissioned to create a visual record of this collaboration. Seen in this photograph: Michel Espeel, Minister of Culture Luc Martens, Paul Gees and Luc Espeel.

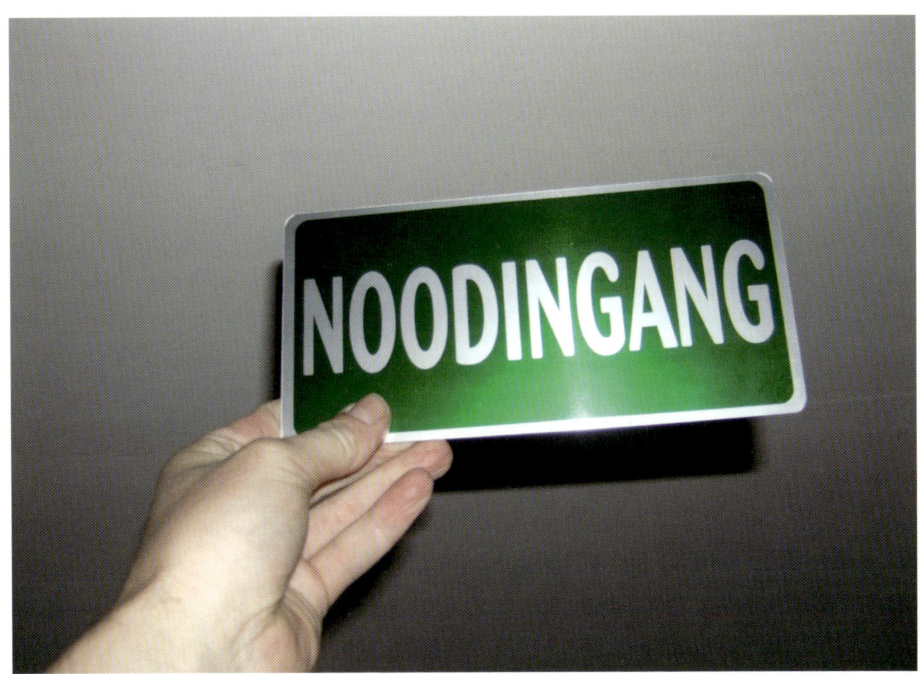

fig. 31

45

fig. 31   Invitation and raffle ticket with which the work entitled *Metalen reis naar de hemel* [Metal journey towards heaven] was raffled off at the opening. Design by Honoré δ'O.

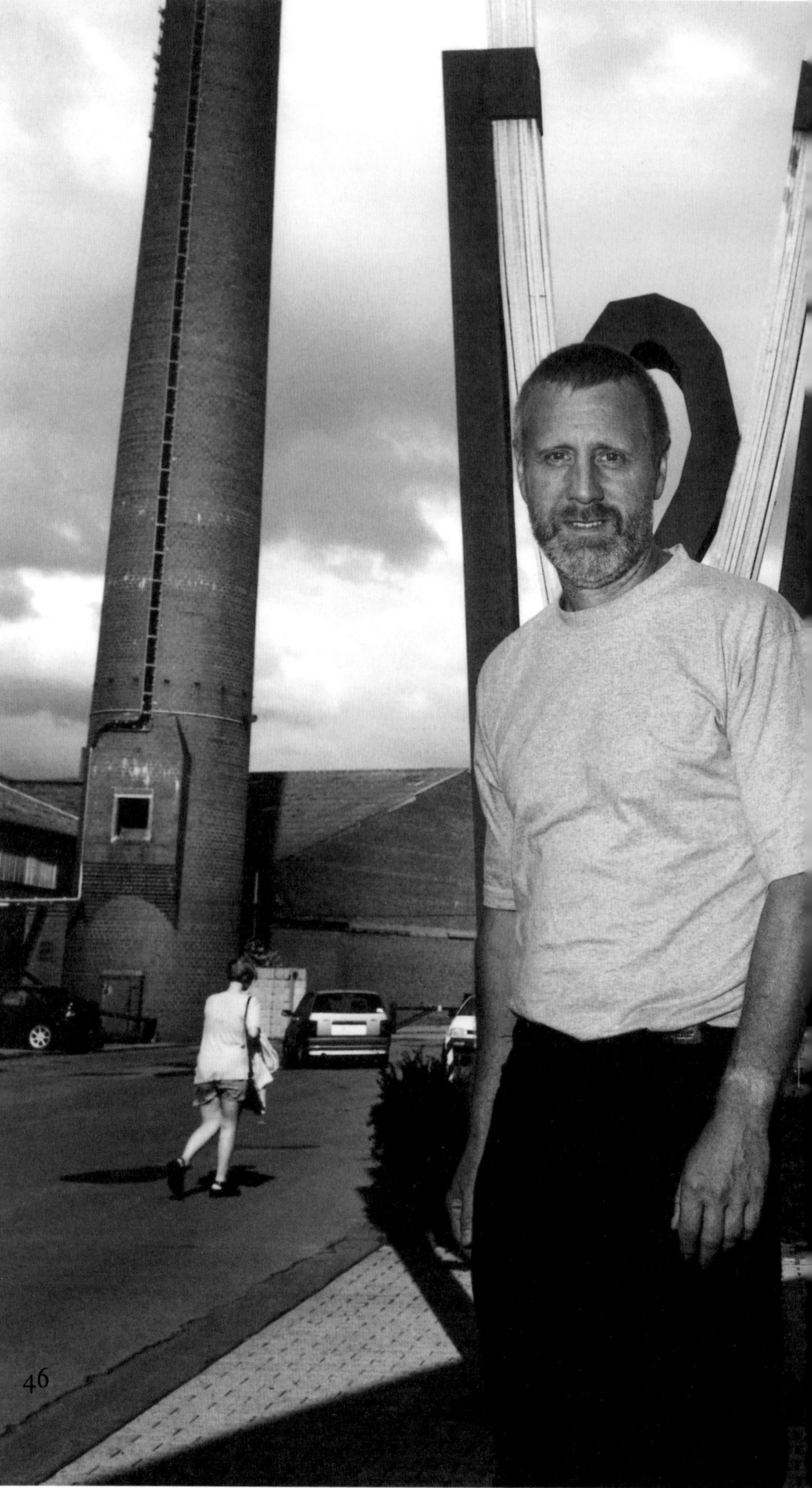

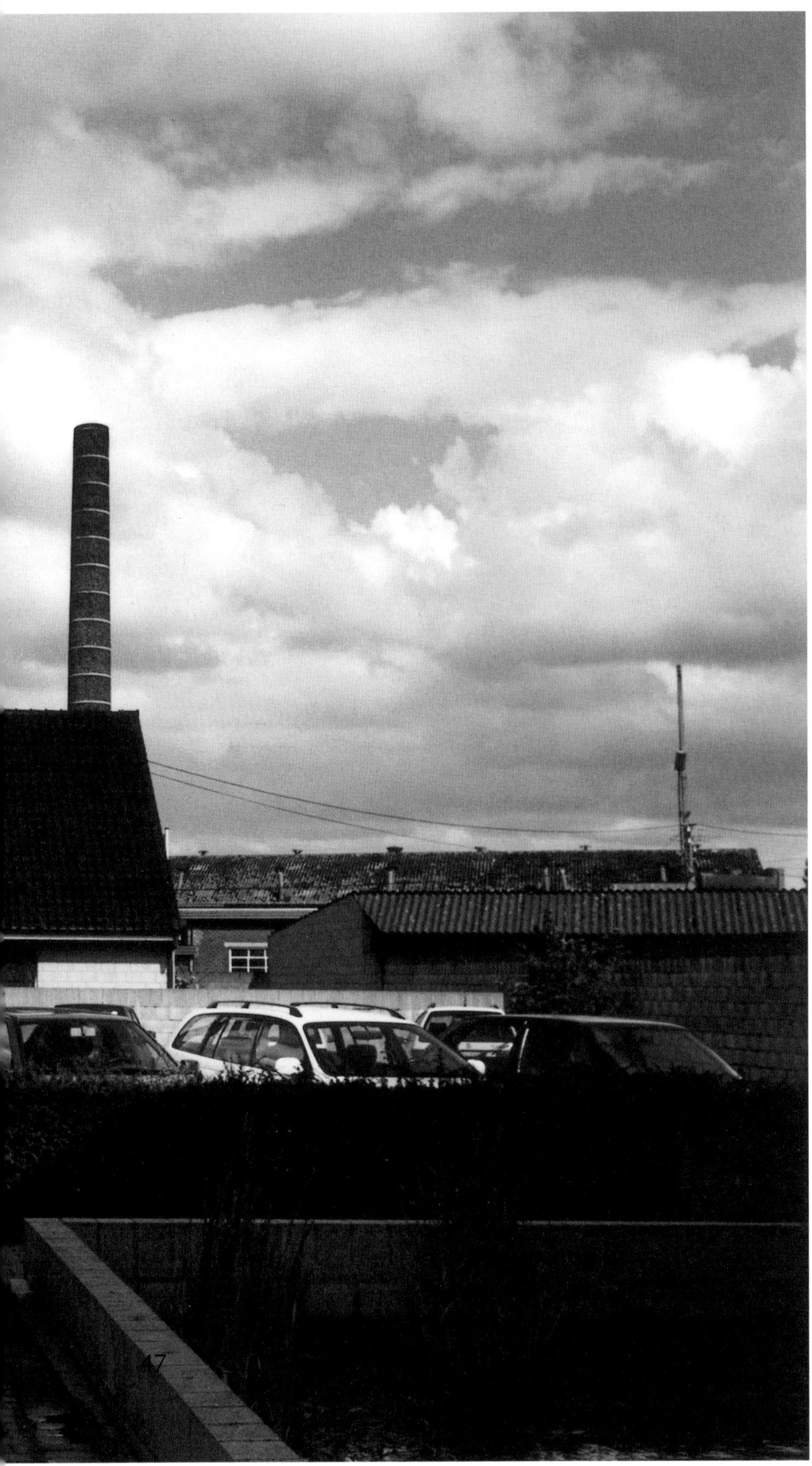

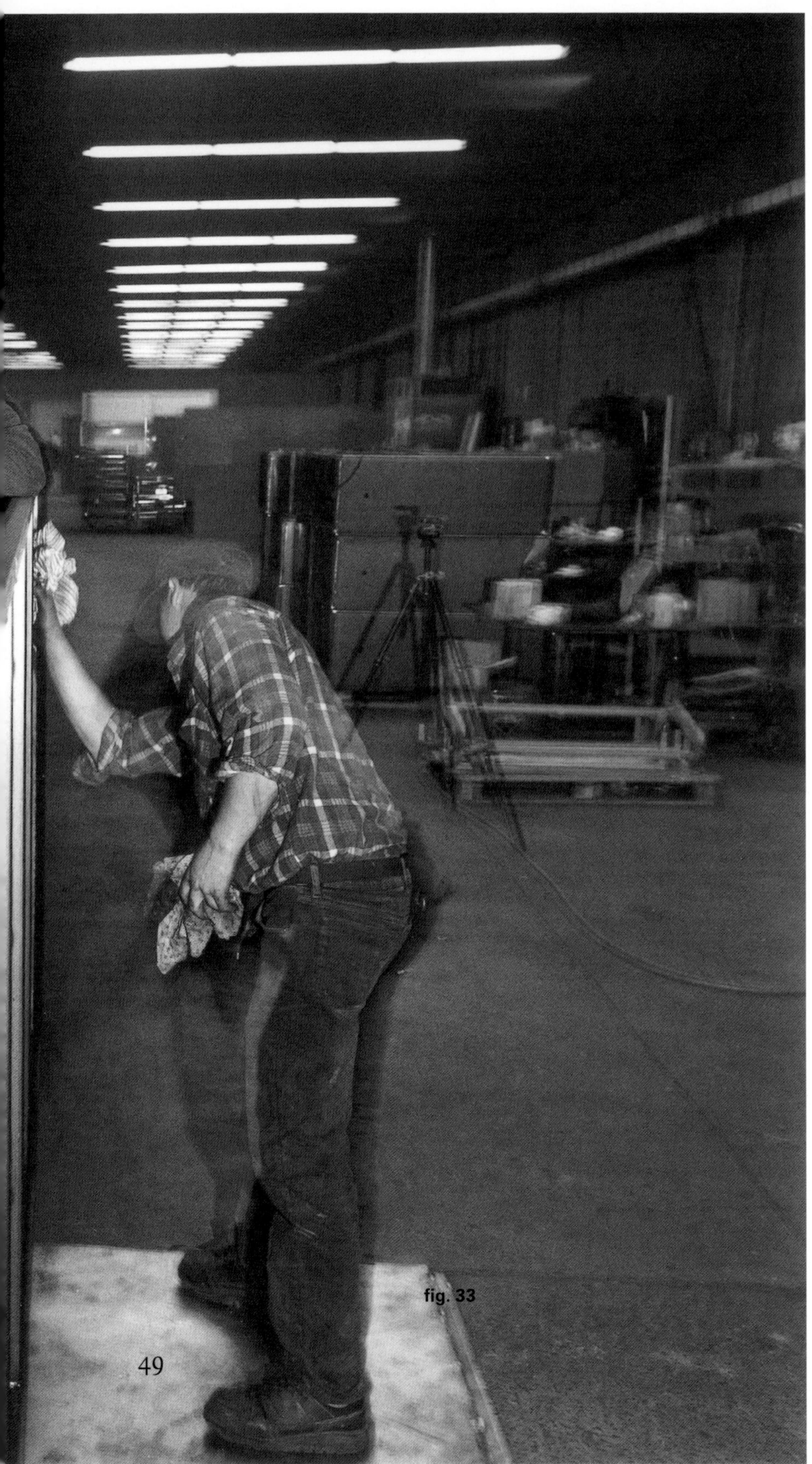

fig. 33

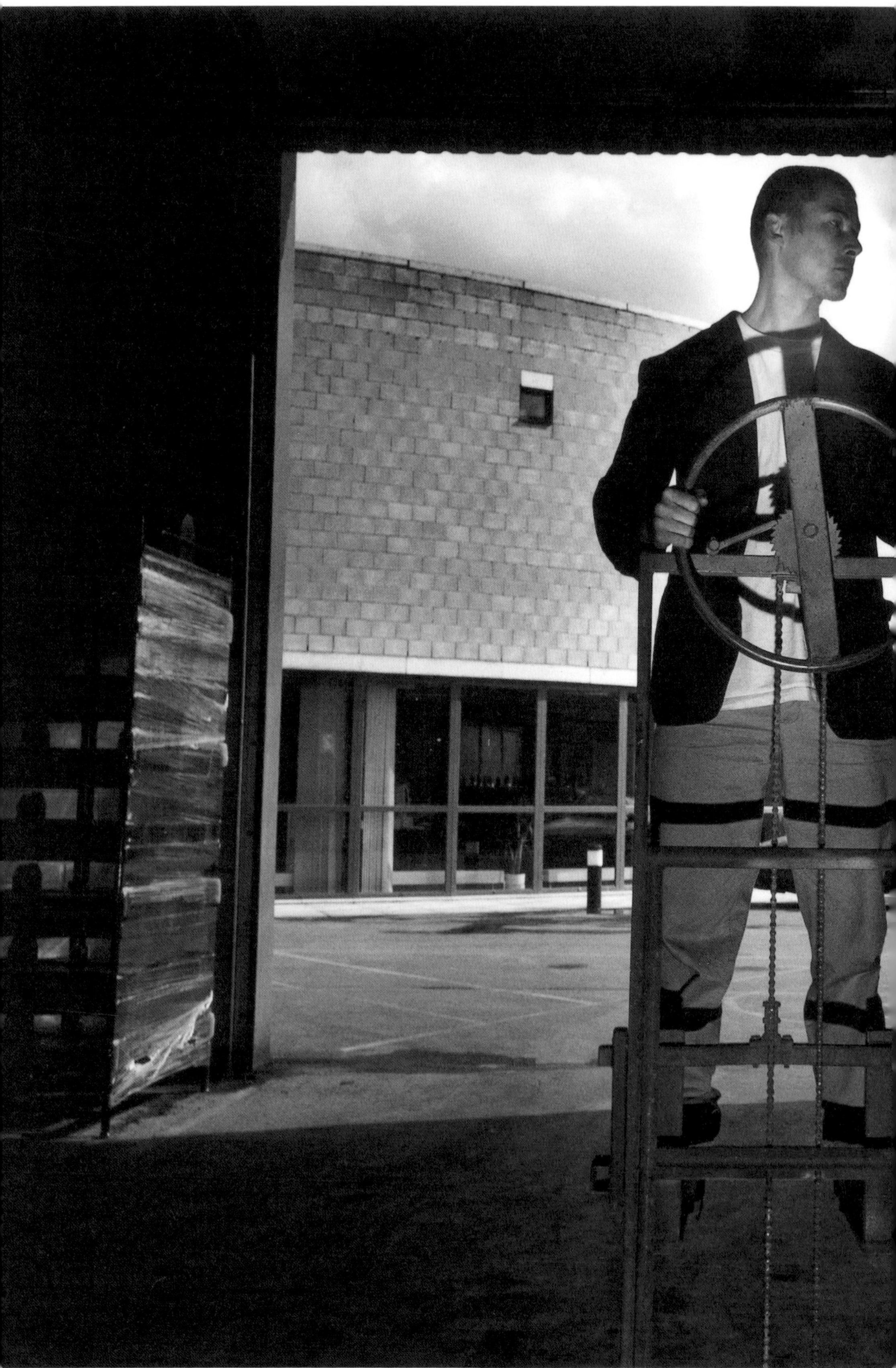

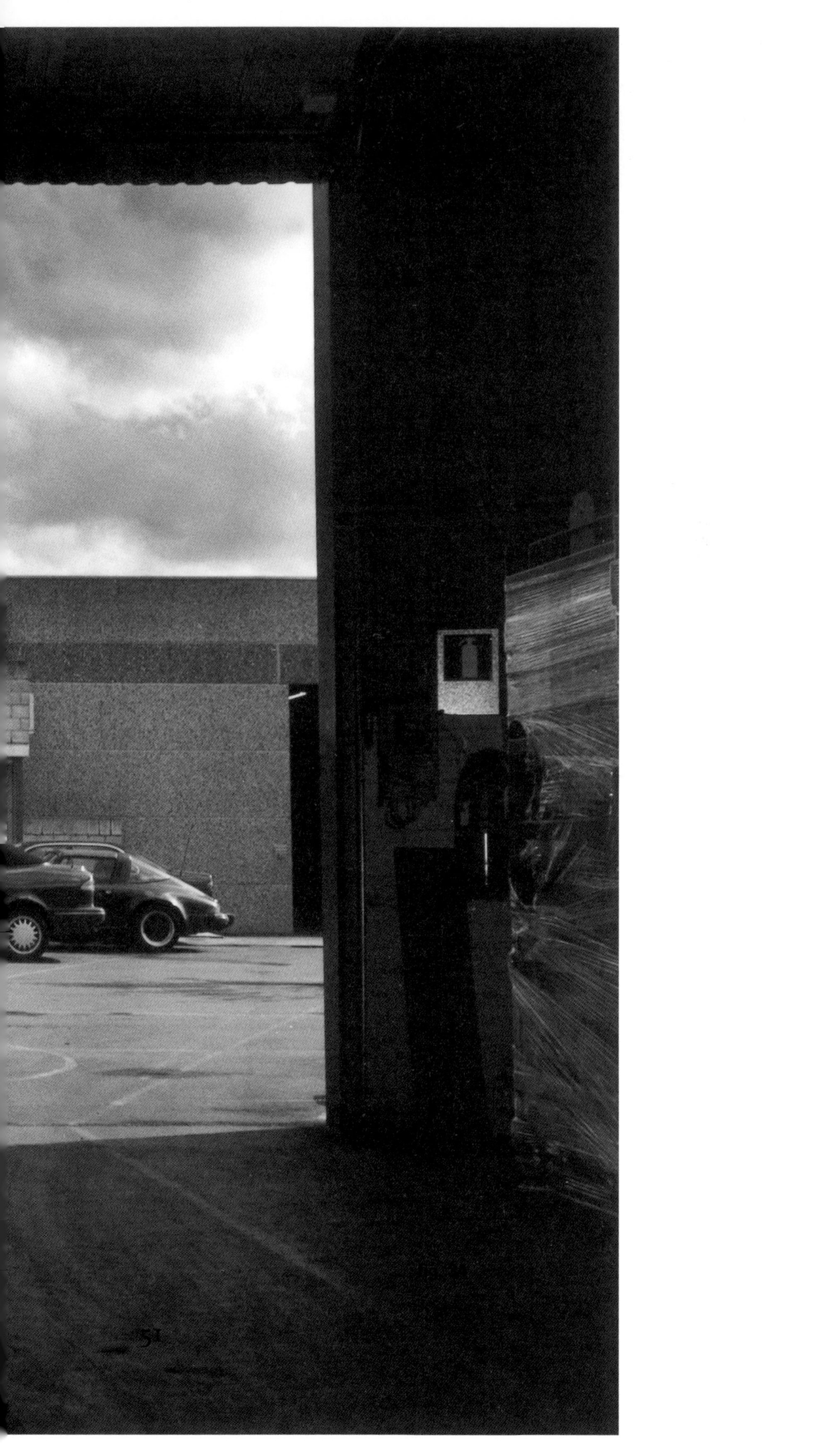

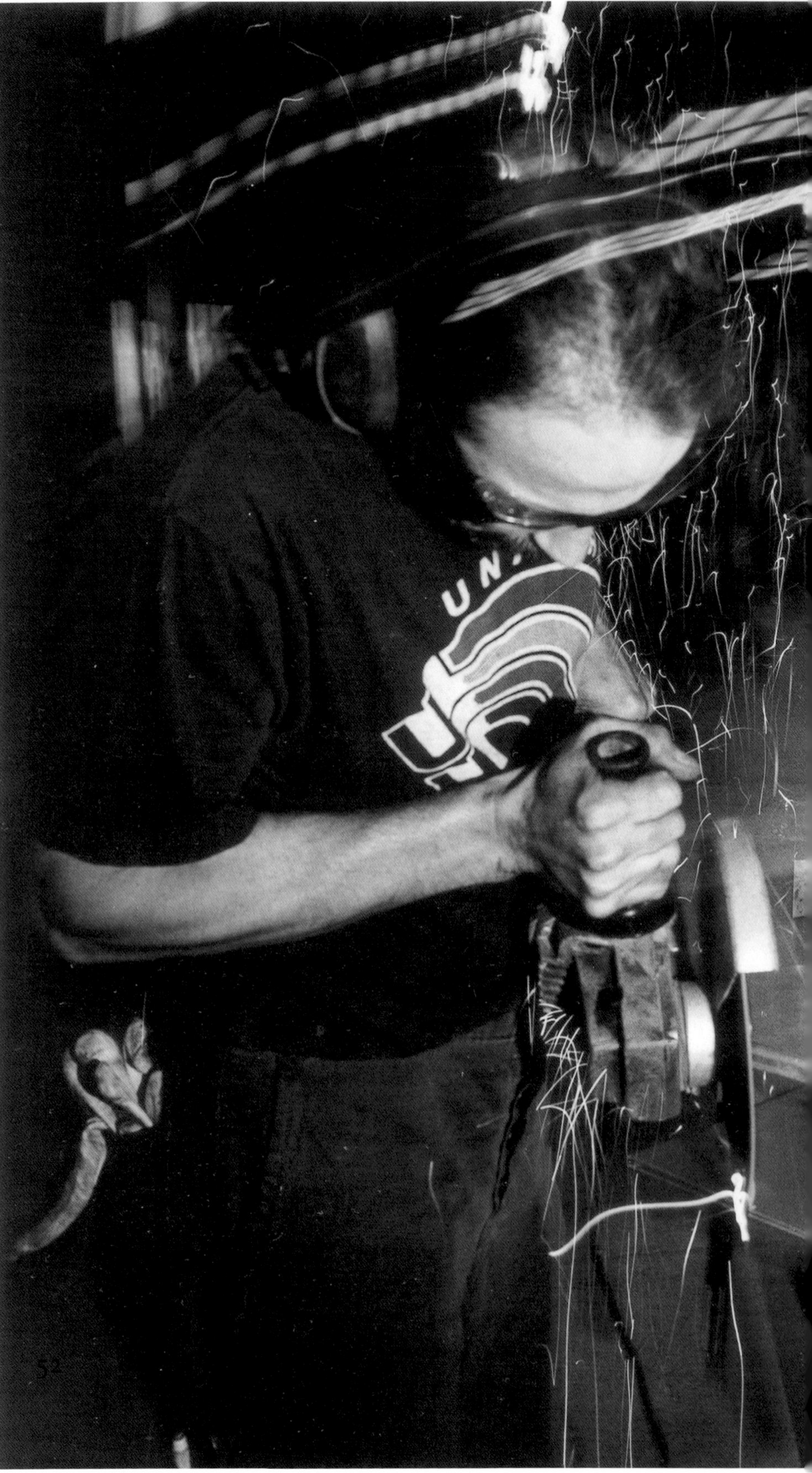

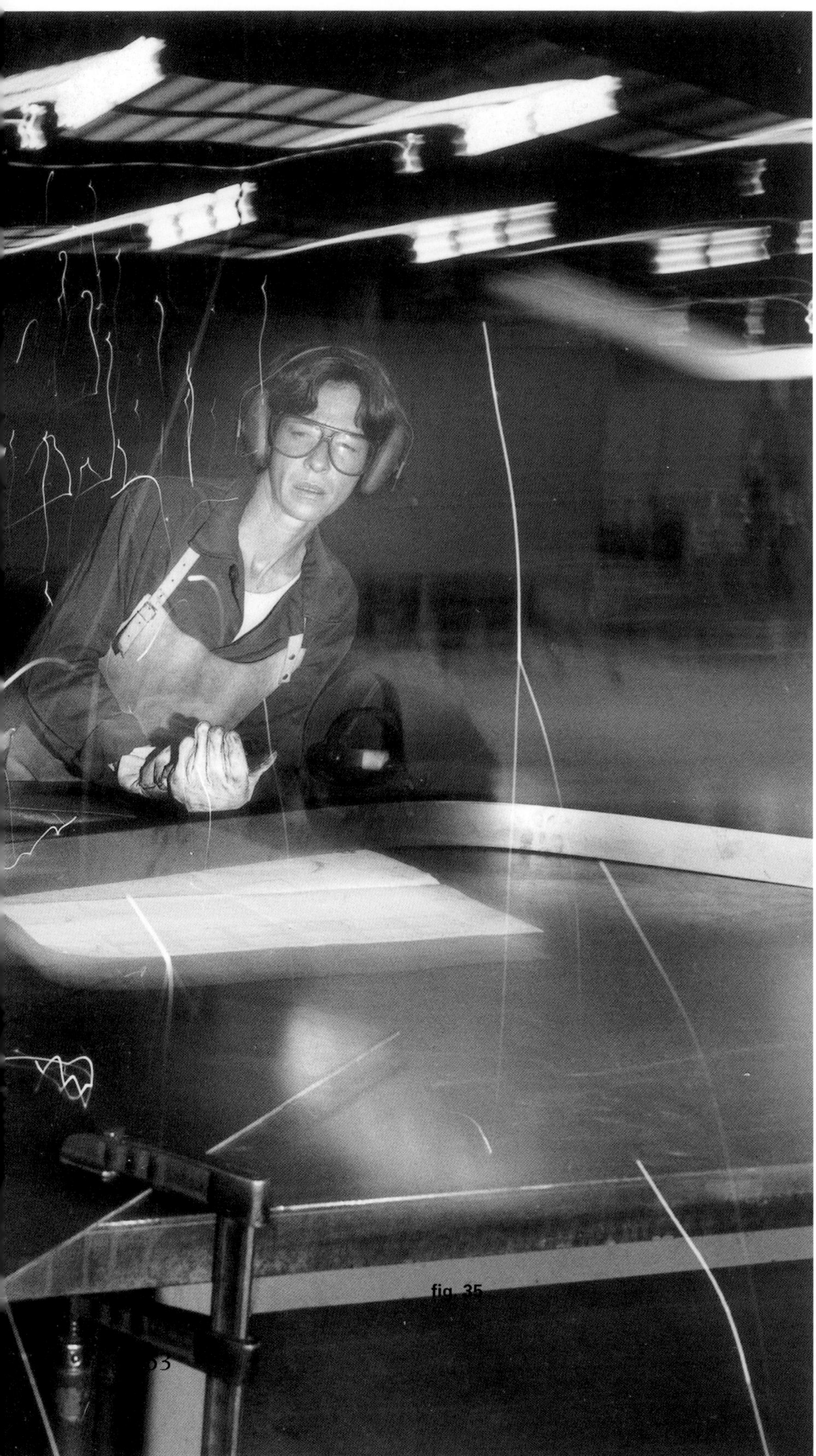

fig. 35

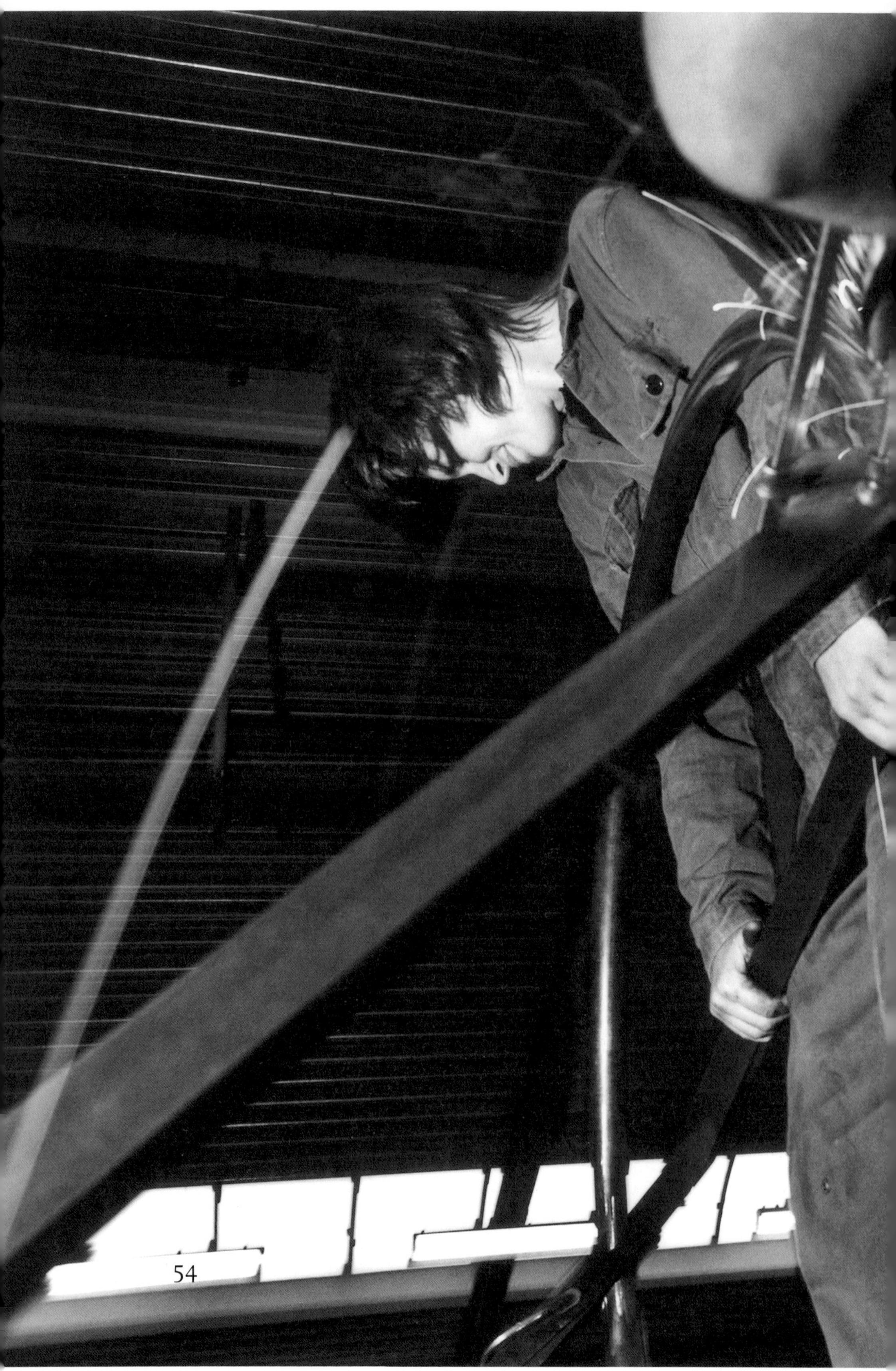

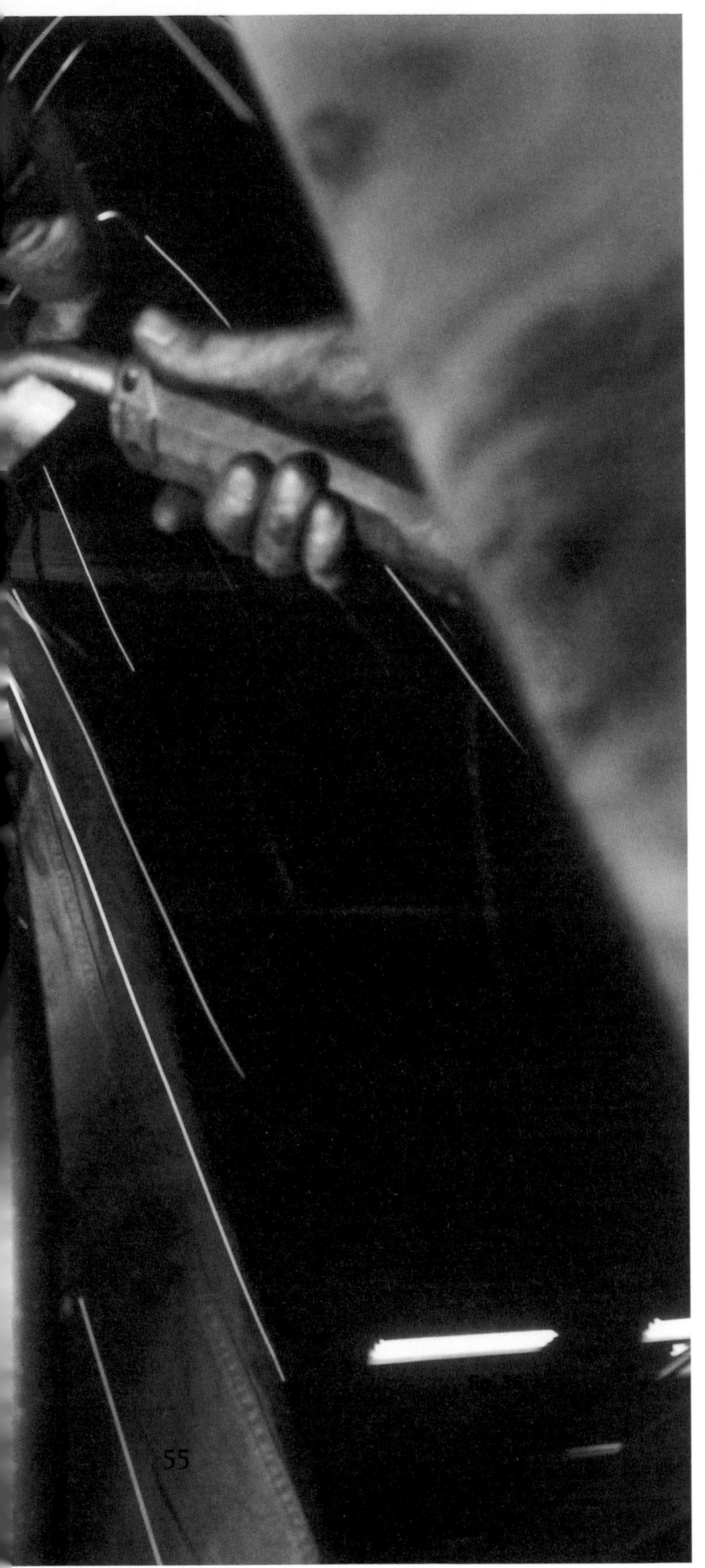

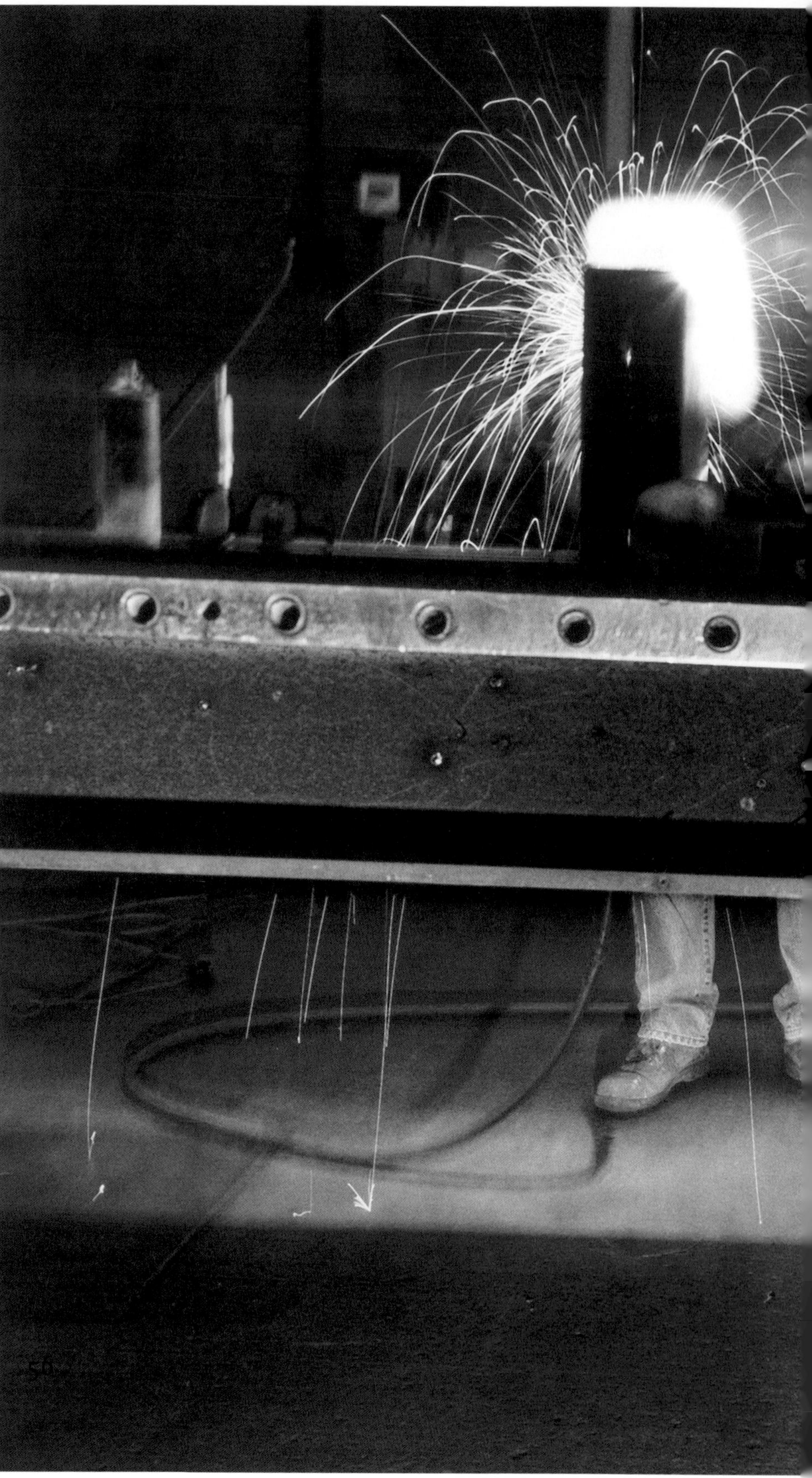

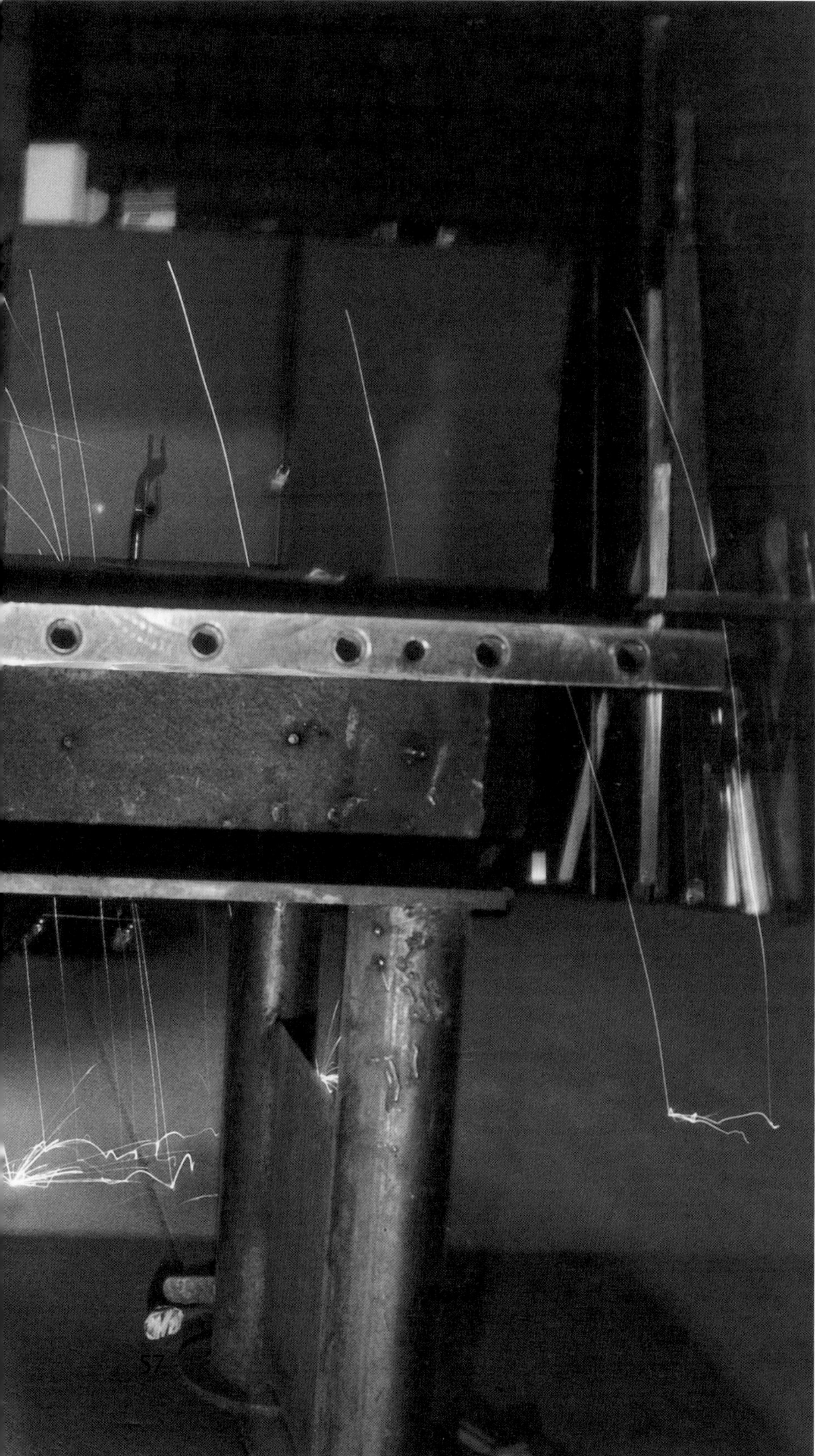

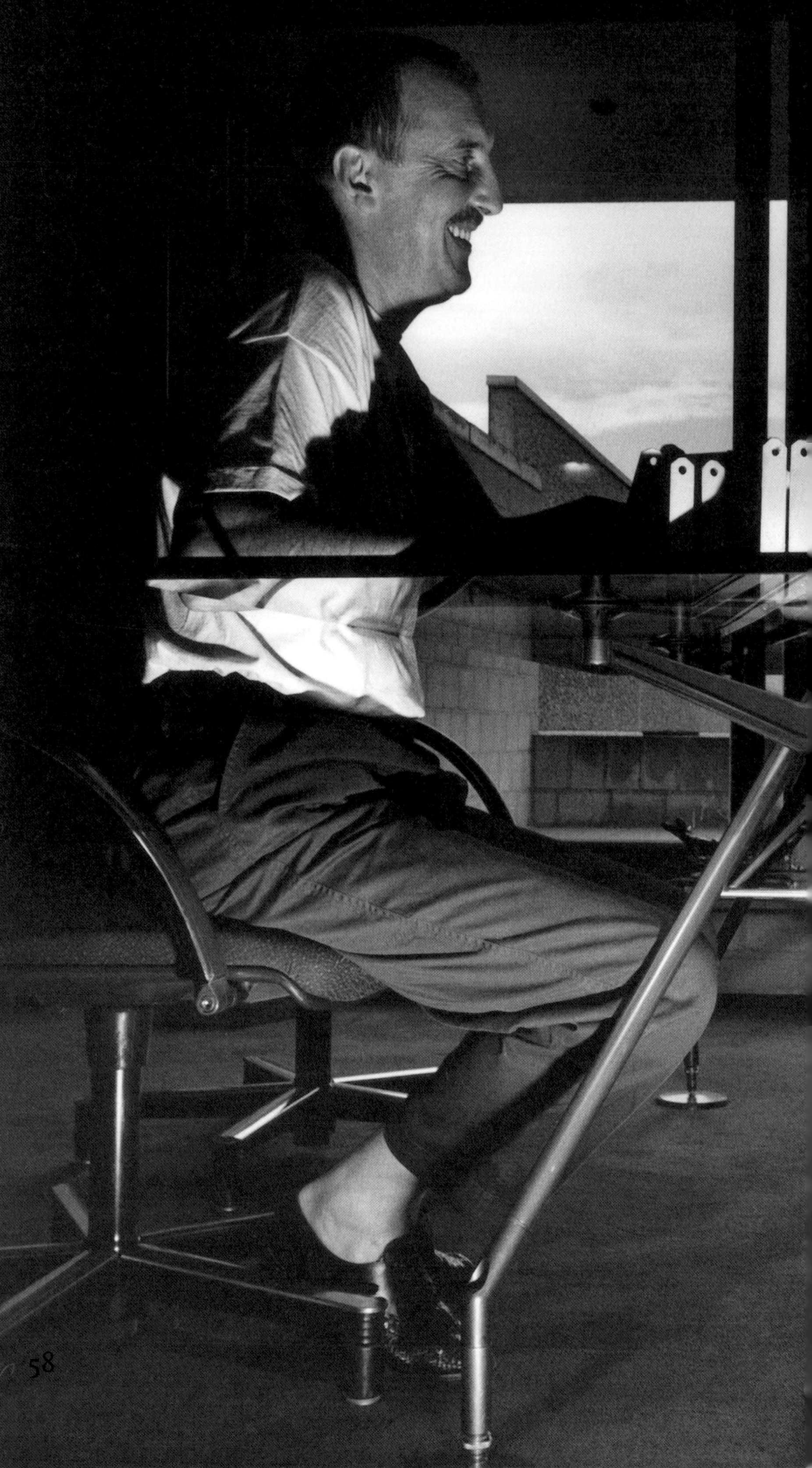

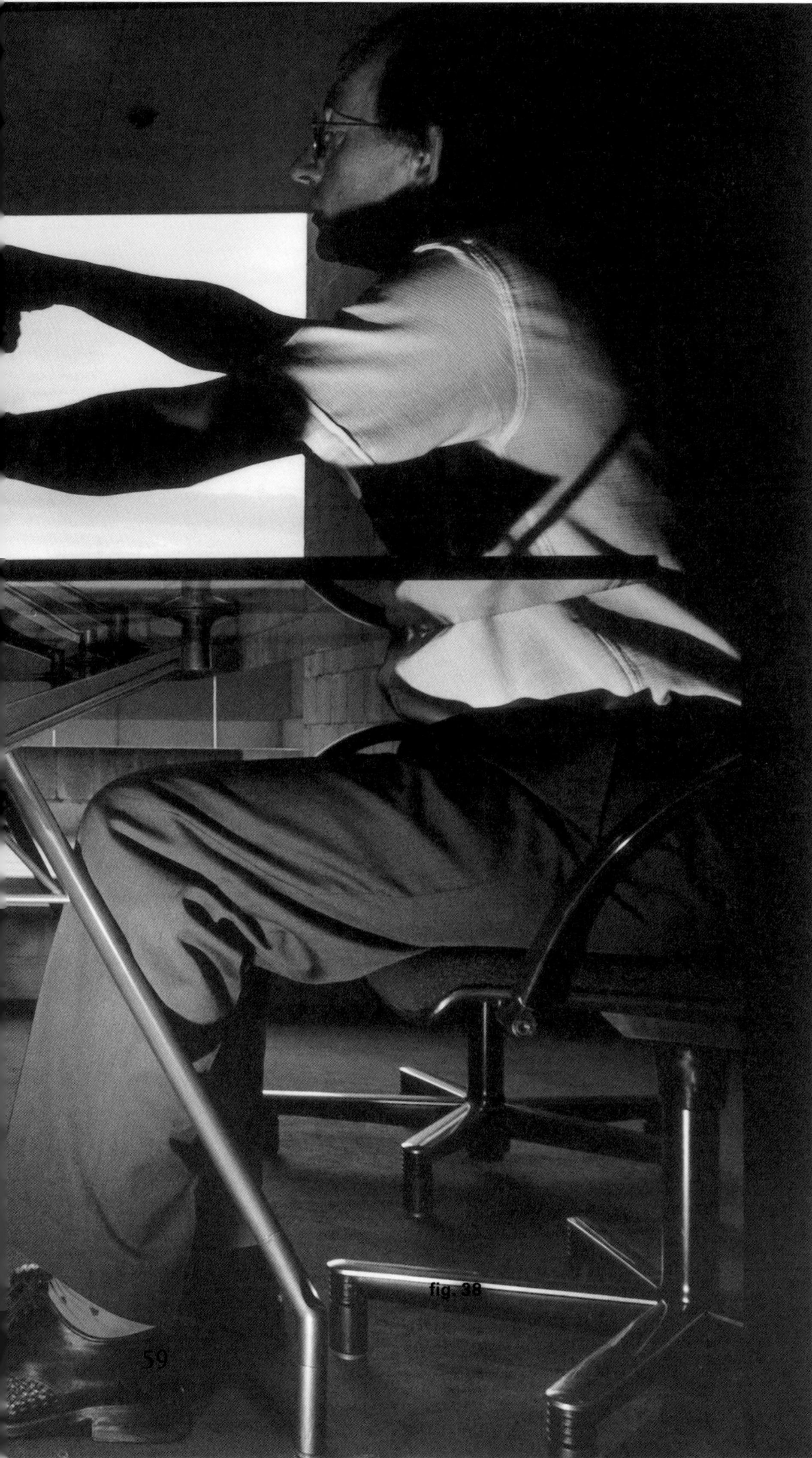

fig. 38

59

Series of portraits by Carl De Keyzer

During *Noodingang*, the exhibition space of *De Spil* remained empty. Leaving them bare showed that it was impossible to exhibit the works there. As an alternative each artist created his own 'emergency entrance', a space framed by his artwork. All the works have a metal element that was made at Constructies Espeel, as Carl De Keyzer's photos attest.

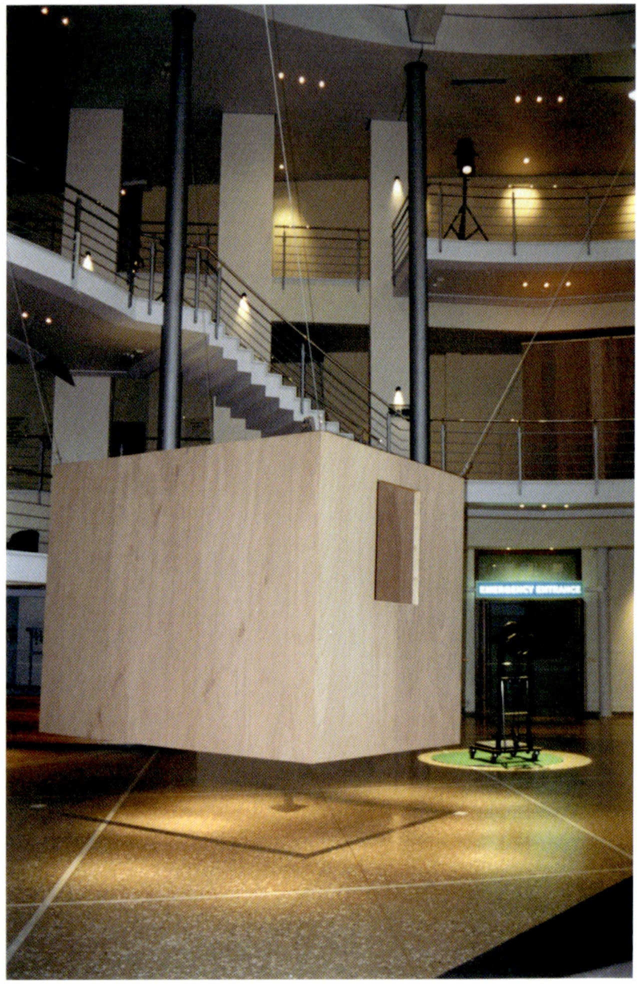

fig. 39

60

fig. 39   Paul Gees, *Untitled*, 1998.

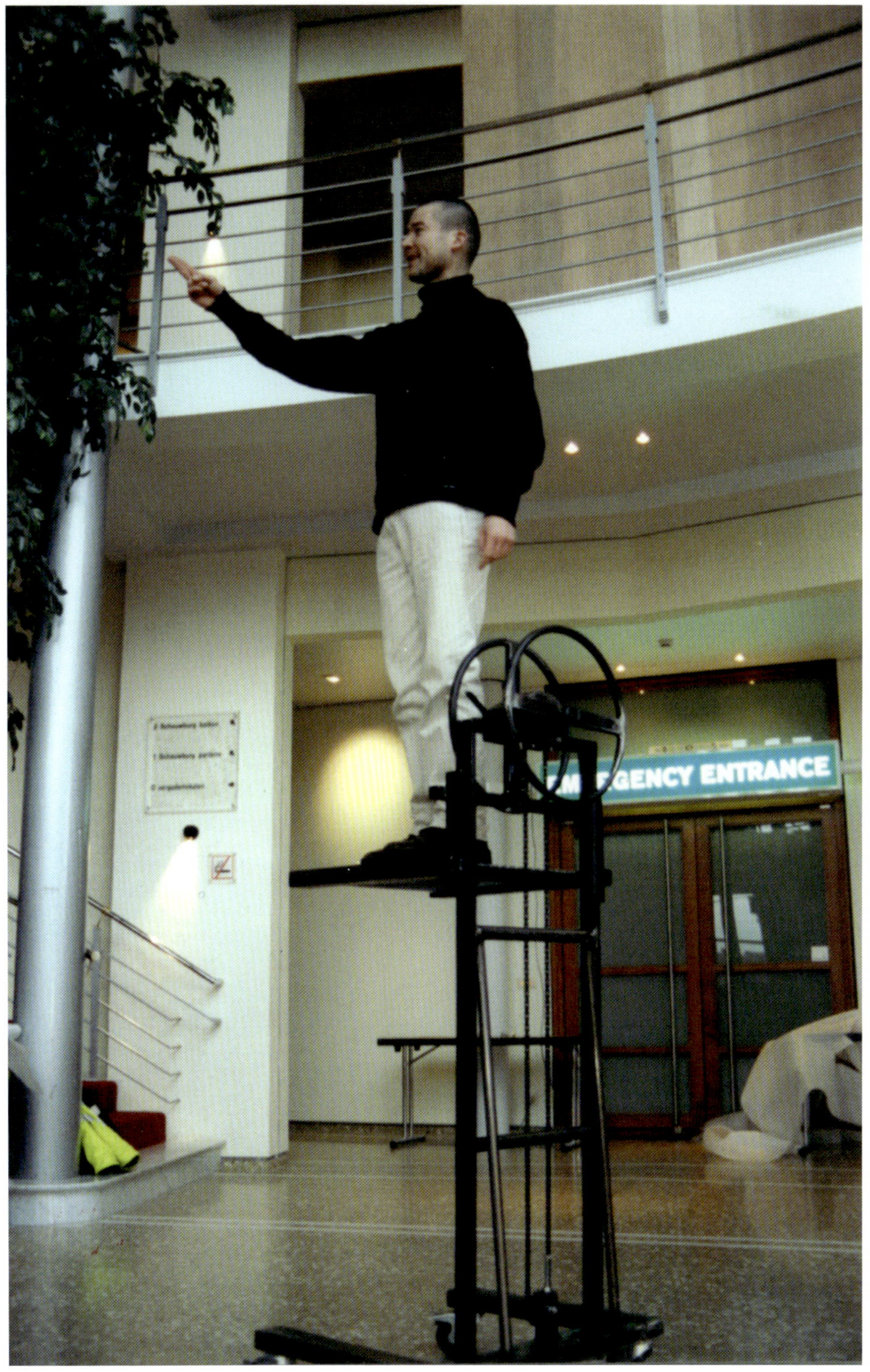

fig. 40

fig. 40   Honoré δ'O demonstrates
Metalen reis naar de hemel [Metal
journey towards heaven].

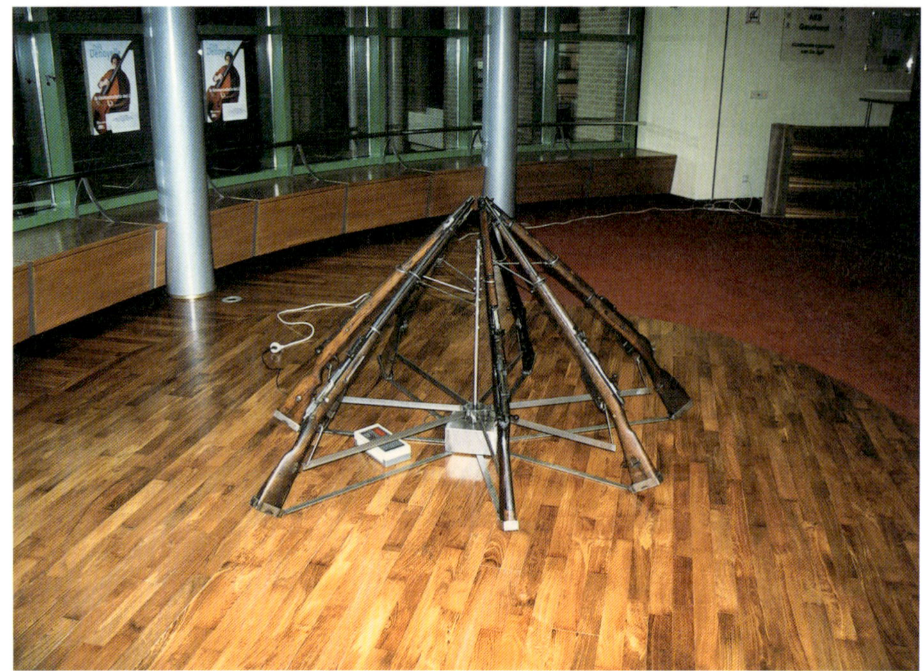

fig. 41

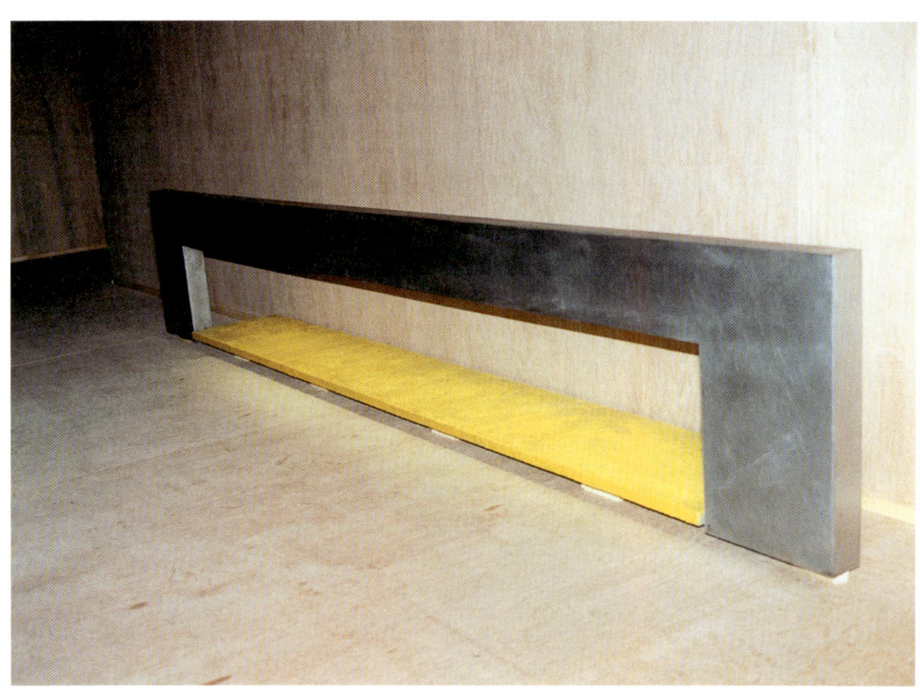

fig. 42

fig. 41   Leo Copers, *Zonder titel
[untitled]*, 1998.
fig. 42   Hans De Pelsmacker, *Zonder
titel*, 1998.

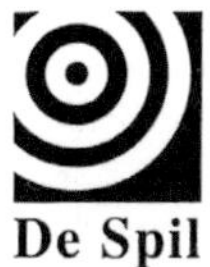

De Spil

CONSTRUCTIES ESPEEL
T.a.v. de heer Michel Espeel
Moorseelsesteenweg
8800   Rumbeke

Roeselare, 28 april 1998

Beste Michel,

Uw ondersteuning van onze hedendaagse dansprogrammatie tijdens dit seizoen was voor ons
een belangrijke stimulans voor ons om artistieke keuzes te maken en financieel enig risico aan
te durven.

Ook naar volgend seizoen willen wij op in onze programmatie deze weg verder inslaan. We
zijn daarom zeer verheugd dat u ook volgend seizoen de hedendaagse dans in De Spil verder
wilt stimuleren.
In het dossier over het seizoen 1998/99, dat wij u vroeger bezorgd hebben, is één optie
weggevallen, nl. Maguy Marin met RamDam. De overige voorstellingen blijven bestaan.
In bijlage vindt u nog eens de exacte data.
Opnieuw worden deze voorstellingen ingeleid door een beknopte lezing vooraf.

Graag willen wij u naar komend seizoen volgend voorstel formuleren:
voor de 5 dansvoorstellingen:

- Constructies Espeel sponsort de hedendaagse dansvoorstellingen voor het seizoen 1998-
  1999 : voorstel : 100.000 fr.
- C.C. De Spil vermeldt telkens "in samenwerking met Constructies Espeel" in de
  seizoensbrochure (oplage 88.000 ex., spreiding 20.000 ex. via Knack abonnees, 20.000 ex.
  via spreiding Het Nieuwsblad, regio Zuid-West-Vlaanderen) en op alle publicitair druk-
  werk betreffende hedendaagse dans.
- C.C De Spil stelt 50 vrijkaarten ter beschikking aan de sponsor, volgens eigen voorkeur te
  spreiden over de 5 voorstellingen hedendaagse dans.
- C.C. De Spil biedt de gelegenheid om tijdens deze voorstellingen extra publiciteit te voeren
  in het cultureel centrum.
- C.C. De Spil stelt zaal de Komedie gedurende een avond gratis ter beschikking.

Graag willen wij dit voorstel met u verder bespreken.

Met vriendelijke groeten,

Bieke Demeester
cultuurfunctionaris

Filip Strobbe
directeur

:l centrum · Vereniging zonder winstoogmerk · Hippoliet Spilleboutdreef 1 · 8800 Roeselare · Tel. (051) 26 57 00 · Fax (051) 26 58 00

fig. 43

**fig. 43   From 1997, thanks to sponsor-
ship, Constructies Espeel has been able
to add contemporary dance to the
programme at *De Spil* cultural centre.**

play on the conventional symbol denoting an emergency exit made the emergency *entrance* recognisable to all.

Carl De Keyzer's black and white images left their metallic traces on the walls. Besides the artists in action, what struck the viewer were the fragments, the welding seams, the cold railings and the grinding sounds. Works by Leo Copers, Tjok Dessauvage, Honoré δ'O, Hans De Pelsmaecker, Paul Gees, Martine Platteau and Tine Vindevogel exuded their metallic odour in the space.

De Keyzer's photos were collected between two sheets of metal on which was engraved the wordplay on the conventional symbol of an emergency exit. Honoré δ'O gave the idea for the cover, the invitations and the raffle tickets. Constructies Espeel took charge of the production and even looked after the sharpest metal edges.

Step two: *Heavy Metal* (12 May – 27 June 1999)[3]

Heavy Metal began with a funeral cortege. It ran from the Villa Eksternest, via the Buro II architectural firm in Roeselare, to the site of Constructies Espeel. In the hearse lay seven hundred and twenty litres of *Proper Water* (Clean Water) that would be buried in a metal coffin. The ceremony was the work of the artist Johan De Wit.

Accompanying the burial was *Dead Water Music* by the composer Philippe de Chaffoy.

This was followed, as a sort of buffet, by *Heavy Metal*, with "video art and photography in the production room. There people wandered on Saturday and Sunday between the silenced bespoke production in order to discover 'silent' photography and 'moving' video art by Belgian artists. These addressed the themes of power, time, rhythm, performance and an exclusively goal-oriented commerce. These concepts are at the forefront of our society and are very closely linked with economic activity."[4] The artists who took part in this event were David Claerbout, Wim Delvoye, Carl De Keyzer, Johan Dewit, Torimitsu Momoyo and De NV n.v. They came to Constructies Espeel for the sole purpose of the exhibition: to expose their existing work to the reality and economic regularity of heavy metal. The anchor was the historic poster of *Modern Times* by Charlie Chaplin. In De Spil, the film entitled *Dial H-I-S-T-O-R-Y* by Johan Grimonprez was screened.

64

During *Heavy Metal*, the Constructies
Espeel company displayed images:
photos and films, mainly by Belgian
artists who call into question the
capitalist definitions of power, time and
performance. Charlie Chaplin's *Modern
Times* set the tone.

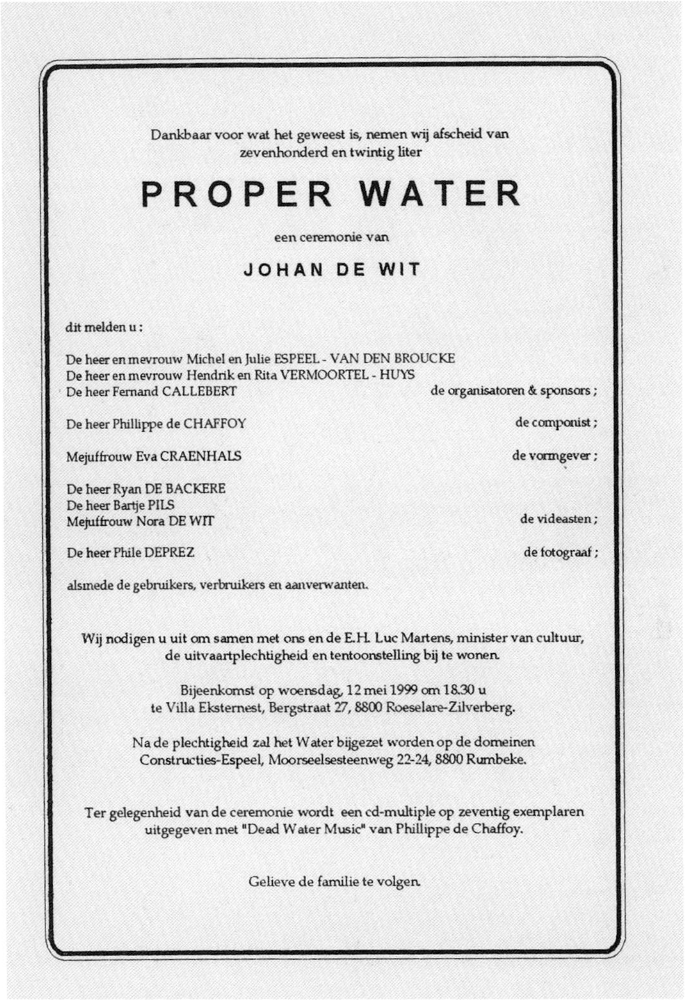

Dankbaar voor wat het geweest is, nemen wij afscheid van
zevenhonderd en twintig liter

PROPER WATER

een ceremonie van

JOHAN DE WIT

dit melden u :

De heer en mevrouw Michel en Julie ESPEEL - VAN DEN BROUCKE
De heer en mevrouw Hendrik en Rita VERMOORTEL - HUYS
De heer Fernand CALLEBERT — de organisatoren & sponsors ;

De heer Phillippe de CHAFFOY — de componist ;

Mejuffrouw Eva CRAENHALS — de vormgever ;

De heer Ryan DE BACKERE
De heer Bartje PILS
Mejuffrouw Nora DE WIT — de videasten ;

De heer Phile DEPREZ — de fotograaf ;

alsmede de gebruikers, verbruikers en aanverwanten.

Wij nodigen u uit om samen met ons en de E.H. Luc Martens, minister van cultuur,
de uitvaartplechtigheid en tentoonstelling bij te wonen.

Bijeenkomst op woensdag, 12 mei 1999 om 18.30 u
te Villa Eksternest, Bergstraat 27, 8800 Roeselare-Zilverberg.

Na de plechtigheid zal het Water bijgezet worden op de domeinen
Constructies-Espeel, Moorseelsesteenweg 22-24, 8800 Rumbeke.

Ter gelegenheid van de ceremonie wordt een cd-multiple op zeventig exemplaren
uitgegeven met "Dead Water Music" van Phillippe de Chaffoy.

Gelieve de familie te volgen.

fig. 44

figs. 44-48   Johan De Wit, *Proper Water*
[Clean Water], 1999. The funeral for 720
litres of clean bottled water with which
Heavy Metal started. The water was
buried in a metal coffin on the site of
the Constructies Espeel factory.

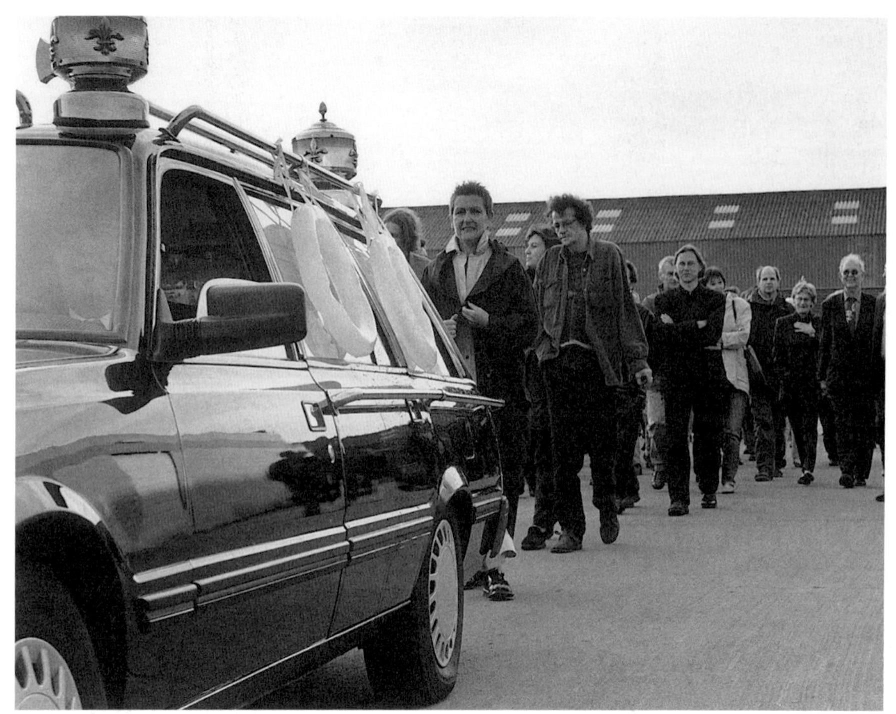

fig. 45

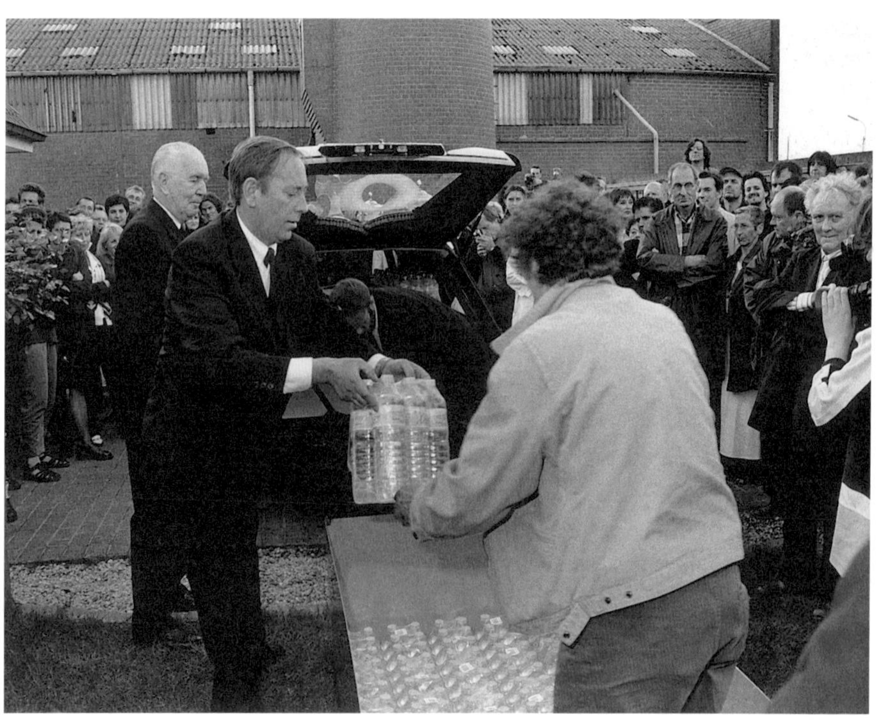

fig. 46

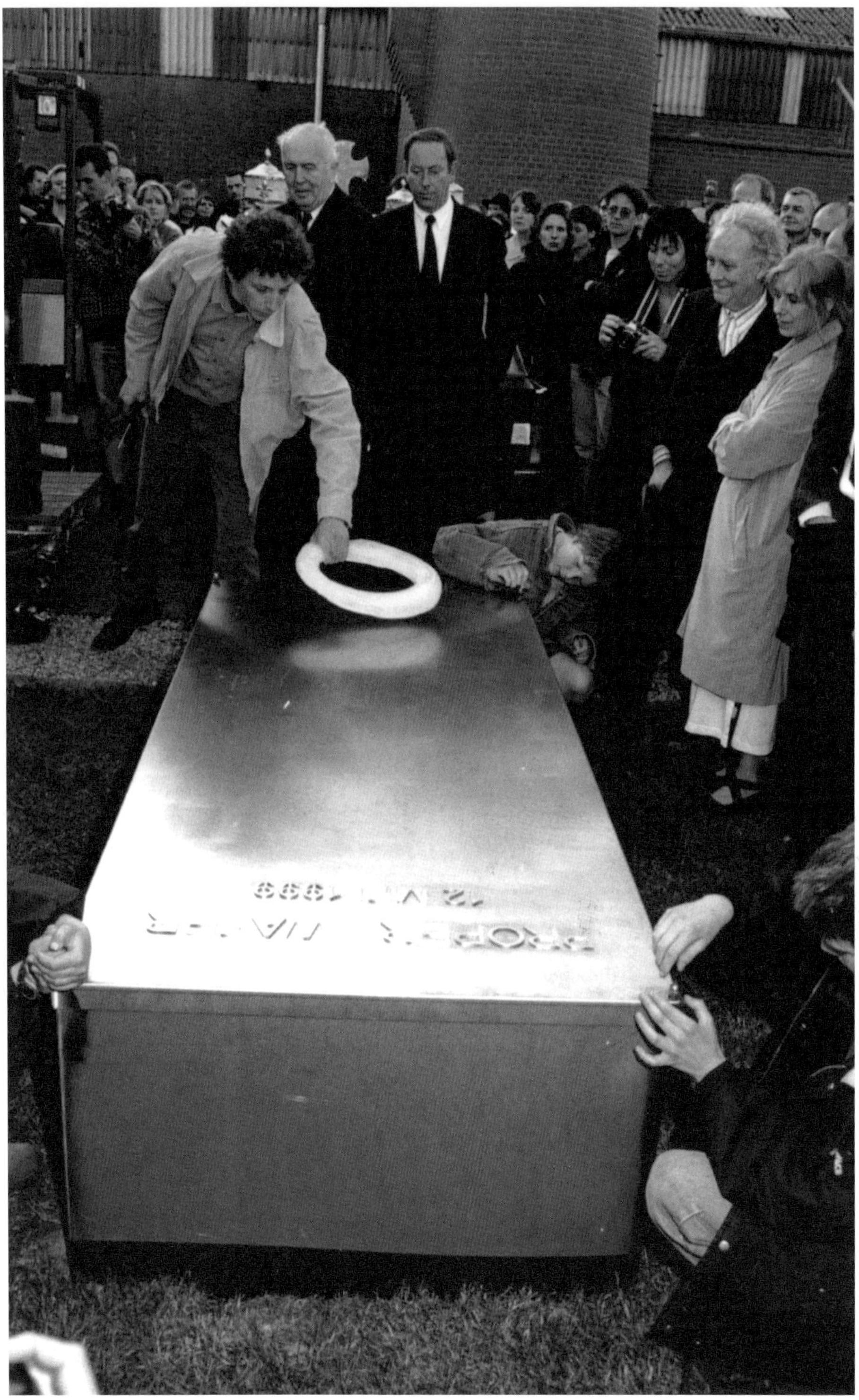

fig. 47

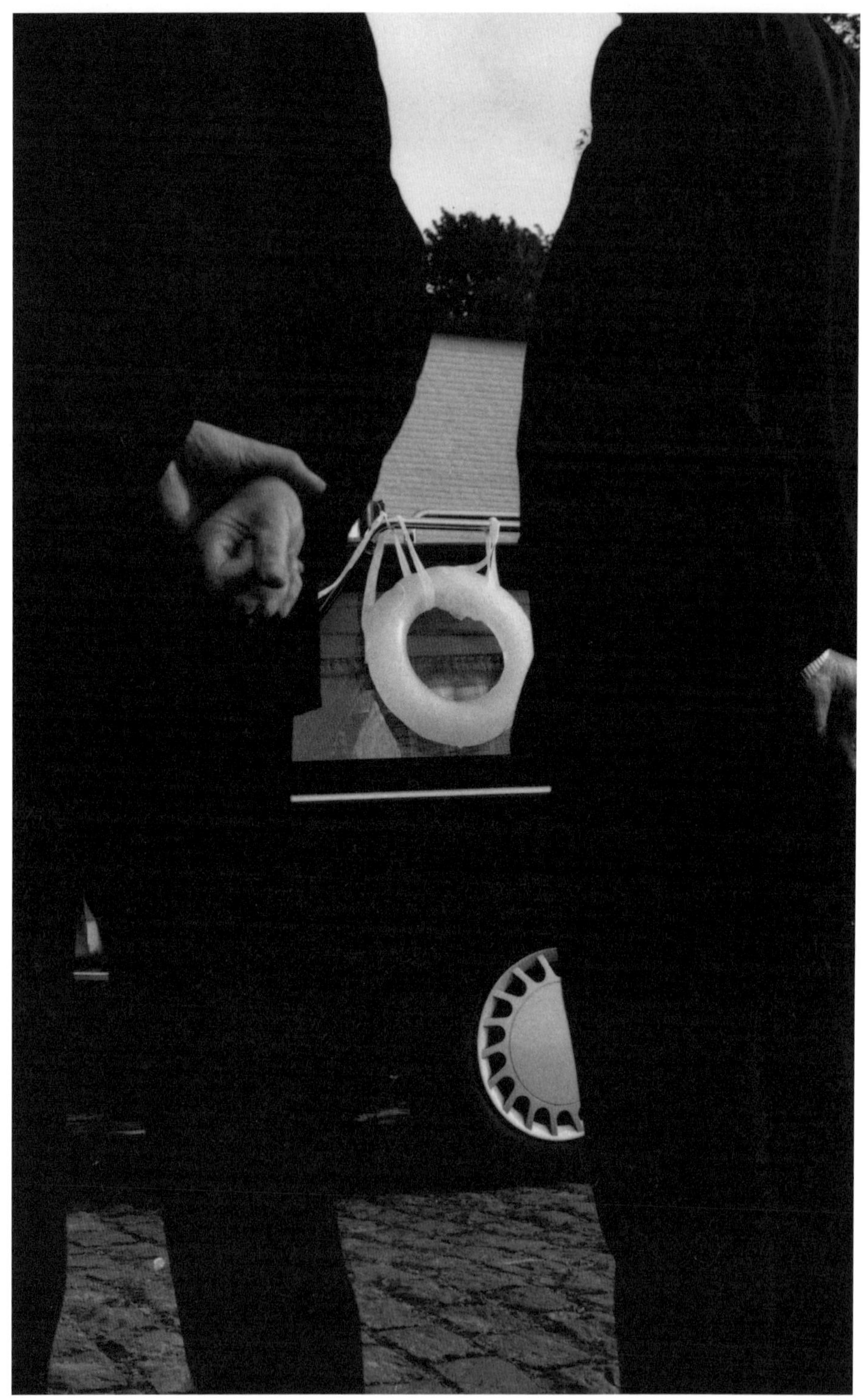

fig. 48

Kunst in de fabriek

Naar aanleiding van een geforceerd Frans-Nederlands-Belgisch circuit van hedendaagse kunst in Roeselare is de actieve productiehal van Constructies Espeel in Rumbeke nu uitzonderlijk op zondag toegankelijk als een begenadigde kunstruimte.

Julie Espeel zorgde hier voor de selectie en het moge onmiddellijk duidelijk zijn dat de vele videoprojecties en foto's in deze hal een perfect en geborgen onderkomen gevonden hebben. Het is trouwens fascinerend om gewoon even rond te slenteren in deze enorme hal, waar ook de vele onafgewerkte metalen constructies (onbewust) opgeladen worden met een verwijzing naar kunst. Een wit gelakte constructie bijvoorbeeld kon net zo goed een onderdeel zijn van een nieuw tuig van Panamarenko. En stapels mooi op elkaar geplaatste stukjes metaal doen meteen denken aan de gloriedagen van de *minimal art*.

Deze kruisbestuiving tussen een bedrijf met een op zondag stilgevallen maatwerkproductie en de aanwezigheid van een aantal zeer goede kunstwerken benadrukt een artistiek surplus, dat vooral qua presentatie van video makkelijker kan worden benaderd dan in de context van een verduisterde witte museumruimte. Dat stemt tot nadenken: net zoals bij de onlangs georganiseerde *Art & Party* in de catacomben van het Brusselse Centraal Station (waar drum & basemuziek perfect samenviel met de projectie van twaalf indrukwekkende video's) wordt de vaststelling hard gemaakt dat kunst goed tot zelfs zeer goed kan gedijen in een actieve productiehal. Het is een doordenkertje voor diegenen die van mening zijn dat er veel geld moet worden gestopt in nieuwe kunsthallen.

Wim Delvoye schittert hier met zijn video *Paper Aeroplane* waarin een hilarische parodie ten beste wordt gegeven op een politieke redevoering die handelt over een speels papieren voorwerpje. Johan Dewit heeft iets met water. Niet alleen zijn schitterende, uitvergrote foto's van liggende waterflessen intrigeren, maar ook zijn video waarin poppetjes langzaam van tussen twee bloedrode lippen worden uitgespuugd. Dit werk doet denken aan het fantastische schilderij *De Kolos* van Goya. Dewit bereikt hier een vergelijkbare, beangstigende visie op de machtsverhoudingen tussen mensen.

De volstrekt onbekende Torimitsu Momoyo presenteert een videoinstallatie waarin een robot, aangekleed als een succesrijk zakenman, zich op beide ellebogen een weg baant door het drukke New York. Het is een fantastische videofilm met surreële knipoogjes, waarin het beeld de kruiperigheid van de macht aan de orde brengt. Naast een nieuwe fascinerende bijdrage van David Claerbout is Carl Dekeyser van de partij met een aantal foto's van een huiselijk decor met daarin een naakte man met erectie, gelardeerd met een computergestuurde projectie waarin beelden worden getoond onder de cynische titel *Ode aan de Macht*.

Al deze boeiende installaties worden als vanzelfsprekend in een historische context geplaatst via de projectie van de filmklassieker *Modern Times* van Charlie Chaplin. Aan de ingang van de productiehal weerklinkt het gesamplede geluid van vallende waterdruppels. Het is een leuke cd in beperkte oplage van Johan Dewit, die bij Espeel ook een grafmonument maakte met of voor (?) zuiver water.

(LL)

> ## Een actieve productiehal als begenadigde kunstruimte

'Heavy Metal' als onderdeel van '3 countries - 3 plekken - 3 arts': nog op zondag 27 juni (van 14.30 tot 18 uur) in de Productiehal van Constructies Espeel, Moorseelsesteenweg 22-24 in Rumbeke/Roeselare. Inlichtingen: tel. (051) 26.51.00.

fig. 49

69

fig. 49   The critic, Luk Lambrecht, reviewed *Heavy Metal* in the newspaper De Morgen of Monday, 21 June 1999.

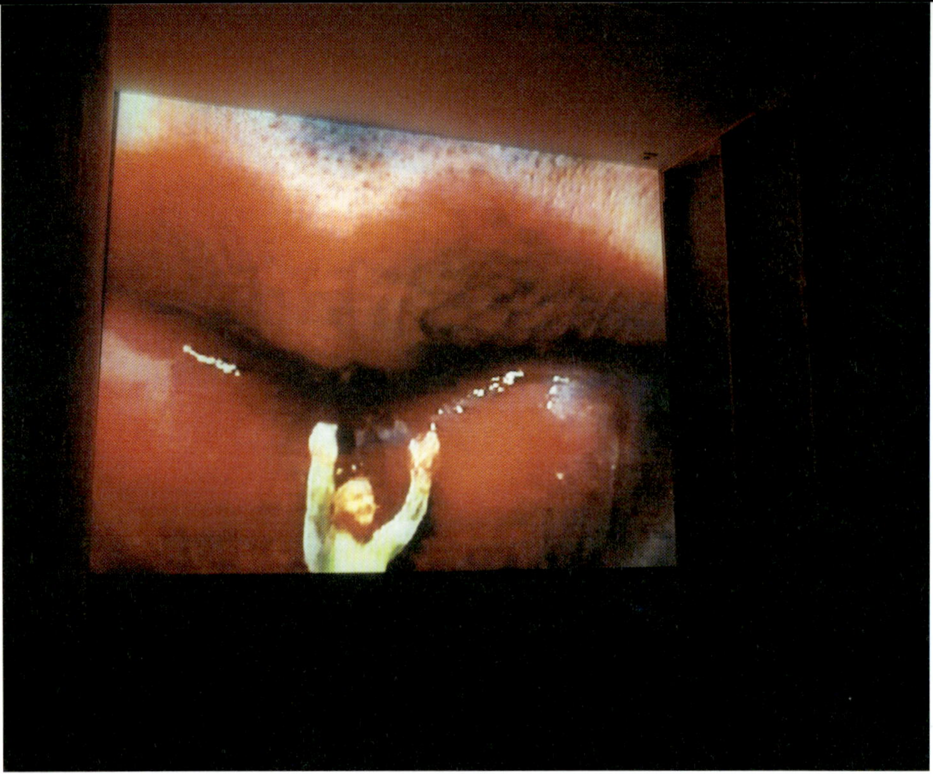

fig. 50

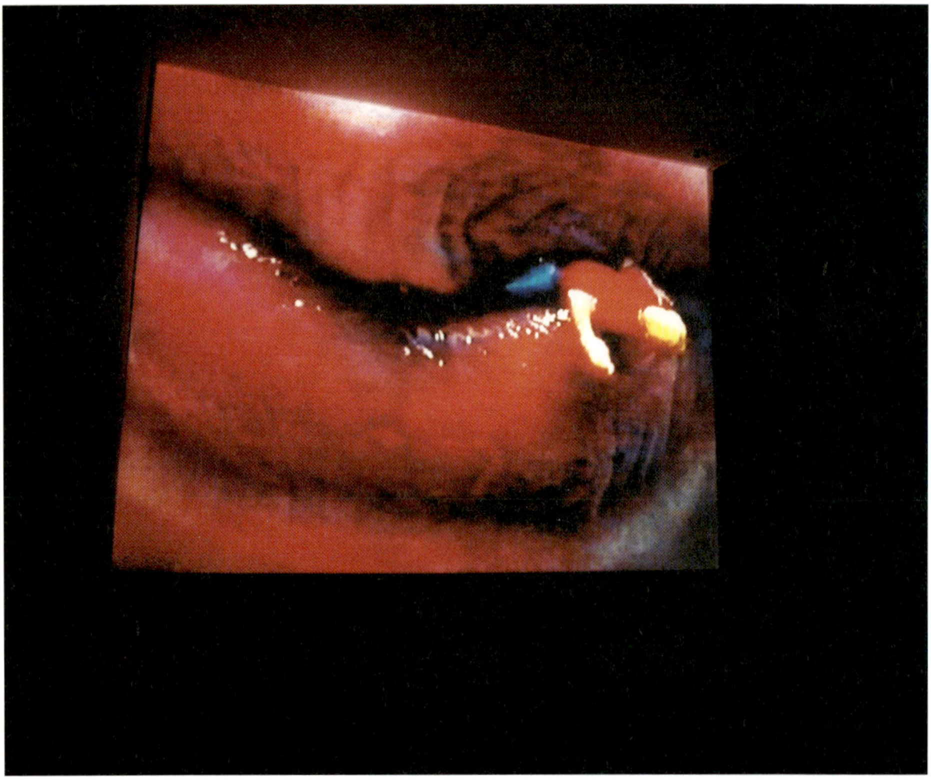

70

fig. 50   Johan De Wit, *Endless Composition*, 1999

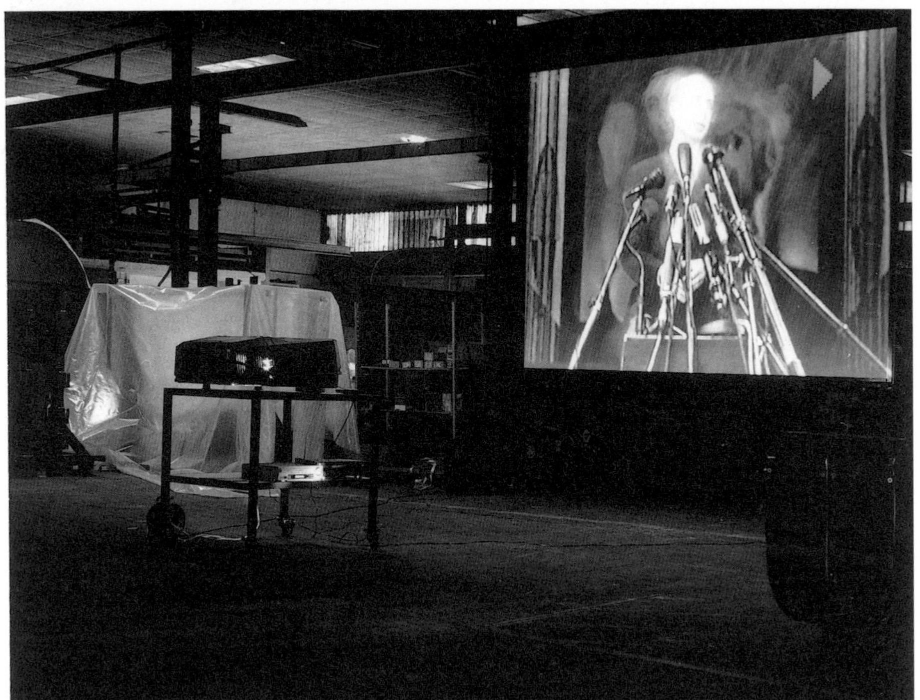

fig. 51

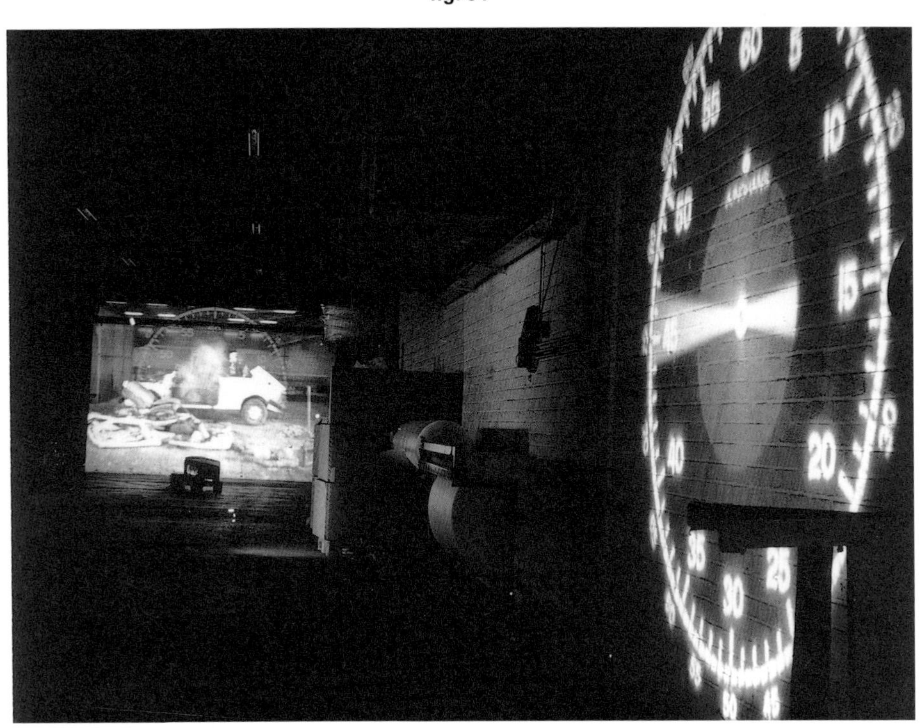

fig. 52

fig. 51 Wim Delvoye, *Paper Aeroplane*, 1999.
fig. 52 NVnv, *1 hour is much more than 60 minutes or 3,600 seconds; 1 hour has content, volume and movement*, 1999.

Step three: *Touch Me* (10 & 11 February 2001)[5]

During the weekend event entitled *Touch Me*, Constructies Espeel's production hall was the port of call for a tangible experience of the physical aspect of contemporary art. Video installations, performance art, readings, dance performances, music and DJ sessions inspired the approximately one thousand pilgrims who had followed the art world all the way to Rumbeke. *Touch Me* left powerful impressions as it played on the idea of the vulnerability of a person in an industrial environment. However, economic matters were not addressed. The employees were present but the factory was kept in an artificial coma for the duration of the weekend.

After these three steps, Julie remarked that the effect on the company was different. It is not unlike a town where the bicycle tour of Flanders (De Ronde van Vlaanderen) passes through. If the race comes through only once, it is celebrated with bells and whistles. A year later, people still talk about the strange people who came through, but the experience gradually fades from memory. But if the cyclists come by every year, the race becomes a solid value with which residents and visitors can identify. In their wake, all sorts of things can spring up, such as a shop or a little museum where locals can get involved and be fulfilled by the experience.

No one prevented her from moving forward, but Julie felt intuitively that she wanted a change of direction. She stood at an important crossroads and took a glimpse backwards. She reflected on how far they had travelled, and understood that the combination of collaboration, events and influences from the outside had brought changes to the employees and transcended a purely economic logic. A one-off event did not achieve the same effect.

The cradle of Arteconomy

The road movie now takes an important turn. Constructies Espeel continues to support the production of art works, but Julie has moved on from home base. In the form of a legal entity as a non-profit association, she sets up an organisation that bears the name Arteconomy. Her journey becomes a veritable mission: "Arteconomy searches for relations between art and economy and their meaning."[6]

For Arteconomy, 'relations' refers to encounters that bring art and economy together. Encounters take place in a group, from person to person, from artist to entrepreneur or vice versa. In its investigation of the relationship between art and economy, Arteconomy is a nomad, moving from one company to the next. With its accumulating baggage, it hopes to cross-pollinate these two fields.

Arteconomy ultimately seeks to reach and influence the public policy-makers in cultural and economic spheres. With the practical example of Constructies Espeel in tow "... and an overarching conception, Arteconomy hopes to formulate a new 'draft law'. This approach seeks to anchor in the solid relationship between art and the economy. The advantage of such a collaboration for both parties can be measured in hard Figures, art is given freer rein in which to find refreshment and inspiration – and workspace [...] The 'status' of creativity slips into the steel cage of the economic landscape, which fortunately becomes acquainted, not a moment too soon, with tenderness. The economic world is all the better for it, where capital fulfils its social obligation [...] and, as a by-product, makes room for the highest good, namely art."[7]

Moving together

Meanwhile, back at Constructies Espeel. The company had been in existence for half a century and it was time for a major celebration. Friend and foe, customers, artists and entrepreneurs were invited. An assortment of guests. The two worlds that met at Constructies Espeel rivalled each other in elegance. The (then) Flemish Minister-President, Yves Leterme, arrived in a tailor-made suit. Dancer Lisbeth Gruwez, by contrast, performed a poem by Peter Verhelst wearing nothing at all.

Two more remarkable events took place at this celebration. One was the presentation of the Espeel Case Study. This was "a sociological case study of the collaboration between Constructies Espeel and artists", carried out by the University of Ghent. It showed, in black and white, how art had benefited Constructies Espeel.

In the second event, employees presented Michel with a work by Paul Geest as a gift, and Michel gave his company a new logo with a motto that, like this book, serves as an invitation: *Moving Together*. These two words sum up Michel and Julie's life work. Constructies Espeel sent the guests off into the world with the poem of Peter Verhelst to reread at home and relive the glow of the celebration:

73

Een op het laken gestolde vrouw, vlies
over melk. Even neemt een rilling
de vorm aan van ruggenwervels. Wat is het
dat zich in beweging zet, wat zoekt zich
nu een uitweg, loopt spits op een borst
toe, duwt zich naar dat punt
door een trechtervormige gedachte heen.
Hartslag in de hals, alsof het daar pikt,
een specht. Plots schiet ze uit een slaap overeind
en klampt zich aan me vast
en kijkt me onherkenbaar aan. Ik denk je
lijkt op iemand die onwennig, voor de eerste keer
in mijn aanwezigheid een bril uittrekt, iets
weerloos naakts aanbiedt – op de rug gelegd –
versmolten oogleden – hoofd afgewend – bekken
langzaam opgeduwd – de eerste vingertop
en de eerste tepel die naar elkaar toe groeien.

[A woman, as if frozen on the sheet, flesh
over milk. A shudder takes on
the form of vertebrae. What is it
that sets itself in motion, what is now
in search of a way out, tapering off into a breast,
pushes itself towards that point
through a funnel-shaped thought.
The heart beating in the throat, as if something were pecking at it,
a woodpecker. Suddenly, she awakens with a start, bolt upright
and clings onto me,
looking at me unrecognisably. I think you
look like someone who, unusually, removes her glasses
for the first time in my presence, offers something
defenceless and naked – laid on her back,
melting eyelids – head turned away – the mouth
slowly held open – the first fingertip
and the first nipple that grow closer to each other.]

74

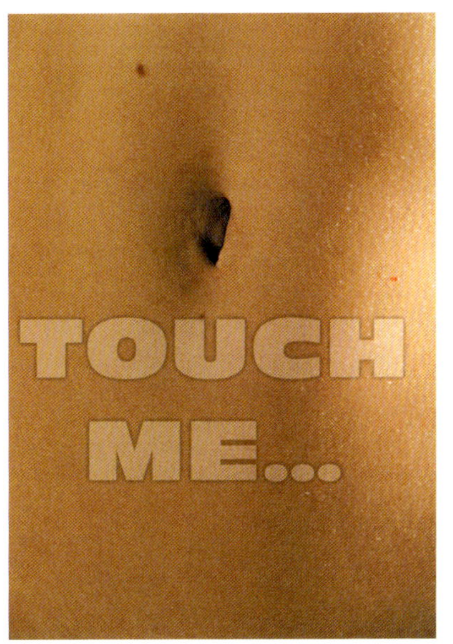

fig. 53

The body is at the centre of *Touch Me*, a two-day happening with a programme of contemporary art, performance, film, dance and movement. That sensual excess is not harmful and is experienced by more than a thousand visitors and the more than fifty artists involved in *Touch Me*. All are prepared to put their bodies into the event taking place in this industrial environment.

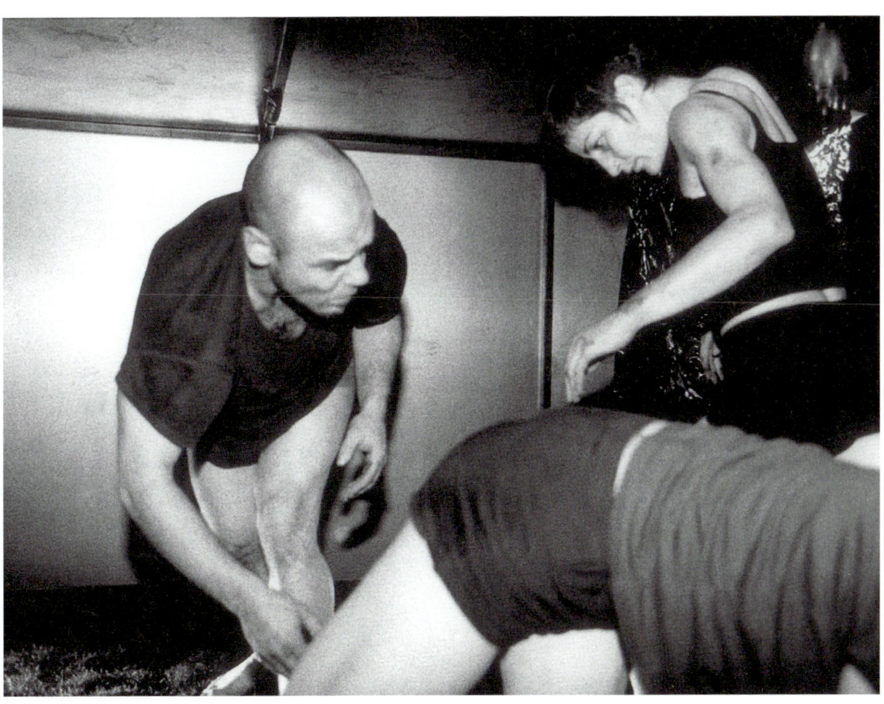

fig. 54

75

fig. 53   "Touch Me" was chosen by the writer Peter Verhelst as the title of the exhibition.
fig. 54   Dance performance by David Hernandez, *Touch Me*, 2001. Photo: Anja Ghesquière & Darry Hellebuyck.

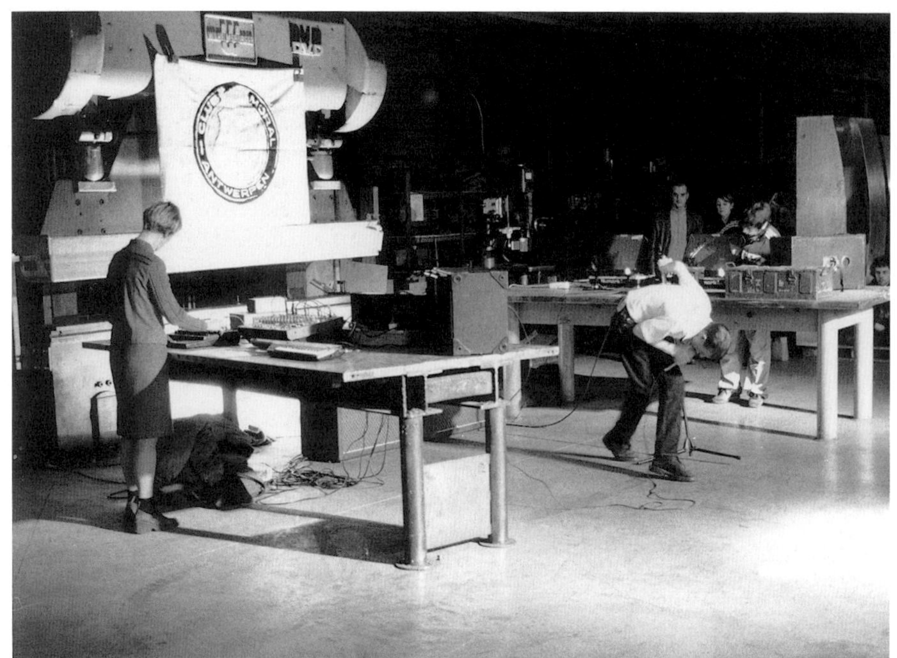

fig. 55

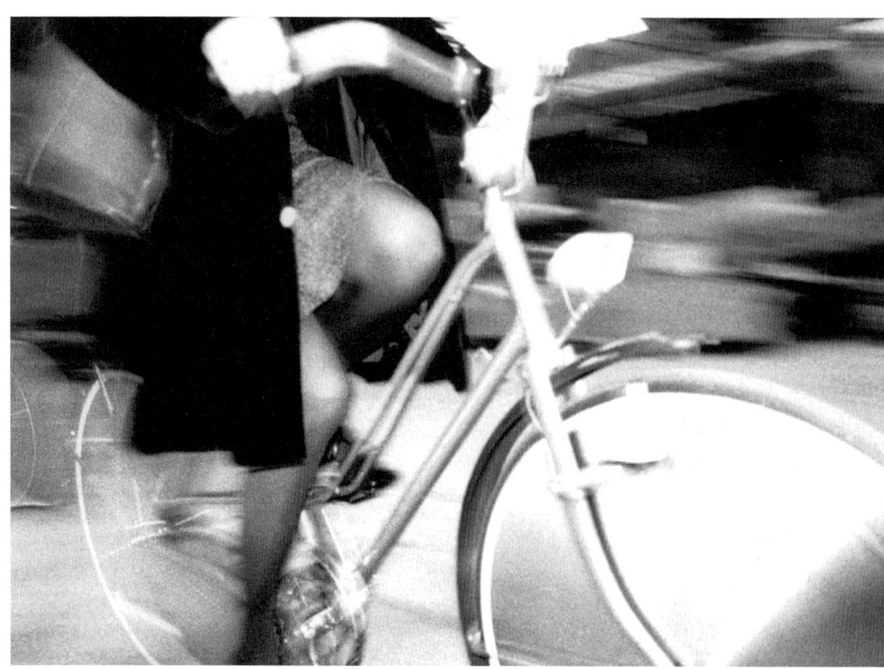

fig. 56

76

fig. 55　Club Moral (Danny Devos &
Marianne Van Kerckhoven), performance
during *Touch Me*, 2001. Photos: Anja
Ghesquière & Darry Hellebuyck.
fig. 56　Ann Veronica Janssens,
Untitled, bicycles with aluminium
hubcaps, 2001. Photo: Anja Ghesquière &
Darry Hellebuyck.

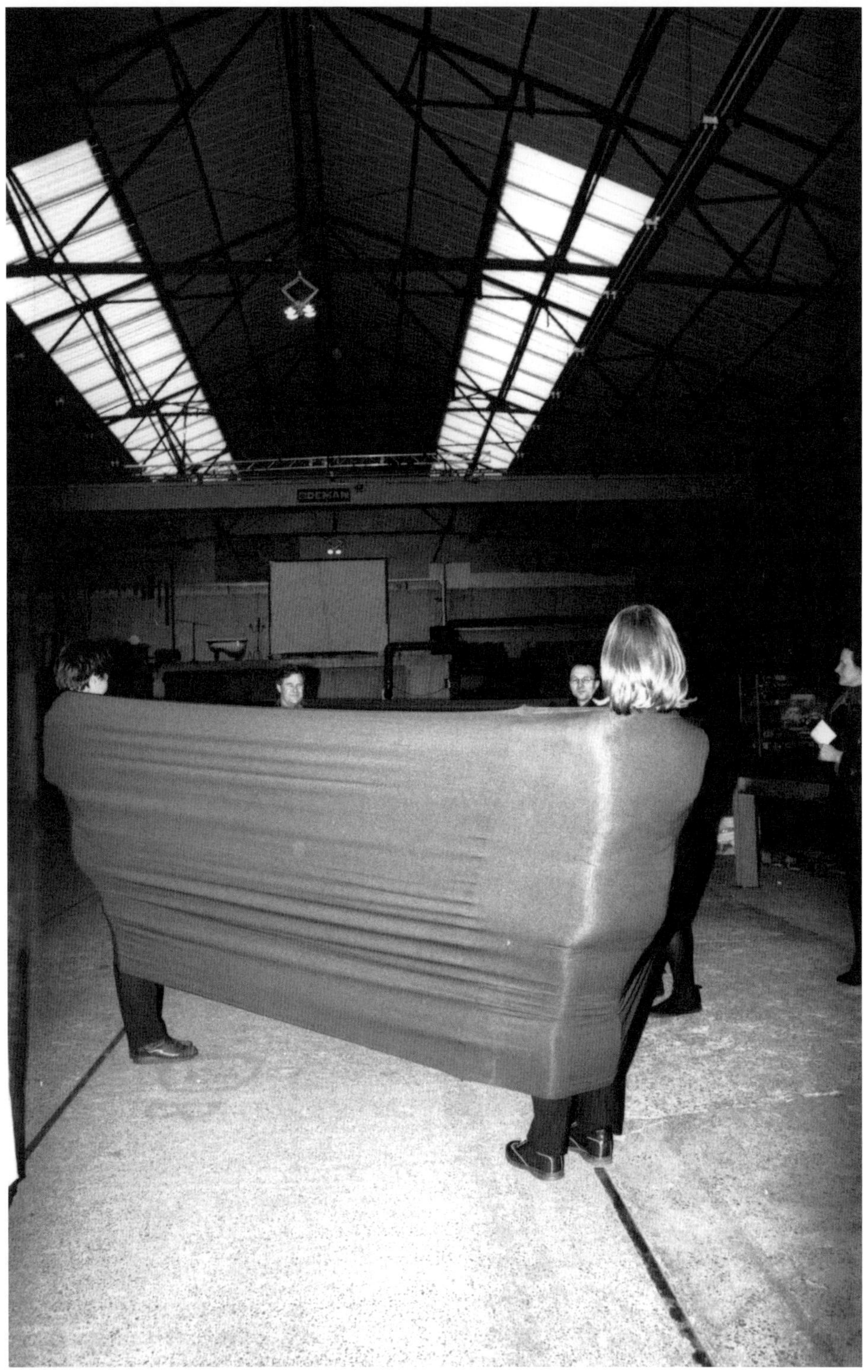

fig. 57

fig. 57   Elastic textile art by Fabien
Lerat worn during *Touch Me*, 2001.
Photo: Boris Saverys.

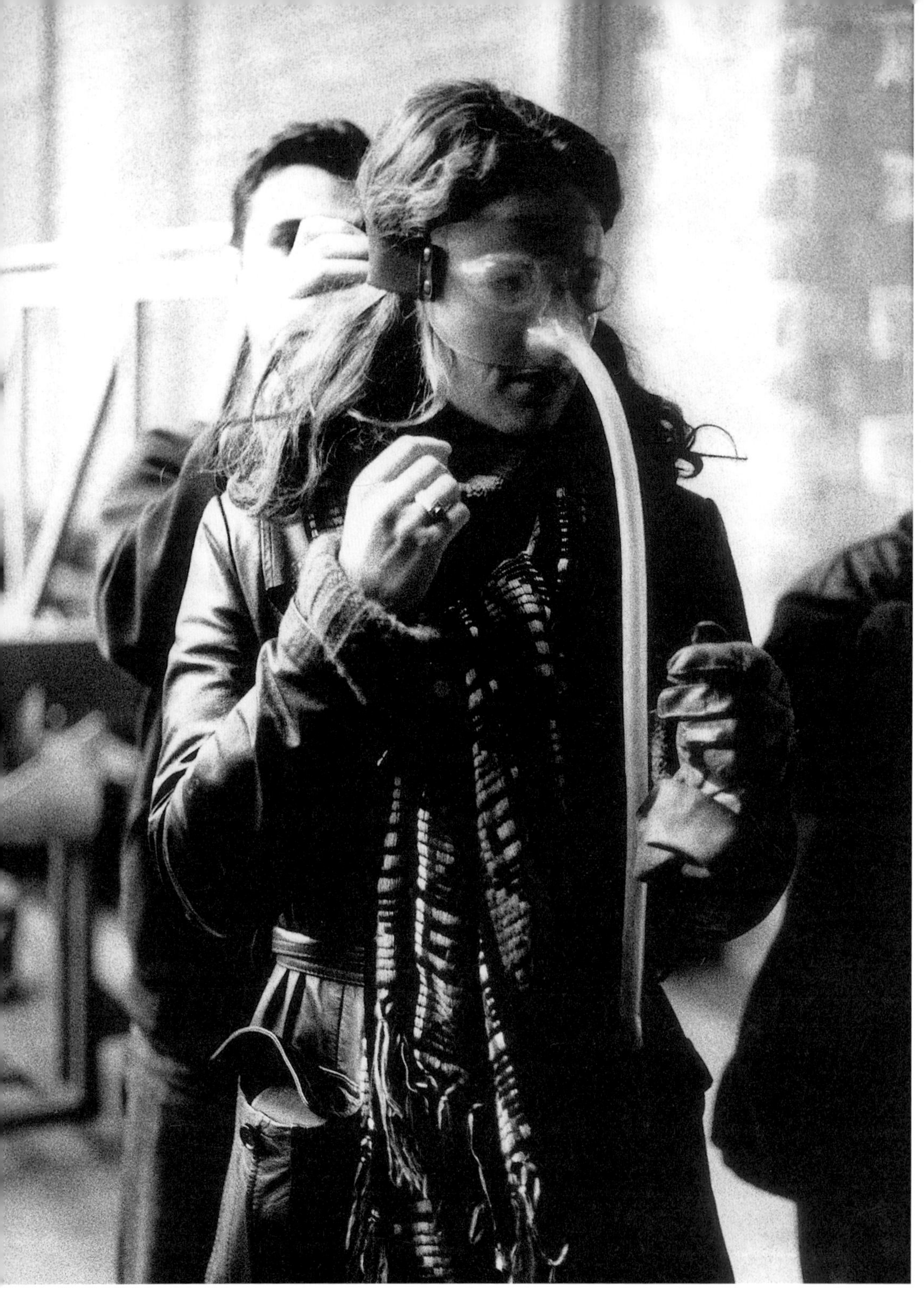

78

fig. 58   Laurent Duthion, nose and eye
installation at *Touch Me*, 2001. Photo:
Boris Saverys.

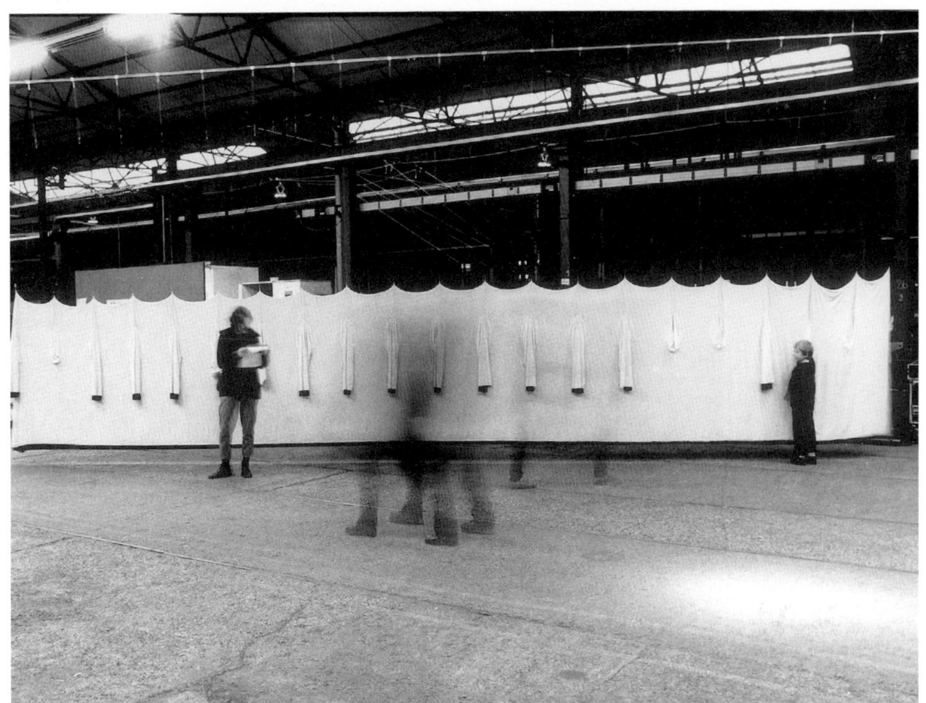

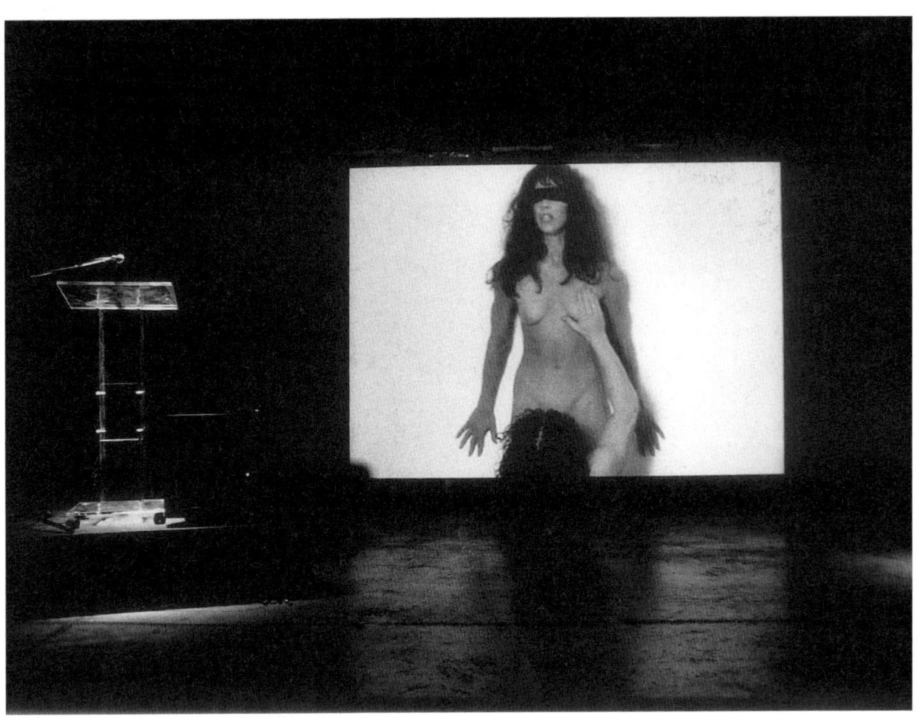

79

fig. 59   Trial installation by Fabien Lerat, 2001. Photo: Anja Ghesquière & Darry Hellebuyck.

fig. 60   Paul McCarthy & Mike Kelley, *Fresh Acconci*, at Touch Me, 2001. Photo: Anja Ghesquière & Darry Hellebuyck.

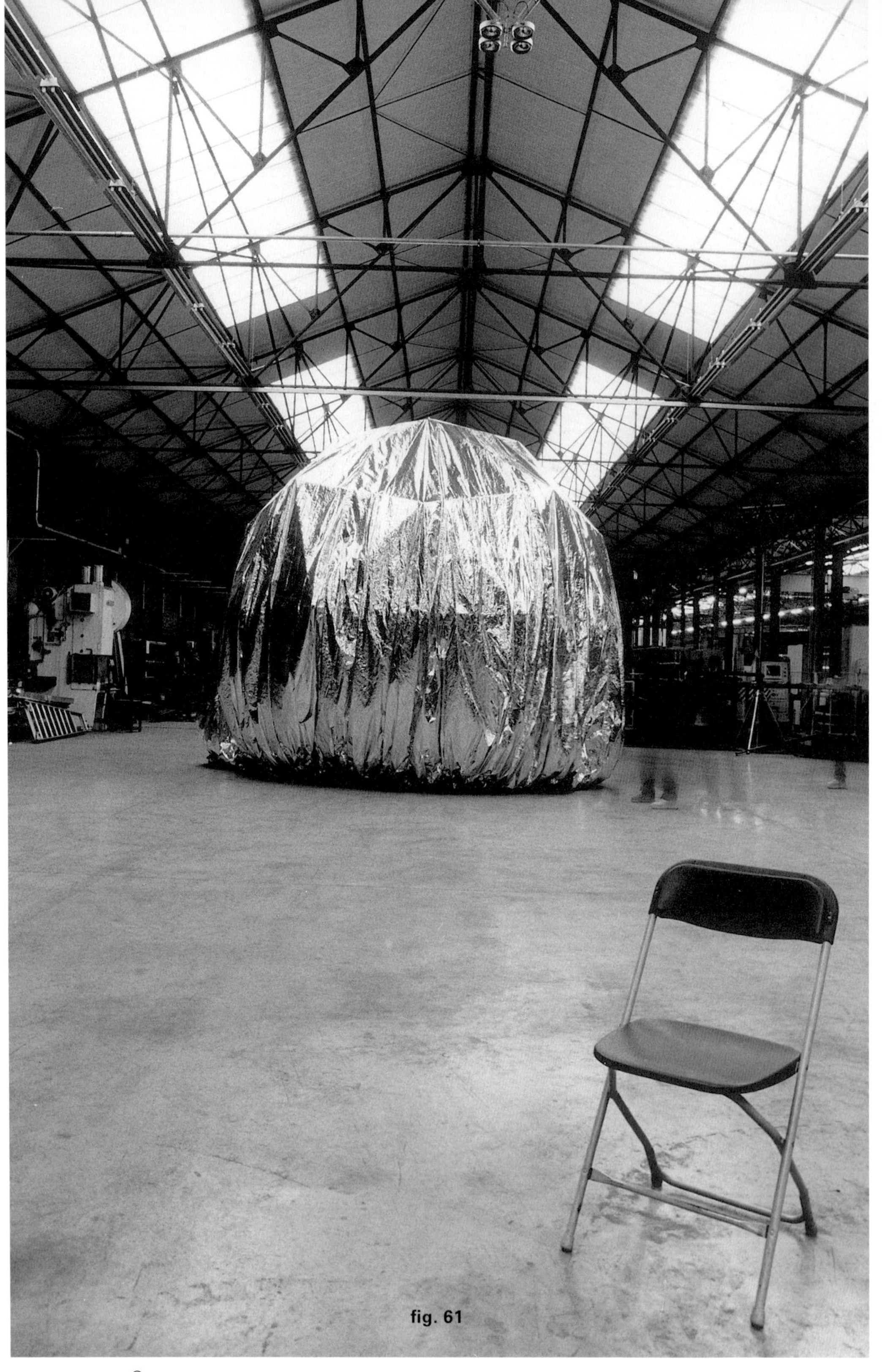

fig. 61

80

fig. 61   Marie-Ange Guilleminot,
L'oursin [The urchin], installation at *Touch
Me,* 2001. Photo: Boris Saverys.

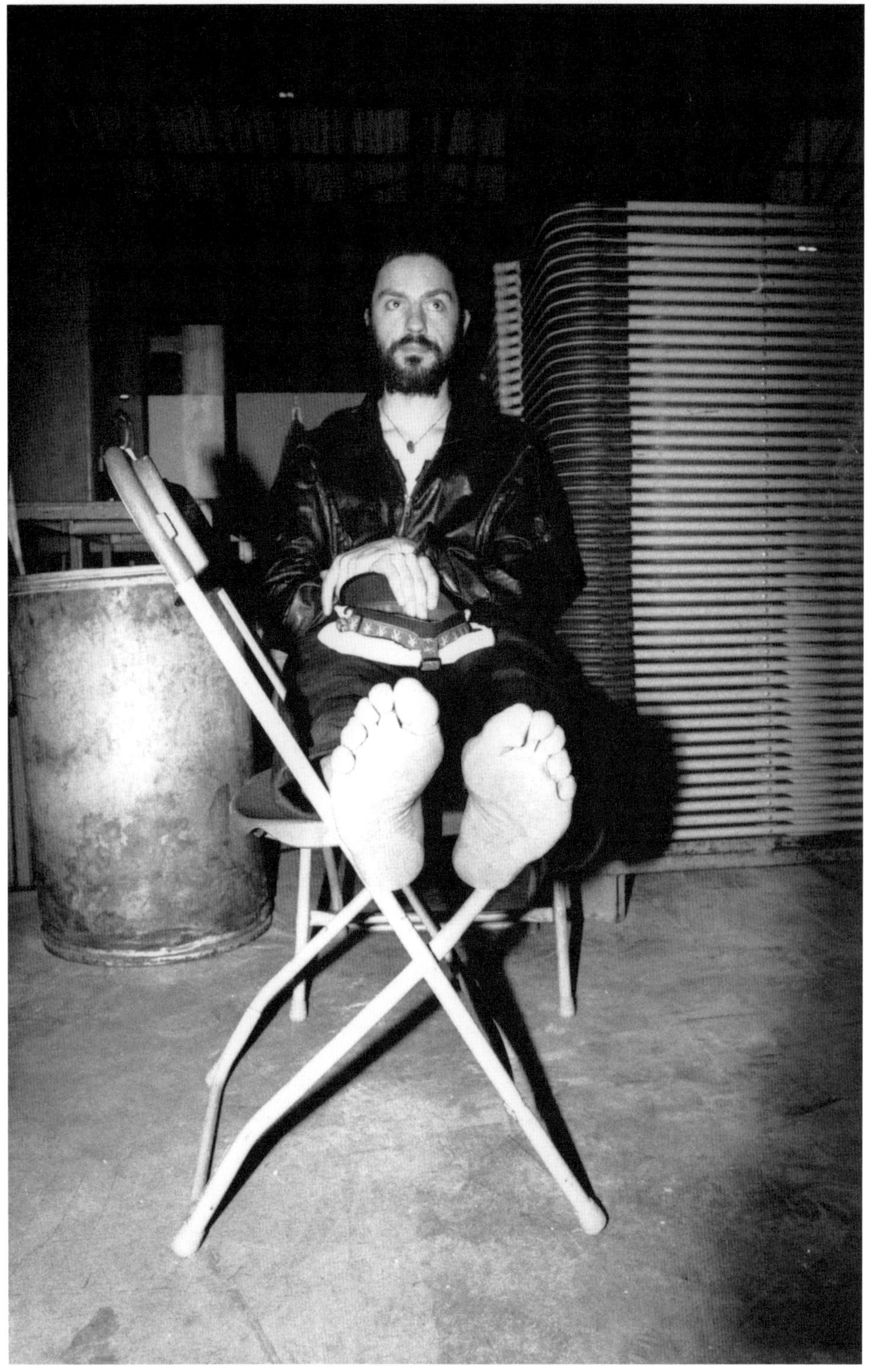

fig. 62

81

fig. 62   Inanna (Johan Derycke),
performance during *Touch Me*, 2001.
Photos: Anja Ghesquière & Darry
Hellebuyck.

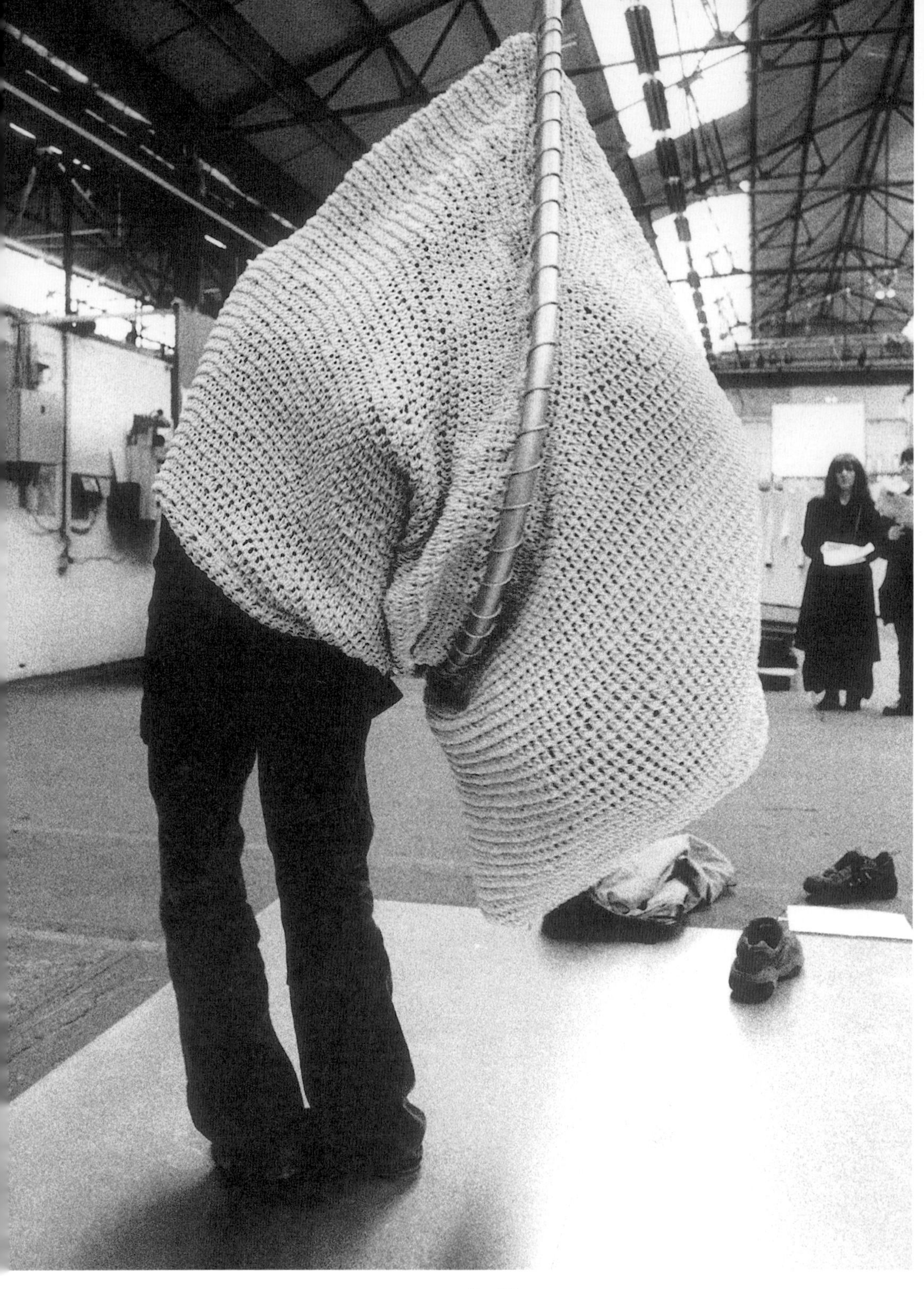

fig. 63

fig. 63   Christelle Familliari, installation
at *Touch Me*, 2001. Photo: Boris Saverys

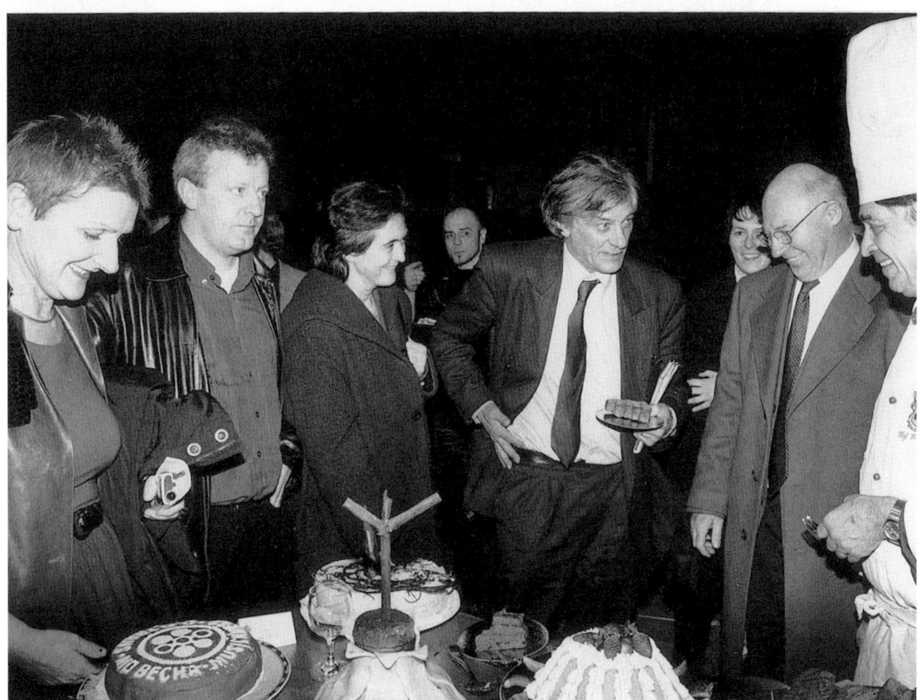

fig. 64

83

figs. 64, 66   *Touch Me* also thinks of the
inner man. Each participating artist
designed a cake that was then baked at
the hotel school in Kortrijk. After an
intervention in which the Liege artist
Jacques Charlier got under the skin of
Belgium's renowned pie thrower, Noël
Godin (the man who threw a pie at Bill
Gates), these artworks were cut up by
Jan Hoet and as a finale, eaten – without
any cutlery, of course. Photo: Anja
Ghesquière & Darry Hellebuyck.
fig. 65   The cake design by artist
Jacques Charlier.

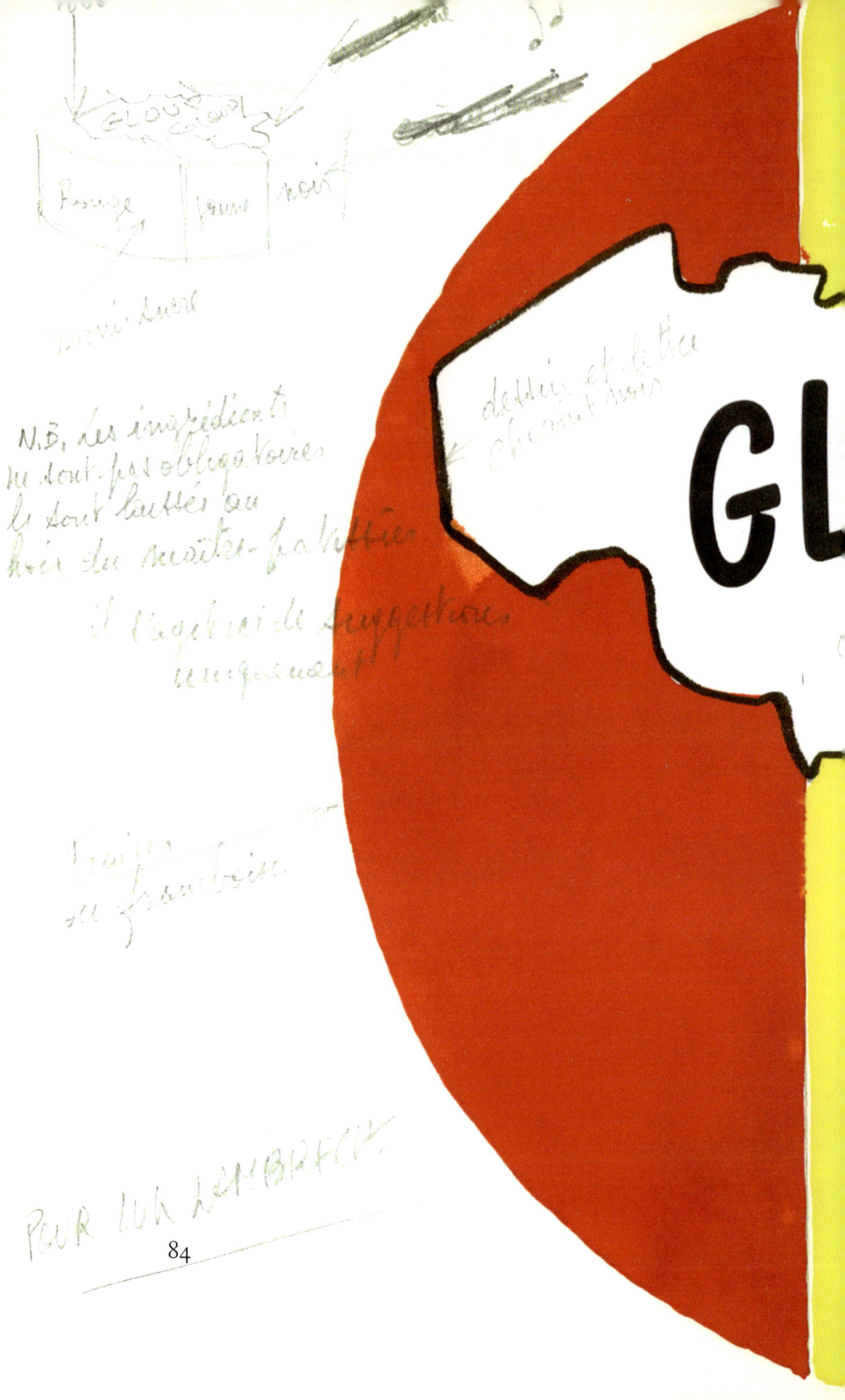

GLOU GLOU

rouge | jaune | noir

panaché sucré

N.B. les ingrédients
ne sont pas obligatoires
ils sont laités ou
hors du maître-pâtissier
il s'agit ici de suggestions
uniquement

dessin et lettre
chemise + noir

... framboise
ou framboise.

POUR LUK LAMBRECHT

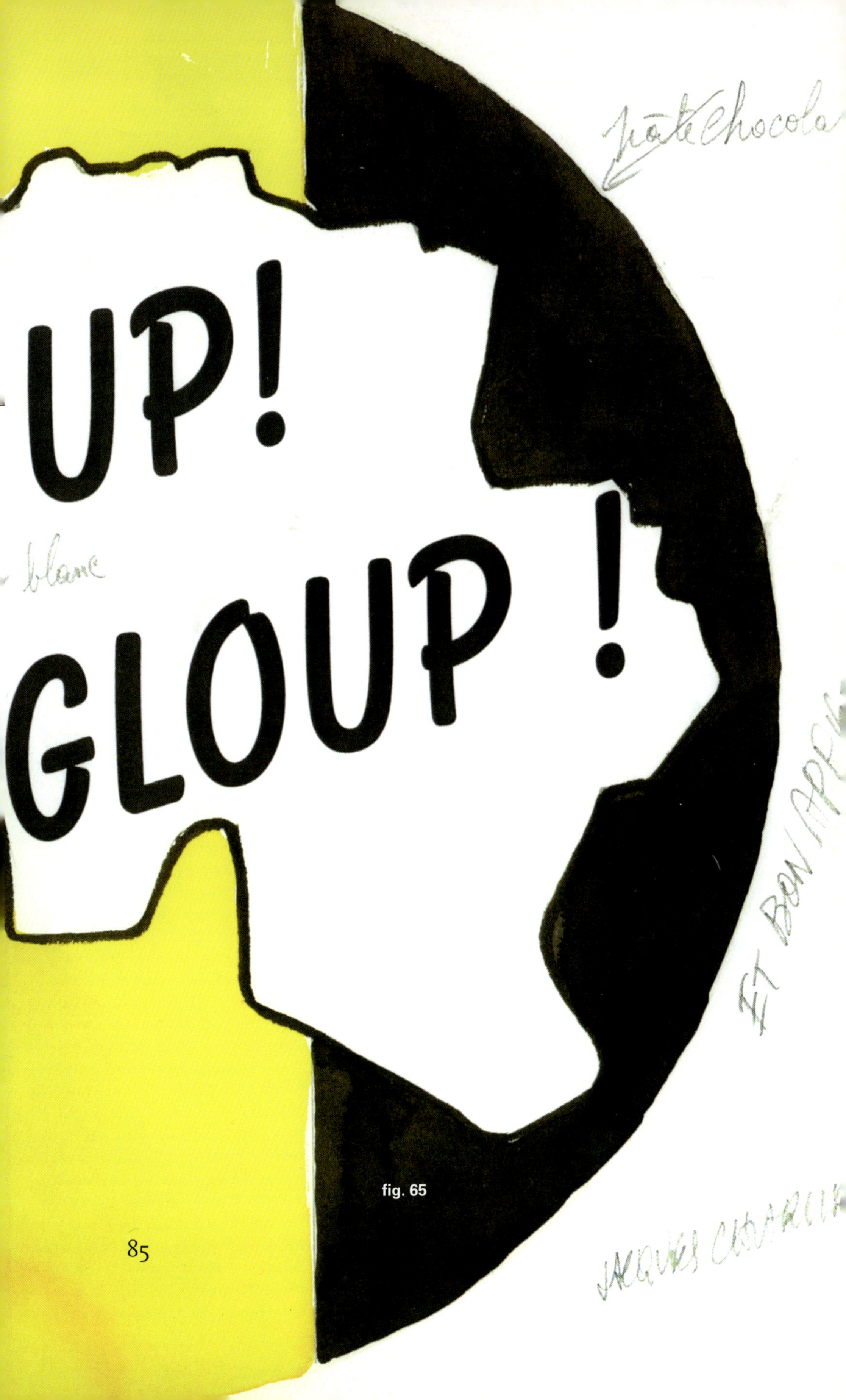

fig. 65

85

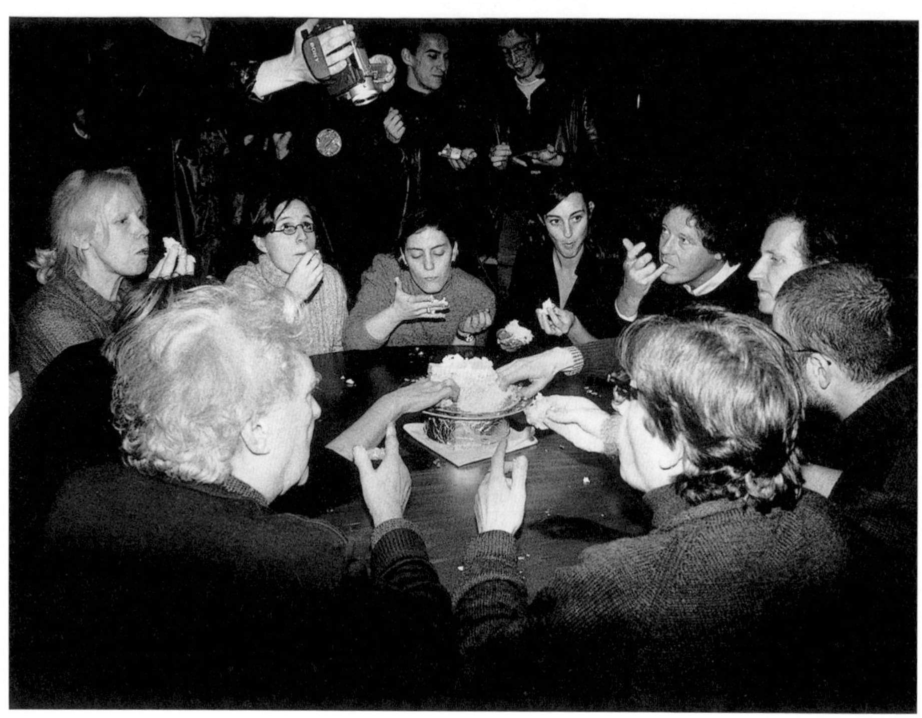

fig. 66

The group known as *Touch Me*: Tine Vindevogel, Ann Veronica Janssens, David Claerbout, Laurent Duthion, Christelle Familiari, Peter Verhelst, Hermann Maier Neustadt, David Hernandez, Bart Maris, Marina Abramovic, Pipilotti Rist, Mike Kelley & Paul McCarthy, Vanessa Beecroft, Hans Op de Beeck, Isa Genzken, Elke Boon, Zhang Huan, Mieke Eeckhout, Ruvanti aka Rudy Vantilborgh, HAP (Academie Gent), Inanna, Claire Roudenko-Bertin, Rudi Laermans, Trees Leroy, Polydans, Marie-Ange Guilleminot, Honoré δ'O, DDTrans & Mo Becha, Club Moral, Mo & Benoelie, École Régionale des Beaux-Arts in Dunkerque, Valie Export, Fabrice Hyber, Fabien Lerat, Pierre Berthet, Jacques Charlier as Noël Godin, the Kortrijk Hotel School, Ria Verhaeghe, Ria Pacquée, Marie-France & Patricia Martin, Ans Nys & Maria Gabrielle, Jan Hoet, Bieke Demeester, Patricia Maes, Julie Vandenbroucke, Luk Lambrecht

September 2004. Constructies Espeel celebrates a half-century of its existence. The discoveries of a sociological study of the added value that collaboration with artists generates in an industrial environment is discussed. Yves Leterme wished Espeel happy anniversary, Lisbeth Gruwez performed a naked version of The Emperor's Clothes. Gifts were exchanged. Michel endowed his company with the dynamic motto *'Moving Together'*, and his employees gave him a gift of a work by Paul Gees; each guest left the celebration with a small piece by Paul Gees and a poem by Peter Verhelst.

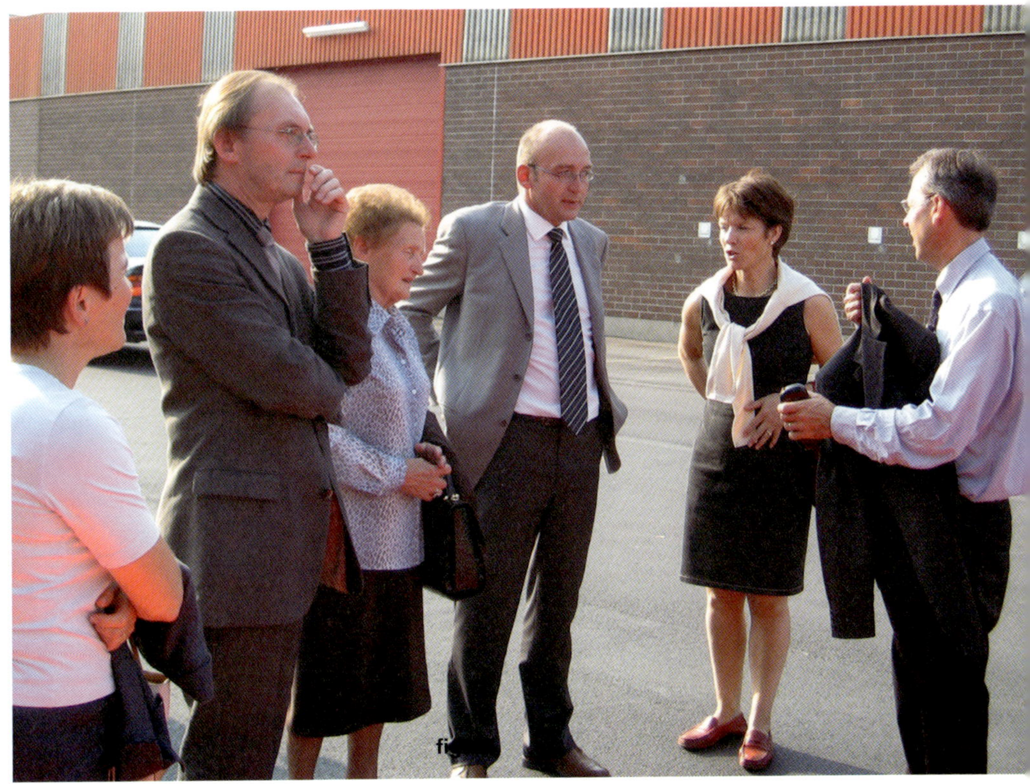

fig. 67   Michel, Luc and their mother, Mrs Espeel.

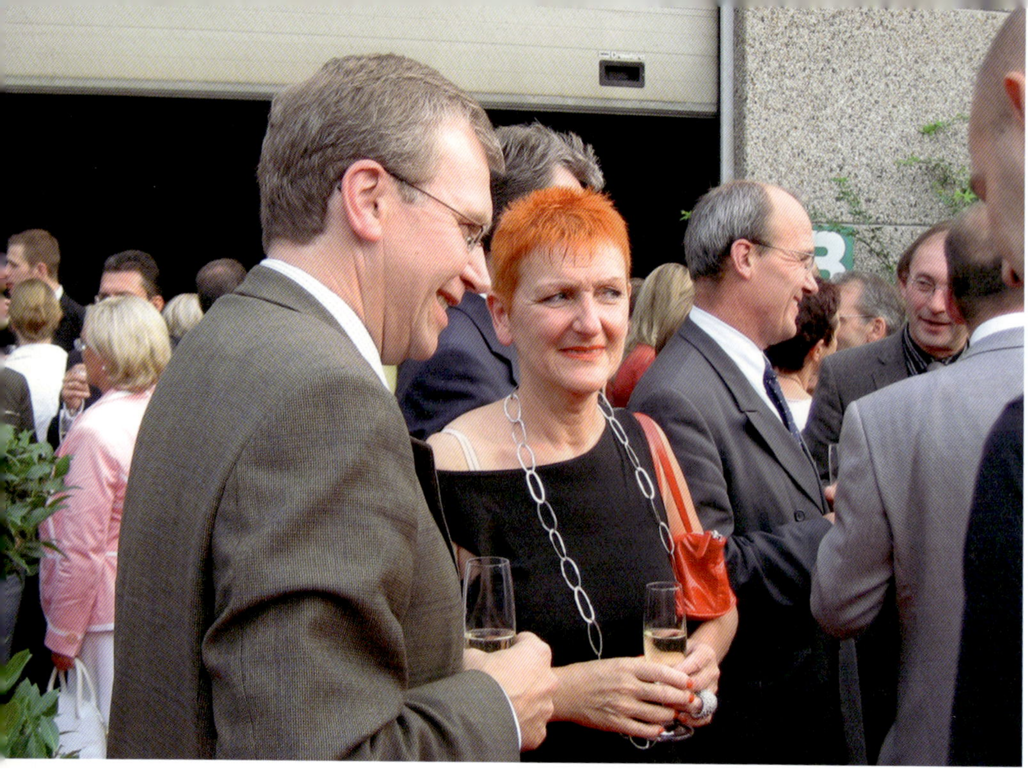

fig. 68

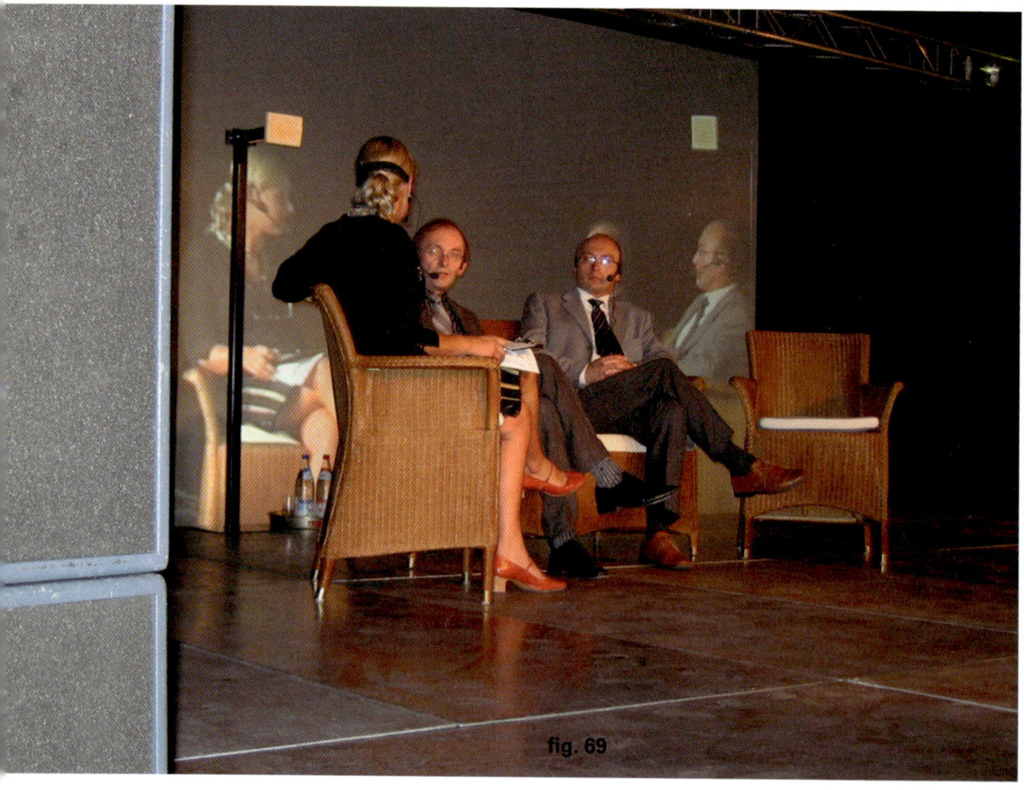

fig. 69

fig. 68   Yves Leterme and Julie Vandenbroucke.
fig. 69   The Espeel Case Study: Chantal Pattyn
in conversation with Luc and Michel Espeel.

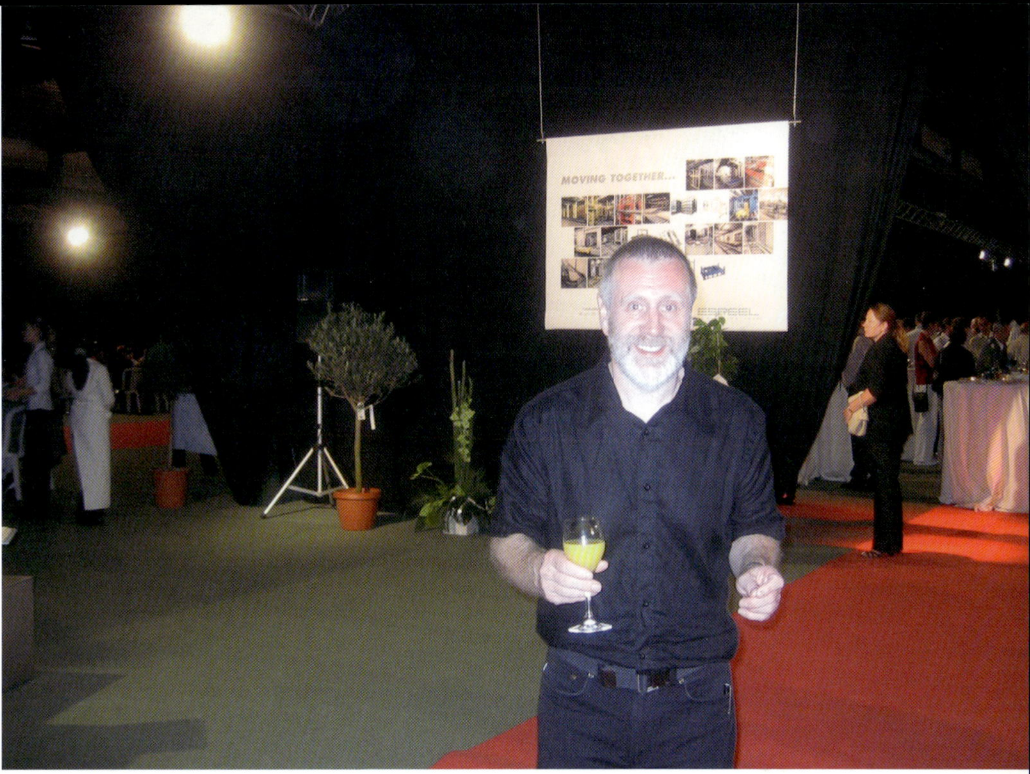

fig. 70

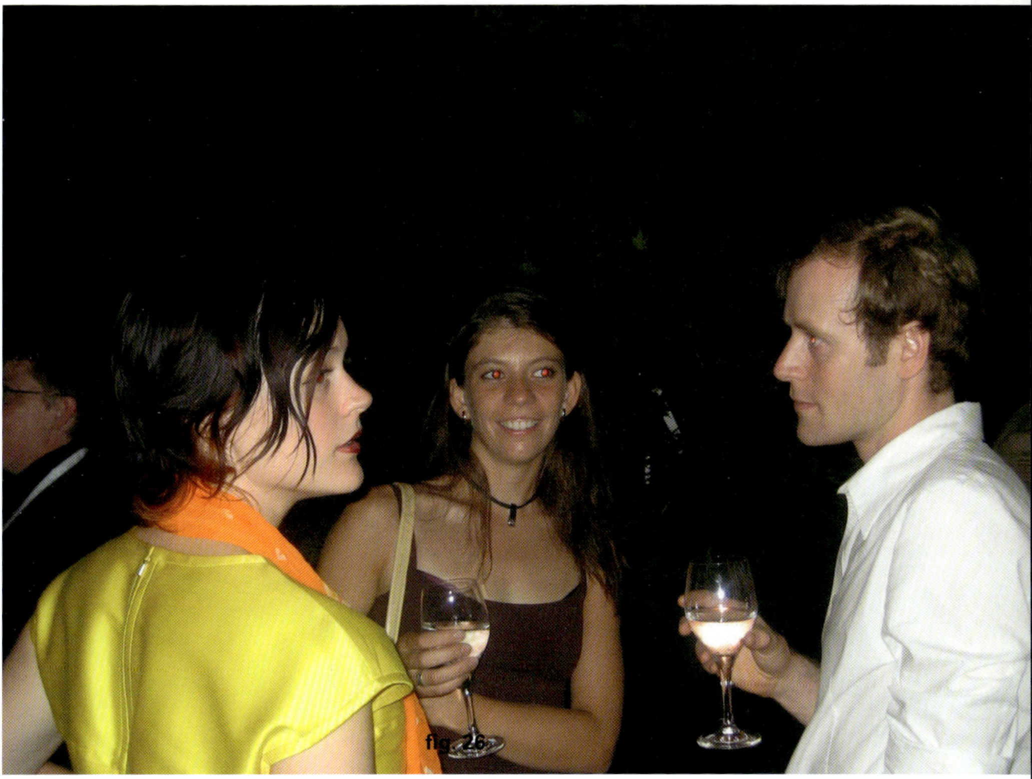

fig. 70   Paul Gees.
fig. 71   Annelies Espeel and Kris Vleeshouwer.

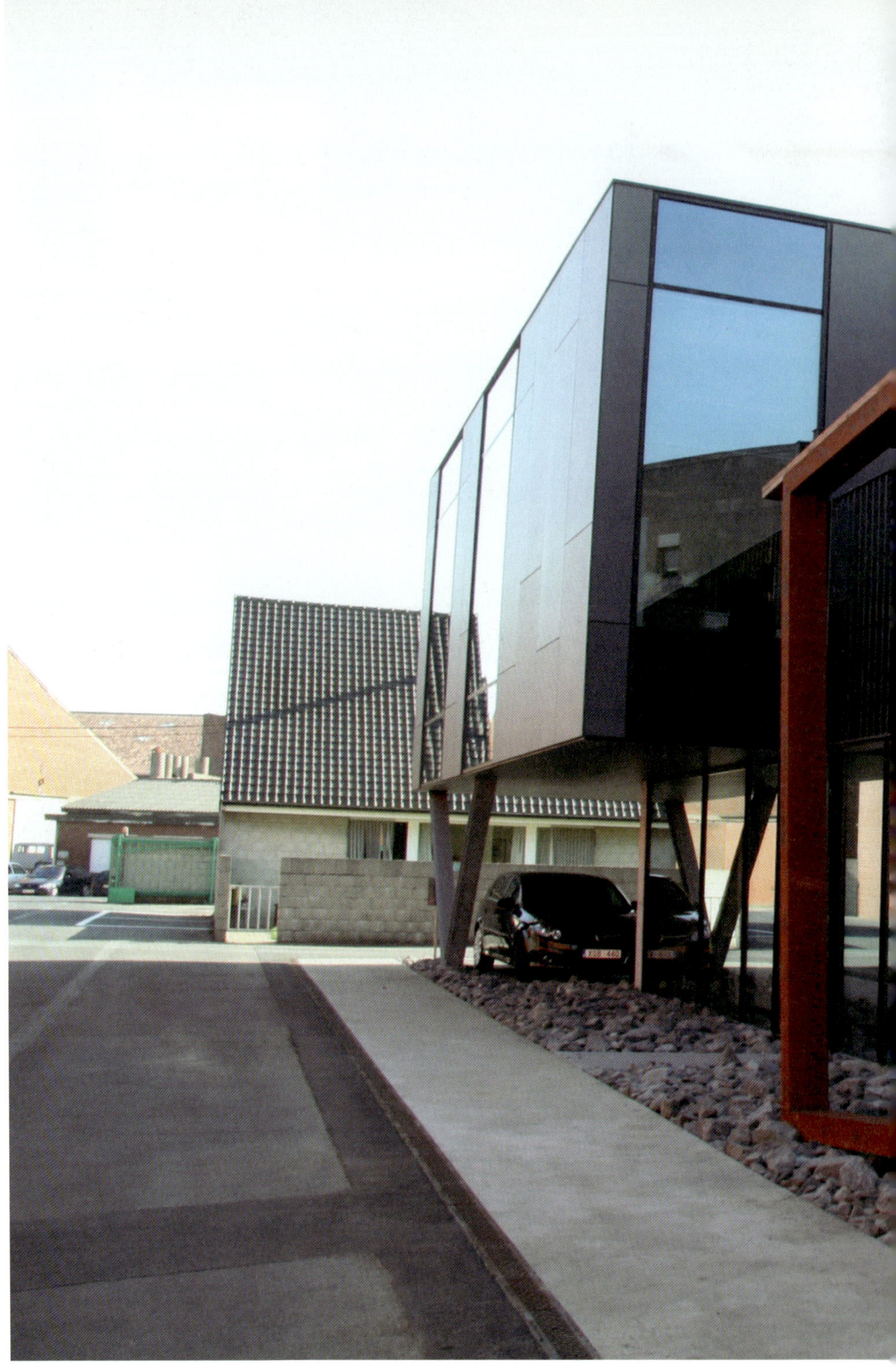

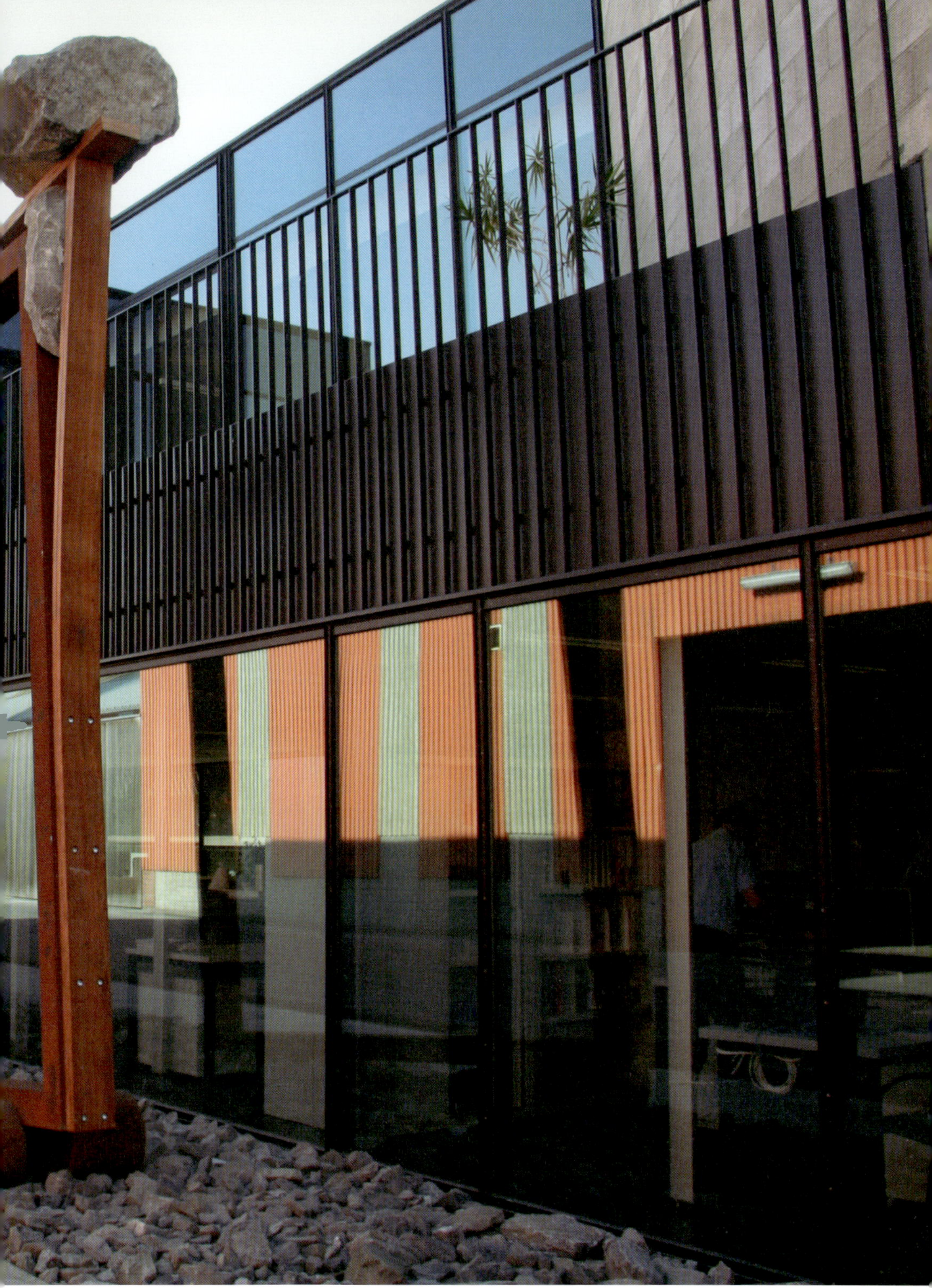

fig. 72

91

fig. 72 Paul Gees, *Hoekstuk* [Corner piece],
2004. A gift in honour of the 50th anniversary of
Constructies Espeel's existence, placed in front of
offices of the Constructies Espeel company.

Part IV

Three travel stories

At this point the narrative shifts in scale. Until now, we have been following the broad outlines from a bird's eye view. But since some of the collaborative ventures went further than usual, it is well worth zooming in on a few of them.

Essential

The collaboration between Constructies Espeel and Paul Gees is exemplary, right down to the last detail. Hans de Pelsmaecker also came knocking at the door, first of all as a sculptor. Constructies Espeel helped him create a number of monumental sculptures for his solo show in the city park at Lokeren (1994). But the result was meagre and De Pelsmaecker was disappointed. He decided to change track and went into teaching. He built a house and designed all its furniture and lighting fixtures.

Constructies Espeel was supplying products to Perfero, which was specialising in the interior finishing of construction sites. When Perfero ran into trouble, Constructies Espeel took it over. But Perfero was not well placed in the market. Construction sites were constantly running over budget, and those at the end of the process were the ones that lost out. Michel, therefore, tried to find a new purpose for the company. At that point, Hans de Pelsmaecker came to Constructies Espeel with a design for a minimalist breakfast table in aluminium. The link with Perfero was an obvious one. A series of five samples were produced under the Constructies Espeel umbrella. Less self-evident was the commercial investment that Hans de Pelsmaecker made in the venture: the artist entered the company – renamed *Essential* at his suggestion – and was to assume, in a Figurative sense, part of the risk. The new company name was intended to reflect what furniture ought to be: essential. The table seemed to be hewn from a single massive piece of aluminium. The design was so pure that there were no seams. In theory, the venture should have run like clockwork: a dream design, a company that combined creativity and sales Figures, the patronage of Constructies Espeel and design guru Max Borka, who lent his support to the project. On two occasions Essential took part in *Interieur*, the biennial design show in

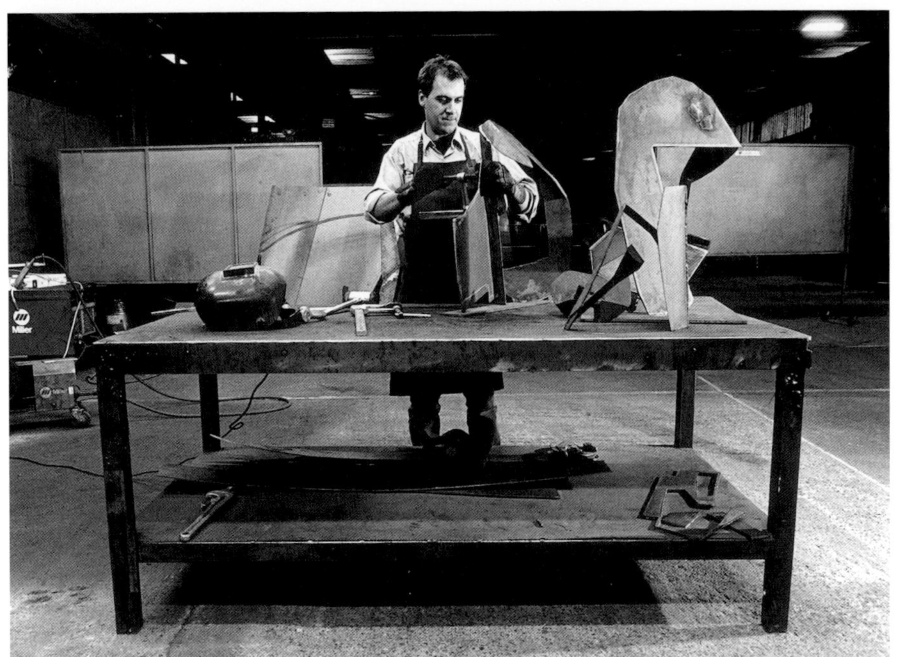

fig. 73

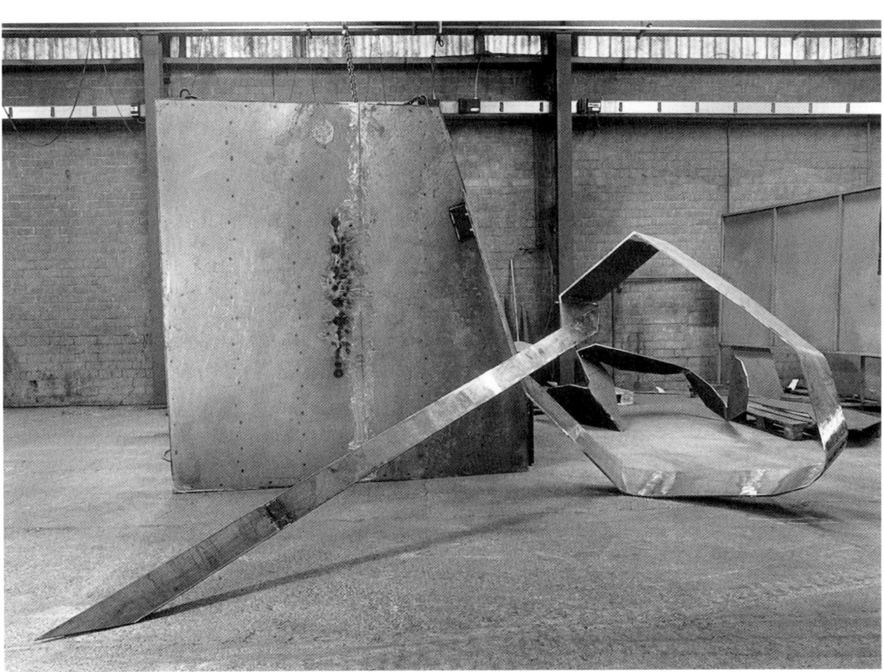

fig. 74

fig. 73   Hans De Pelsmacker. For the exhibition in Lokeren (1994), De Pelsmacker made his own sculptures out of material he found at the Constructies Espeel company. Photo: Griet Blomme.

fig. 74   Hans De Pelsmacker. Finished sculpture in the hall of Constructies Espeel. Photo: Griet Blomme.

93

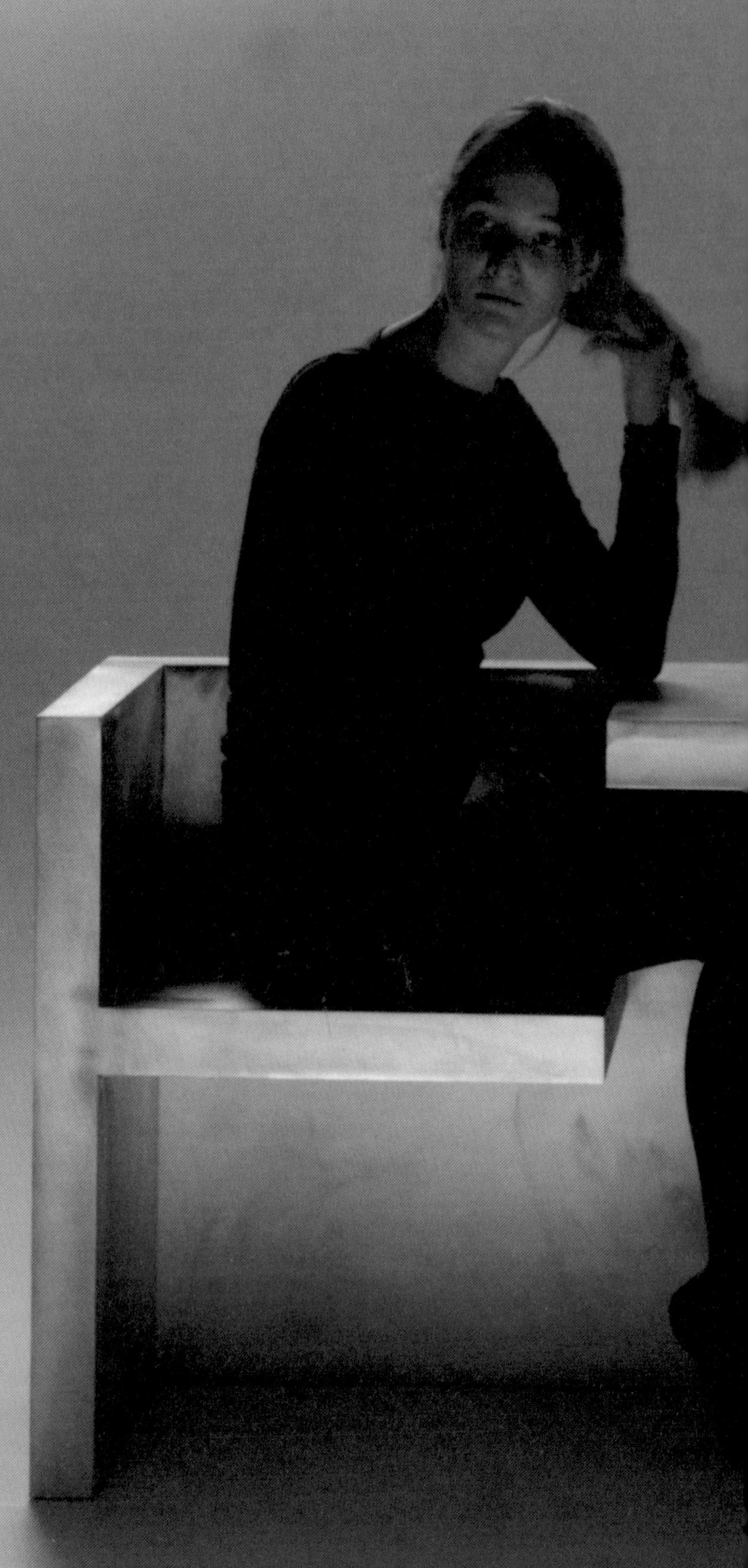

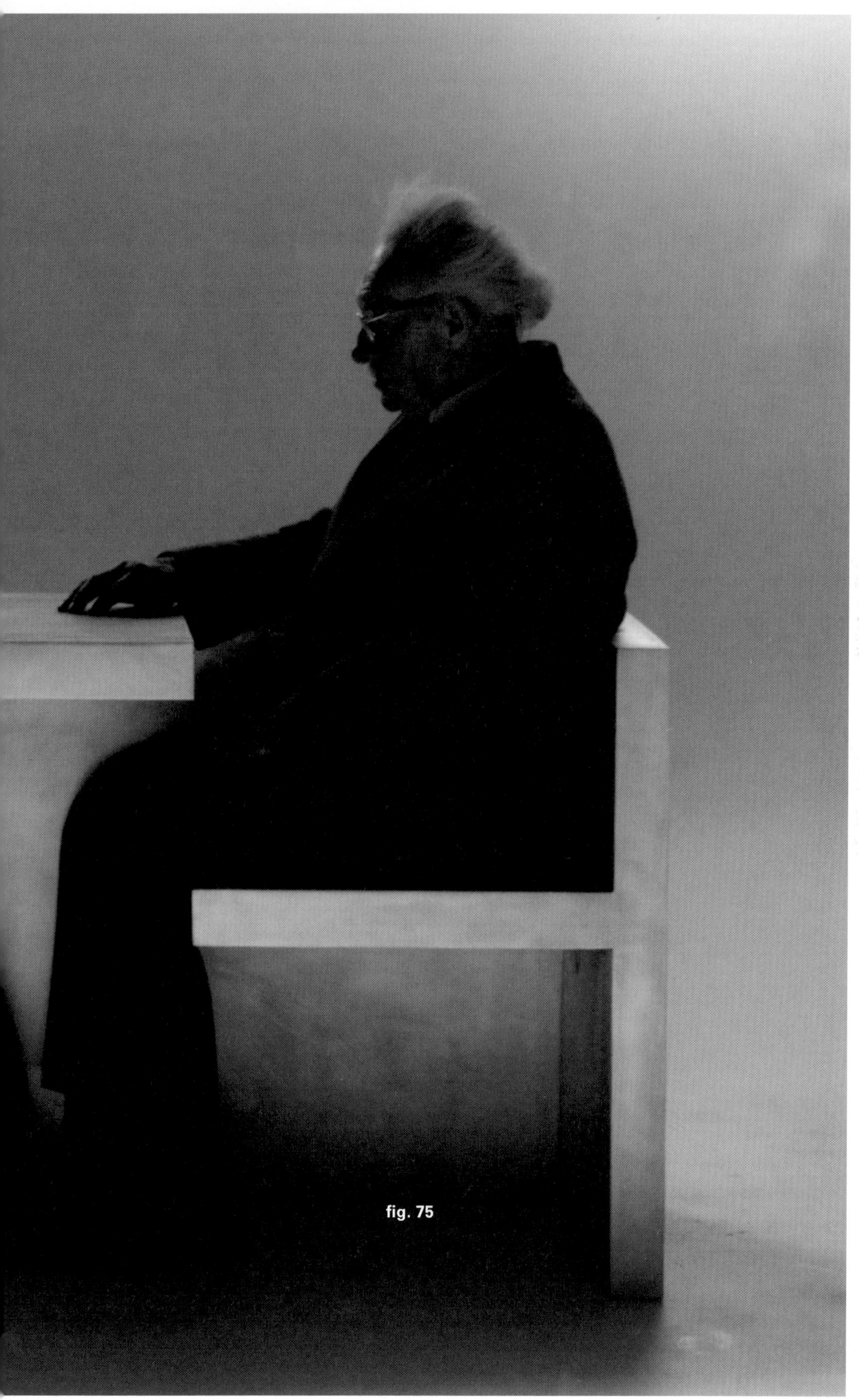

fig. 75

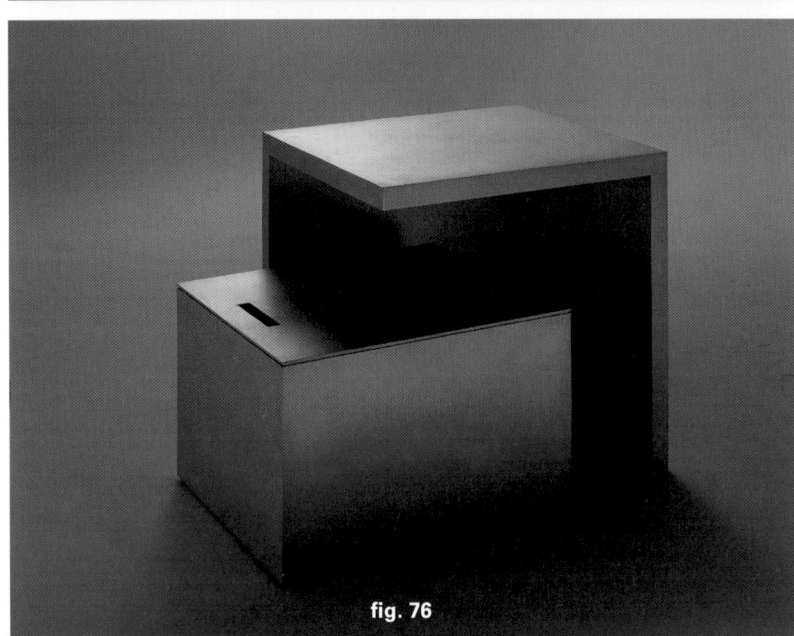

fig. 76

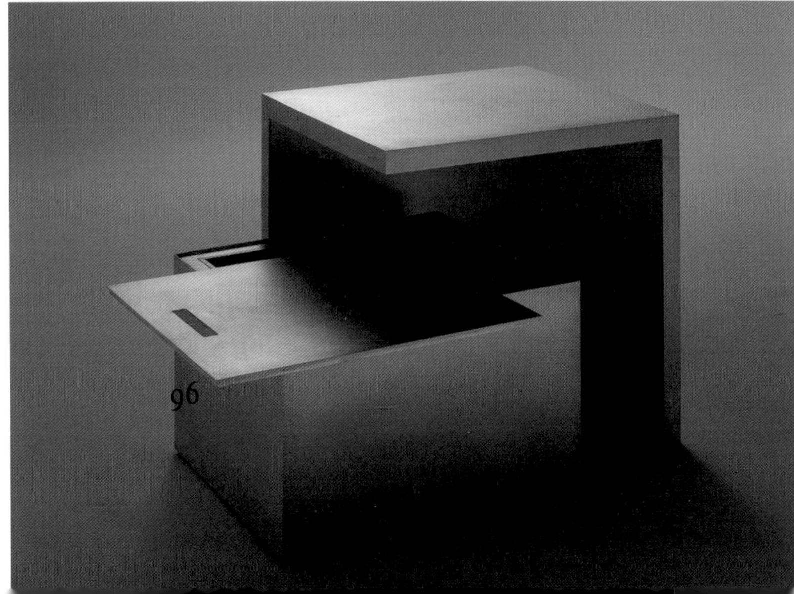

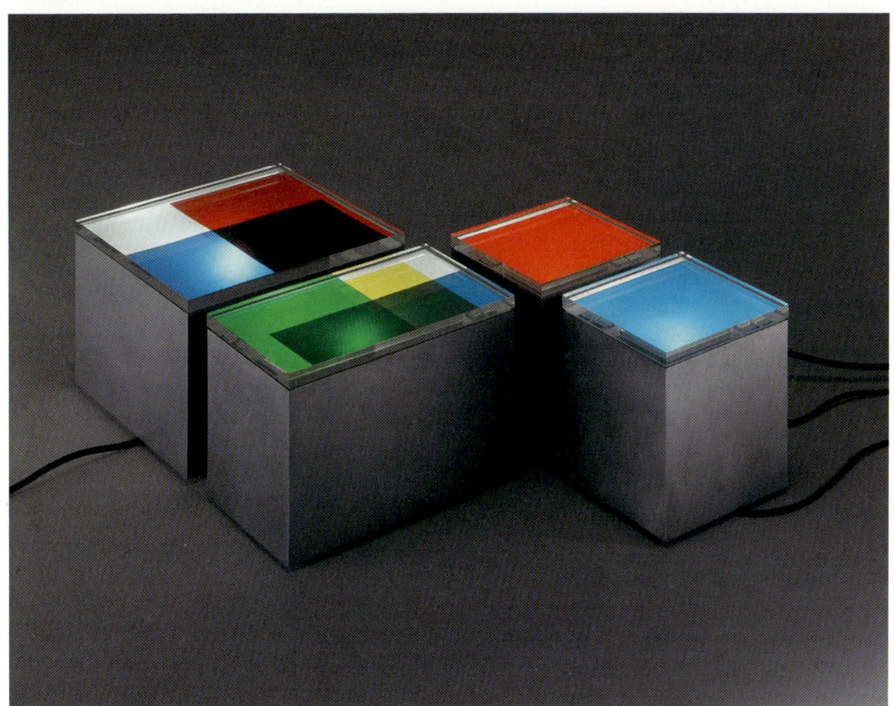

fig. 77

97

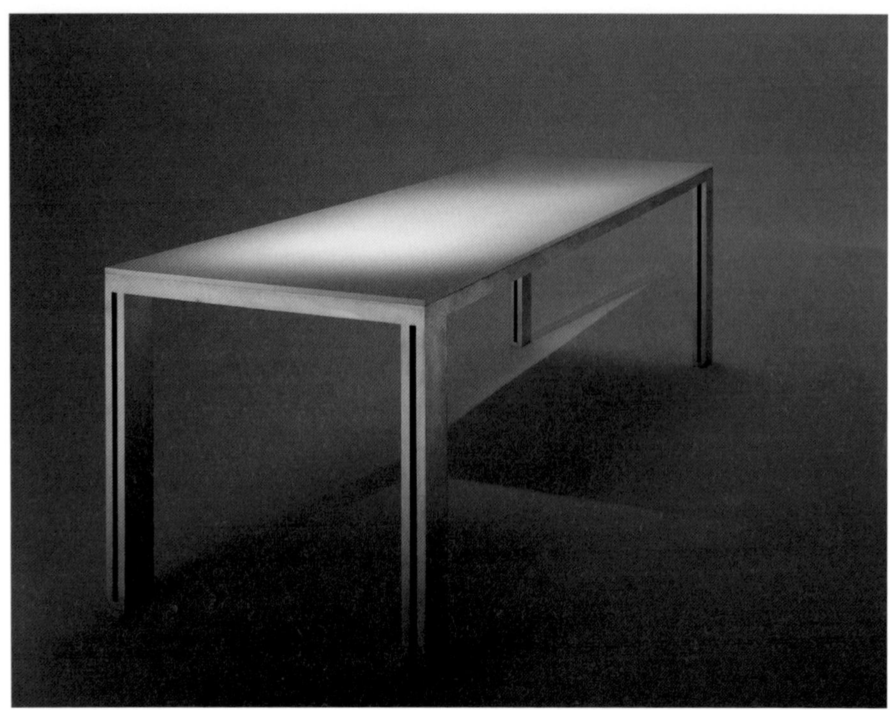

fig. 78

98

fig. 78   Hans De Pelsmacker, *Tafel* [Table] (Essential ESS04). Photo: Pascal Cornet.

Kortrijk. But sales were not ensuing. The price of each piece approached that of an artwork. It was a limited edition with each piece signed by the artist, yet it remained a work of design. That does not justify those kinds of prices.

Constructies Espeel cancelled further productions and Essential fizzled out, but de Peslmaecker's design remained strong. Soon a major design label took this 'coming man' under its wing.

Fragments bring luck

Kris Vleeschouwer had it made. He left the Higher Institute for Fine Arts (HISK) in Ghent, where he had become an artist, and went his own way. He followed the voice on the telephone that invited him to Constructies Espeel. After an initial visit, the contact proved solid. A few months later, when Kris exhibited in the Stroombeek cultural centre, there was a hitch with the technology for his installation. Michel offered him his assistance. From that moment on, the door was open and Kris paid Constructies Espeel further visits.

Kris received help and advice on the shop floor. What more could an artist want? And yet for Kris, the collaboration had yet another meaning. He felt that it meant something for the company, too. In his dealings with the workers and the office, communicating about the production of an artwork posed a greater challenge than just another industrial application. The experience stimulated him as an artist.

Julie introduced Kris to Philip Martens, director of the *Automations & Drives* department of the Siemens plant in the Belgian town of Huizingen. The German head office of Siemens had a longstanding tradition of collaborating with artists, but in Belgium the ice had not yet been broken. Kris, Philip and Julie met a few times, but none of them had a clear vision of what the next step ought to be. That is, until Kris was short-listed for the Young Belgian Painters Award. The modest plan that he had started grew more ambitious in the course of the discussions with Siemens. He has the collaboration with Siemens to thank for the technical elaboration of his work.

For all parties concerned, this was pioneering work. The installation entitled *Glassworks* is an artistic visualisation of the interactive technologies that Siemens was developing. A monumental, industrial shelf loaded with glass bottles was linked up to five monitors. The monitors stood in the Bozar arts centre in Brussels, and were connected to five glass recycling bins in the city. Each time a bottle was dropped into one of the bins, a grip arm grabbed hold of a bottle on the shelf in the Bozar and dropped it on to the floor, where it shattered. This presented Siemens with a challenge that should not be underestimated. The technology had to make the visual language of the artist its own. Right up to the actual opening, they were fiddling with the software. Kris won the Bozar prize for a complex work that was an artistic, social and technological tour de force.

With Kris's story, the road movie takes to the seas. Like a young sailor, he set off from Constructies Espeel in the wake of the habitual collaborative ventures. He displayed a particular sensitivity (thanks perhaps to his youthful years) to the potential of this interaction. And so he sailed into the friendly waters of Arteconomy. Julie grabbed hold of the ropes and steered him into the safe haven of Siemens. In its shipyard, he was able to put together his dream fleet, with which he successfully won his first naval battle. For Siemens, this was an outstanding opportunity to perfect some of its technologies and make them water-tight.

Arteconomy in action

The pioneering work done by Arteconomy in this area deserves special mention. With the expertise it has gradually built up, the organisation aims to set up collaborative projects between artists and companies. The vision of Constructies Espeel serves as a road-map and the Siemens case serves as the first hands-on exercise.

With the knowledge that a joint venture between art and economy will change for the better *along the road*, Arteconomy wants to serve as a sort of travel agent. Its task is not to set out the route, but to mediate and accompany it. In 2006, Arteconomy found five company executives who were willing to go on the journey. The non-profit association linked up each firm with an artist whose personality and approach would fit with the company. This meant that the artist's exposure to reality could serve as a source of inspiration. And conversely, the artist would hold up a mirror to the blind spots in the company.

Arteconomy was now ready and available for the goals it had set out to achieve. While Constructies Espeel and Siemens had in the past responded to requests coming from artists, the demand now was coming from business leaders. What Arteconomy had to offer closely matched the needs of the

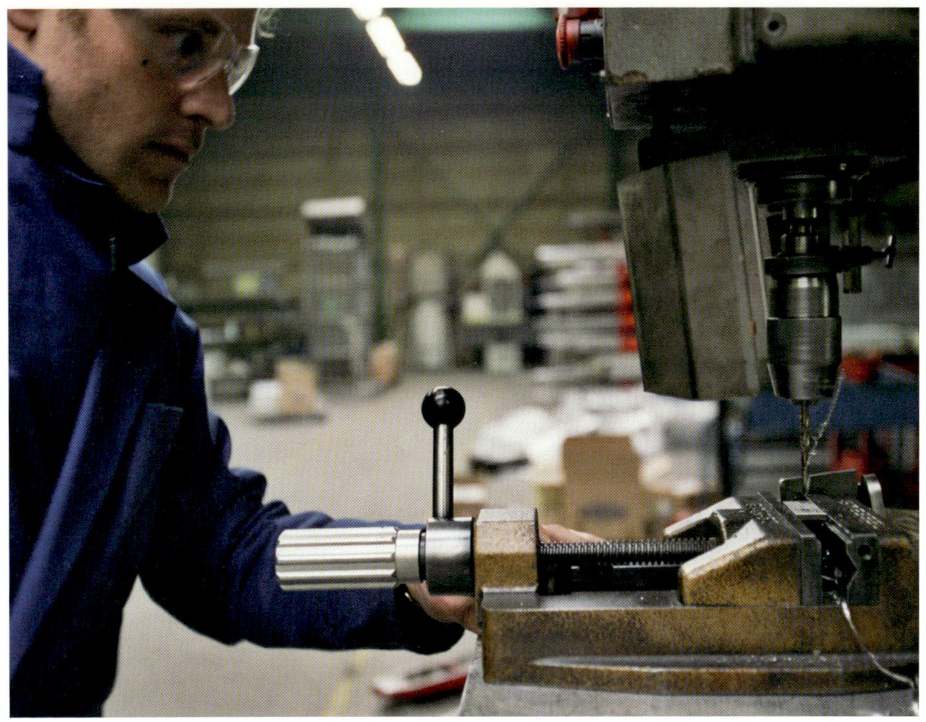

fig. 79

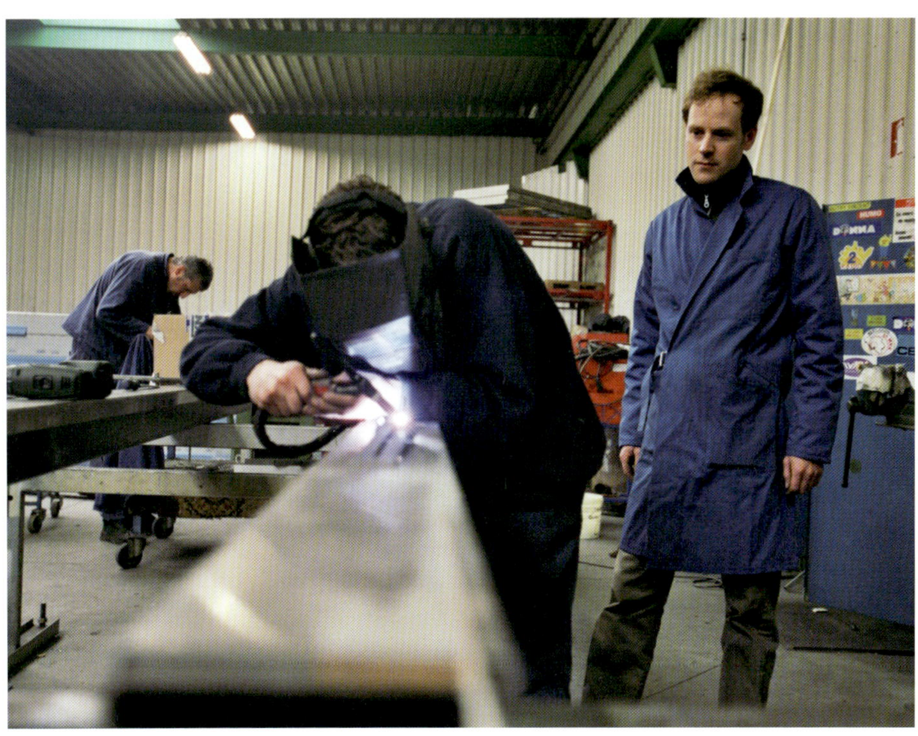

fig. 79   Kris Vleeschouwer at
Constructies Espeel.

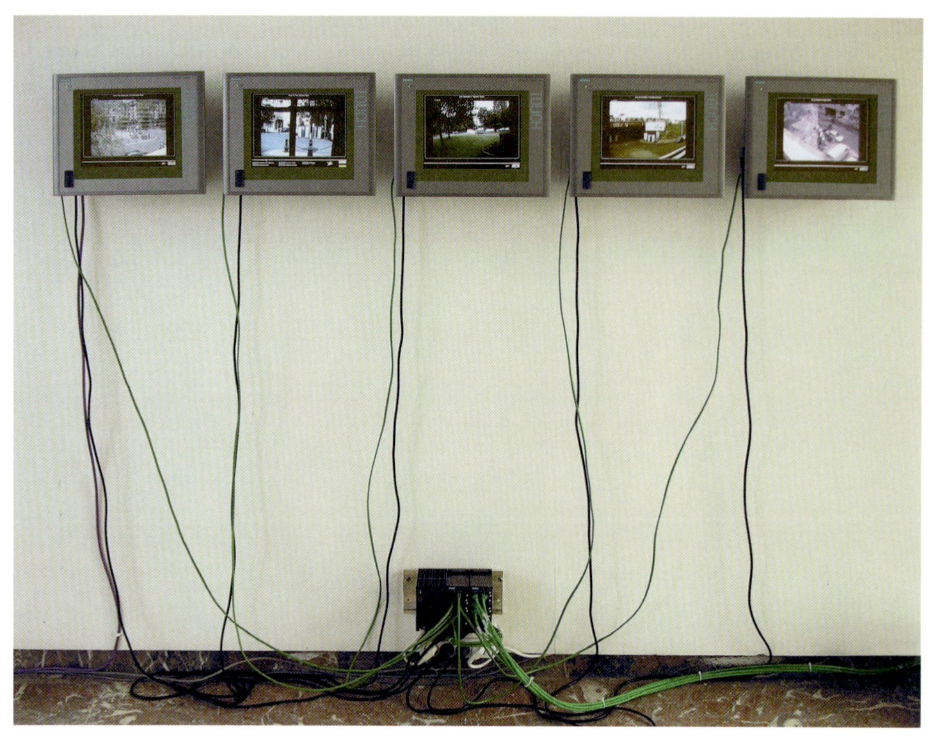

fig. 80

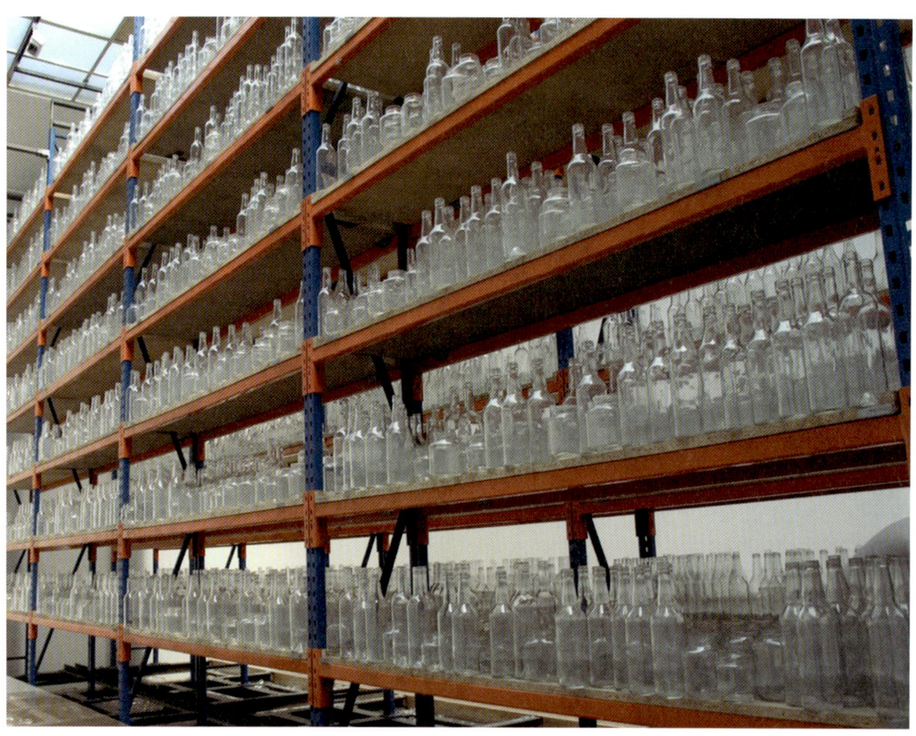

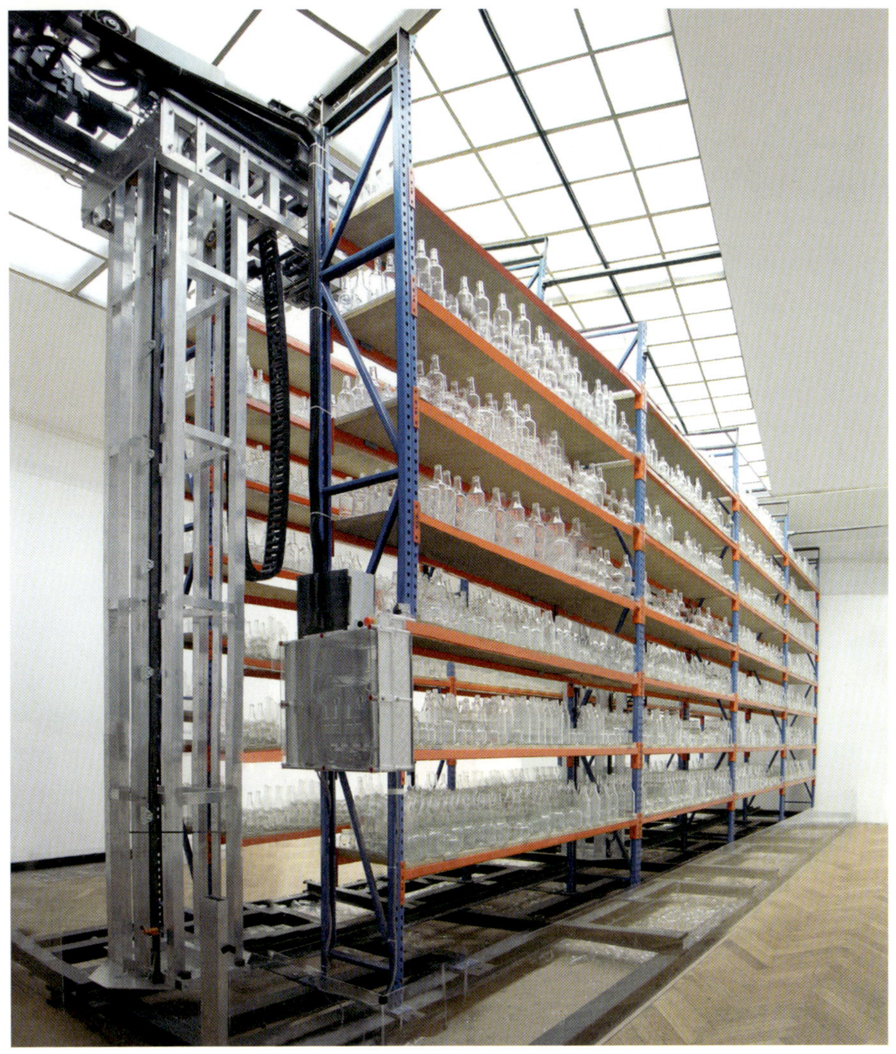

fig. 81

figs. 80-81   Kris Vleeshouwer, *Glass-works*, 2005. Photos of the installation created for the Young Belgian Painters prize, Paleis voor Schone Kunsten (Centre for Fine Arts, now Bozar), Brussels.

modern manager: innovation. Rigidity is the Achilles' heel of every company. Therefore, a process that promotes flexibility finds a ready ear and buyers. Arteconomy says: "Walk with me", we can bring about change. The projects are running while Arteconomy steadily hammers away at paving the way.

Mon usine de fer

Claire Roudenko-Bertin was invited to attend the *Touch Me* exhibition, and she reacted with suspicion. She was fearful of the claws of industry. She doesn't want to take part in the showpiece without at least calling into question the mechanisms of capitalism. During *Touch Me*, Claire gave Michel a contract proposal:

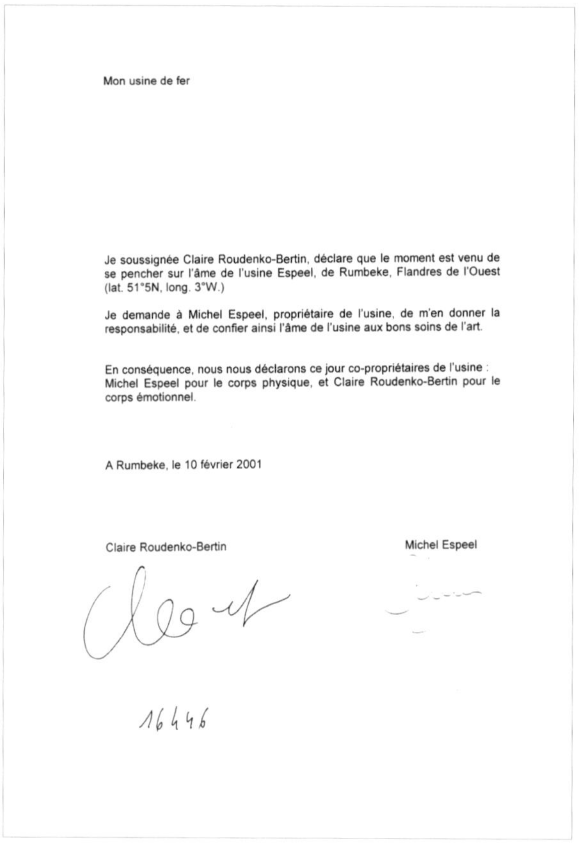

Mon usine de fer

Je soussignée Claire Roudenko-Bertin, déclare que le moment est venu de se pencher sur l'âme de l'usine Espeel, de Rumbeke, Flandres de l'Ouest (lat. 51°5N, long. 3°W.)

Je demande à Michel Espeel, propriétaire de l'usine, de m'en donner la responsabilité, et de confier ainsi l'âme de l'usine aux bons soins de l'art.

En conséquence, nous nous déclarons ce jour co-propriétaires de l'usine : Michel Espeel pour le corps physique, et Claire Roudenko-Bertin pour le corps émotionnel.

A Rumbeke, le 10 février 2001

Claire Roudenko-Bertin   Michel Espeel

How real is this contract? The parodic wordplay on the corporate genre of a 'contract' pokes fun at the economic mentality that treats everything – even the most intangible things – as the subject of a business deal. But both parties, Michel and Claire, sign it in all seriousness. That makes the contract more than mere poetry; it is binding. This is the most radical type of agreement Michel has ever entered into with an artist. From the time of its signing, Michel remained the owner of the firm, while Claire owned the soul of the company. Both undertook to oversee their own domain in the full knowledge that they also needed to rely on each other.

With the soul of Constructies Espeel contractually sealed, Claire had sufficient guarantees to get to work on the 'material side' of the company. She set up her office and meeting room in Michel's old Porsche car, which stood abandoned on the lot. Her mobile home became the intersection of the social systems of art and economy. She was regularly cited for driving against the traffic. She regularly tied the conventions of these two systems to each other like the laces of a pair of shoes.

Claire was invited to put on a major exhibition at the *Musée d'Art Contemporain* of Bordeaux, based in a harbour shed. She could see that the budget was coming from the economy. She used art as a sluice gate to pump money back into the industry via the shortest possible route. Constructies Espeel served as her mouthpiece. She 'purchased' individual items from 'her' Constructies Espeel company, transporting them to Bordeaux. Even the Porsche went along. She thus had the body of the company transported piece by piece. The soul of her exhibition lay in the conceptual aspect of financial transactions: Art that settles accounts with her financial backer.

The company was no longer in its apprenticeship period, but in December 2005 Claire gave it yet another première. The production hall at Constructies Espeel was the site of the first performance of *La Fabbrica Illuminata*, a piece of music composed by Luigi Nono in 1964 for metalworkers in a factory in Genoa. The concert was prepared and performed by the staff of Constructies Espeel. It took place on a Friday afternoon after working hours at 3:30. At the following New Year's reception, each employee received a letter from Claire with a small metal plaque with a calligraphic engraving of an overlapping body and soul.

Claire made her mark on Constructies Espeel. Not in order to set anything right, but to share and nurture the 'life of the soul' with Michel and the staff.

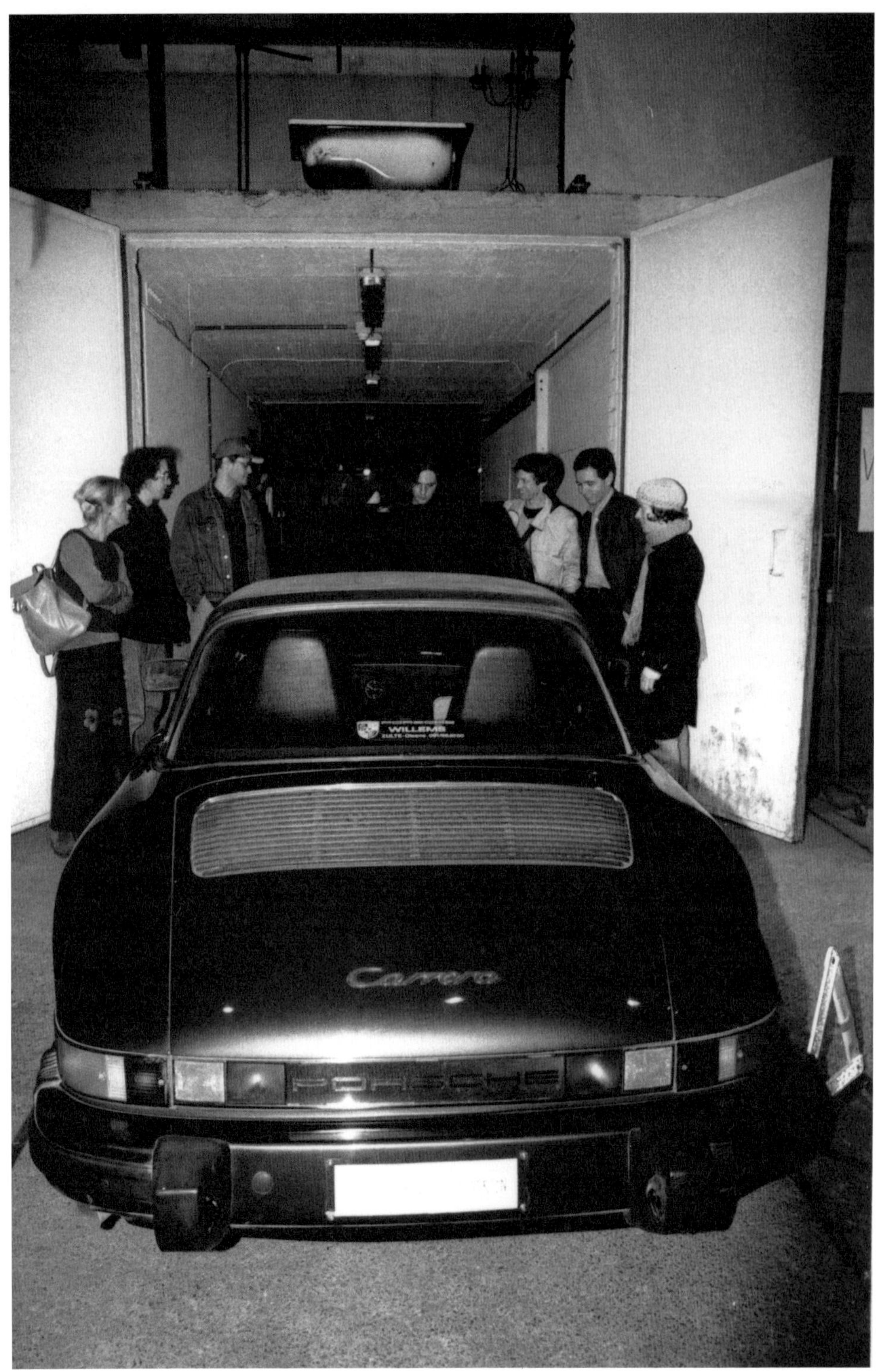

fig. 82

fig. 82   Michel Espeel's old Porsche,
used as an office by Claire Roudenko-
Bertin at Constructies Espeel. Photo:
Boris Saverys.

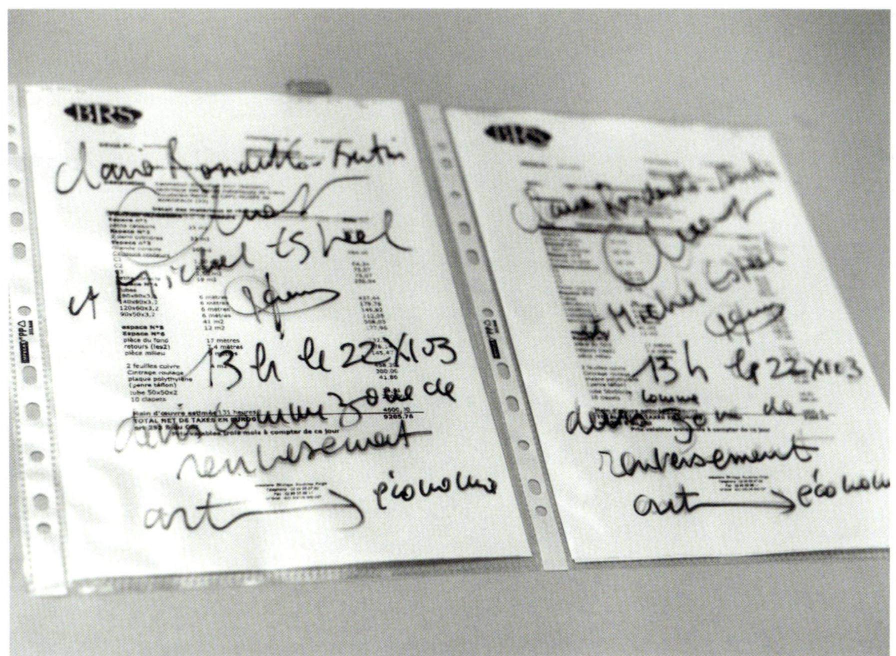

fig. 83

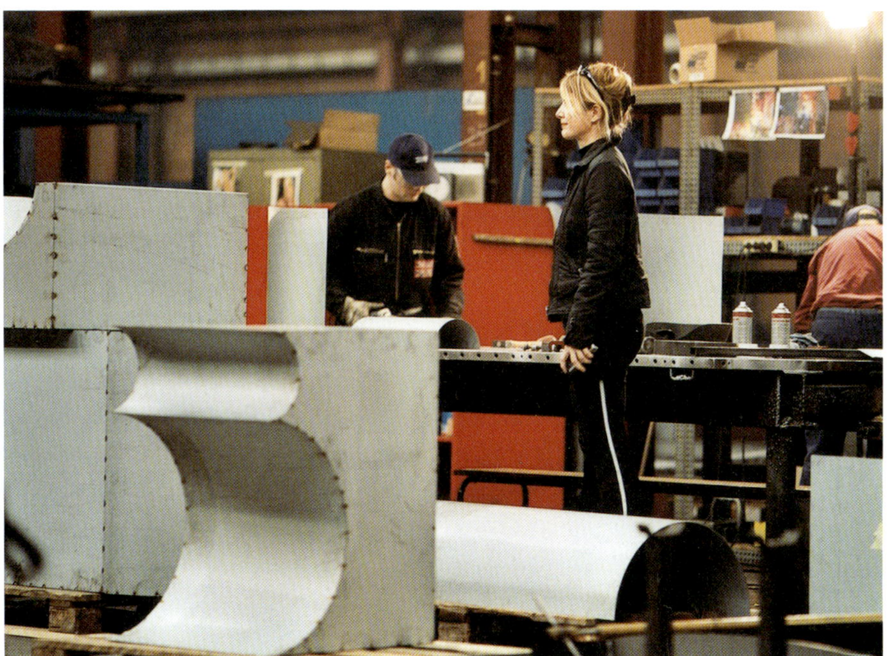

fig. 84

figs. 83-84 Claire brought objects from Constructies Espeel for her exhibition at the CAPC in Bordeaux (2004). Her exhibition budget thus appeared in the company's *cashflow* ledger. This contract sealed the transaction.

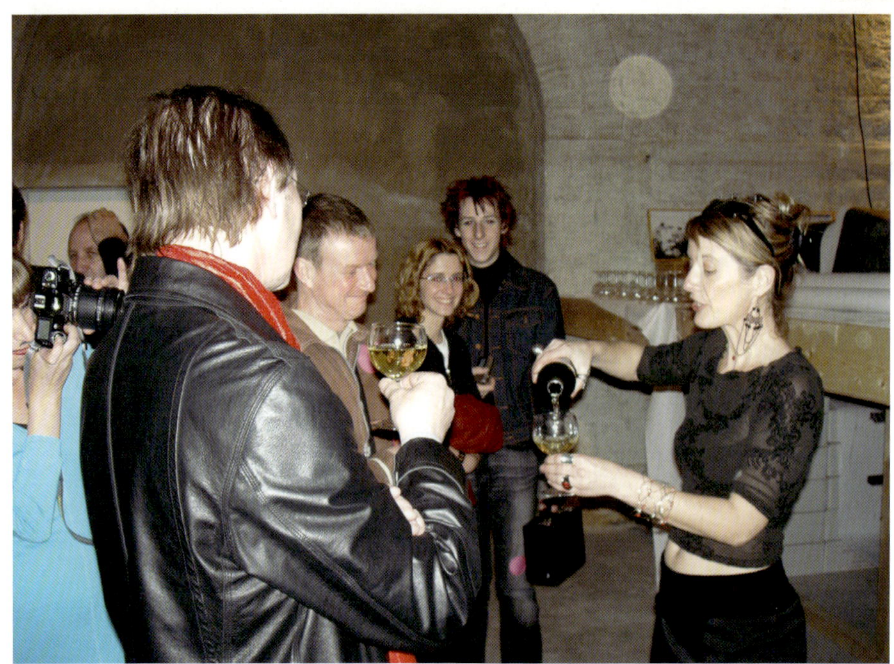

fig. 85

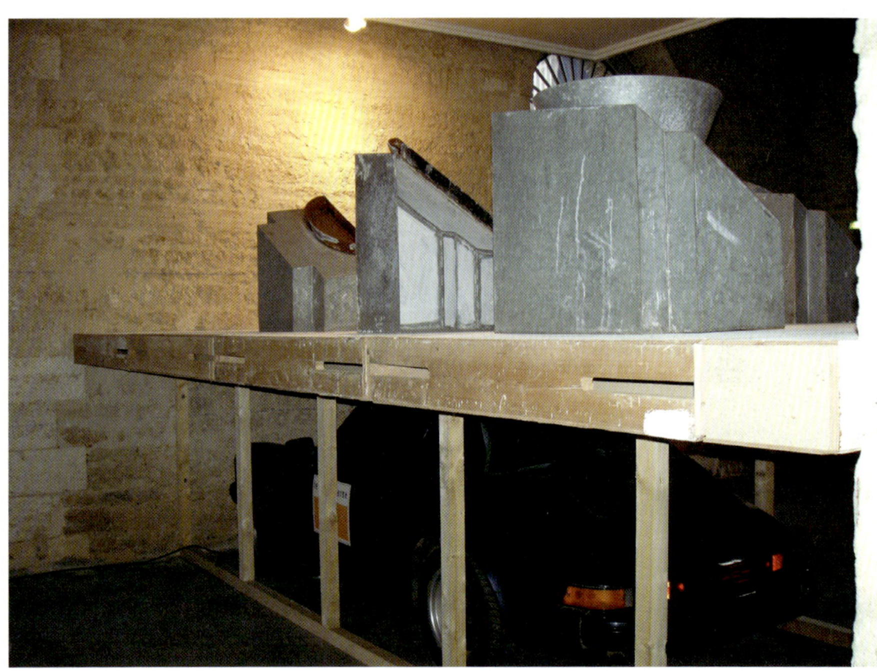

fig. 86

fig. 85 Michel and Claire at the
opening in Bordeaux.
fig. 86 Claire Roudenko-Bertin, *Il est
temps de recommencer à énerver les
dieux*, a view of the exhibition, 2004.

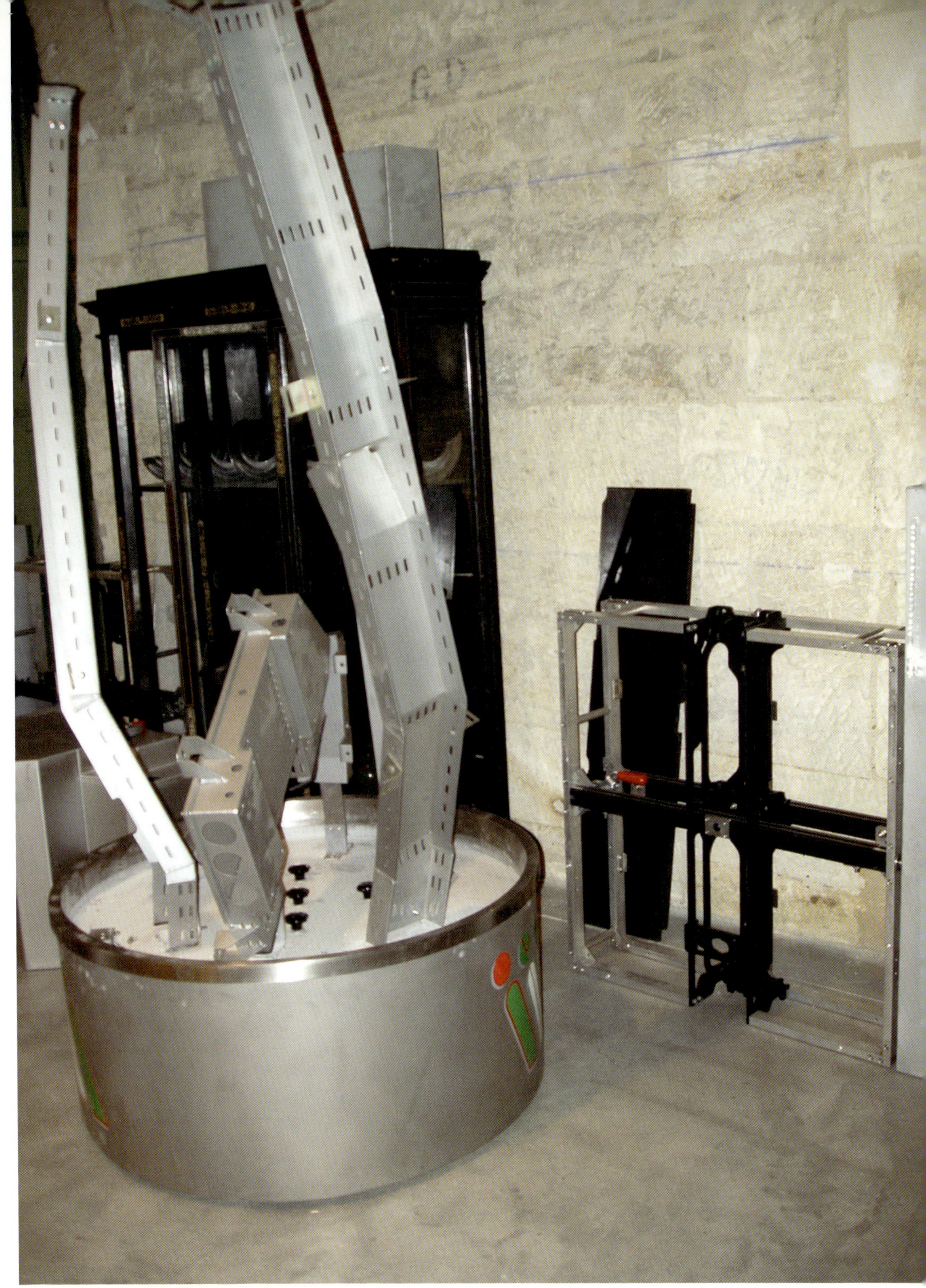

fig. 87

109

fig. 87 Claire Roudenko-Bertin, *Il est temps de recommencer à énerver les dieux,* a view of the exhibition, 2004.

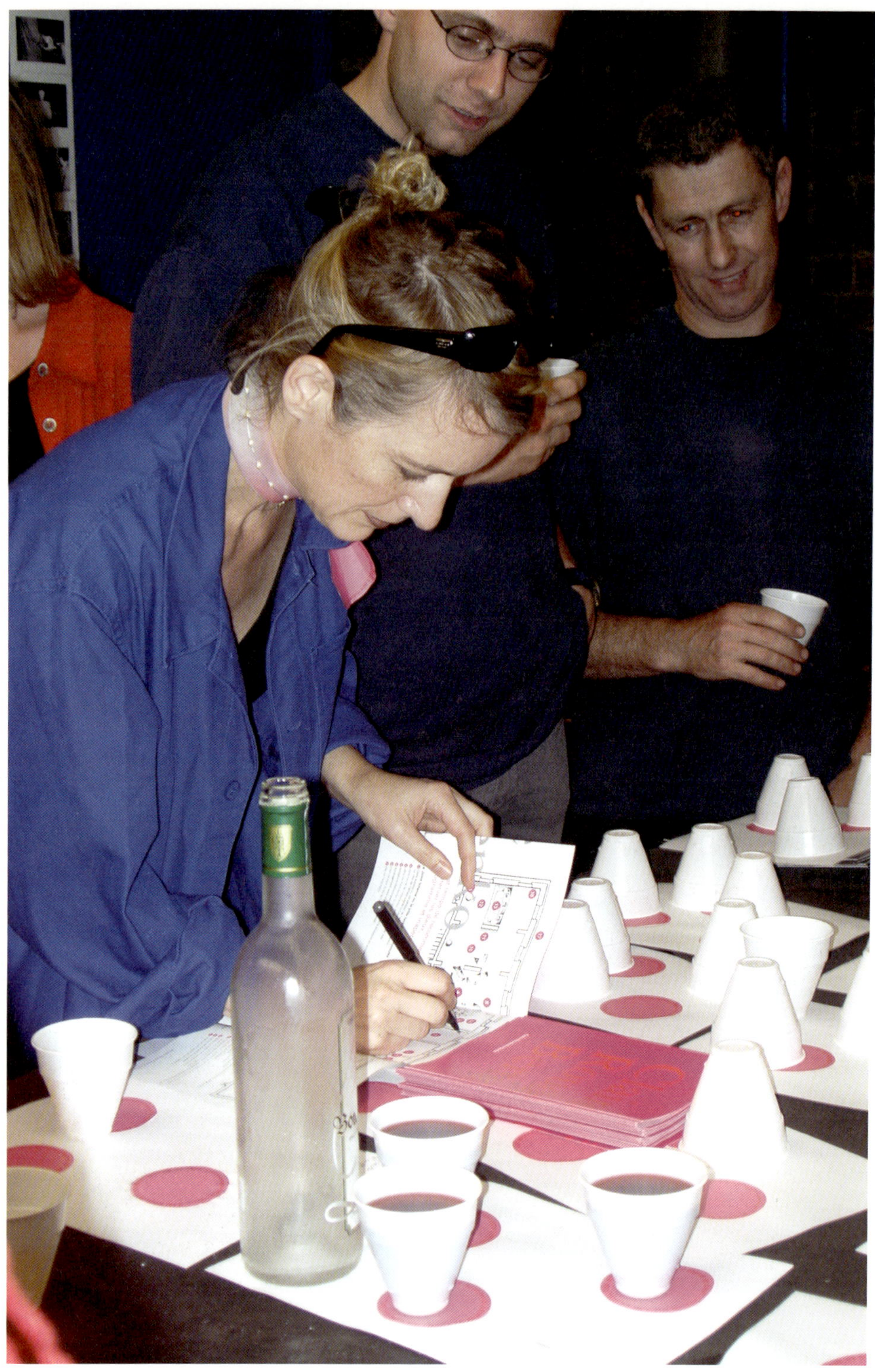

fig. 88

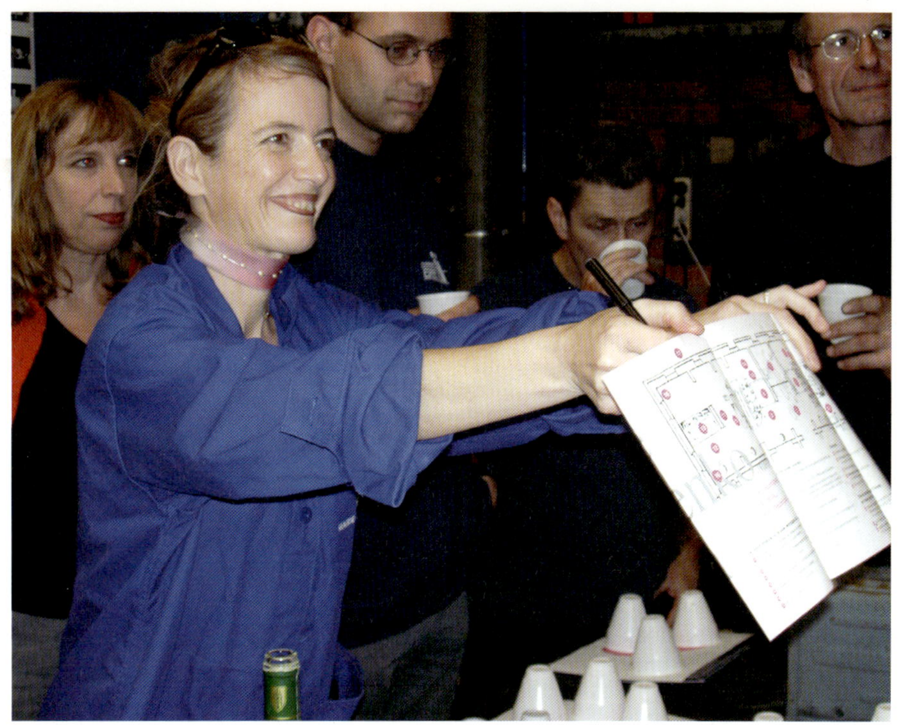

fig. 89

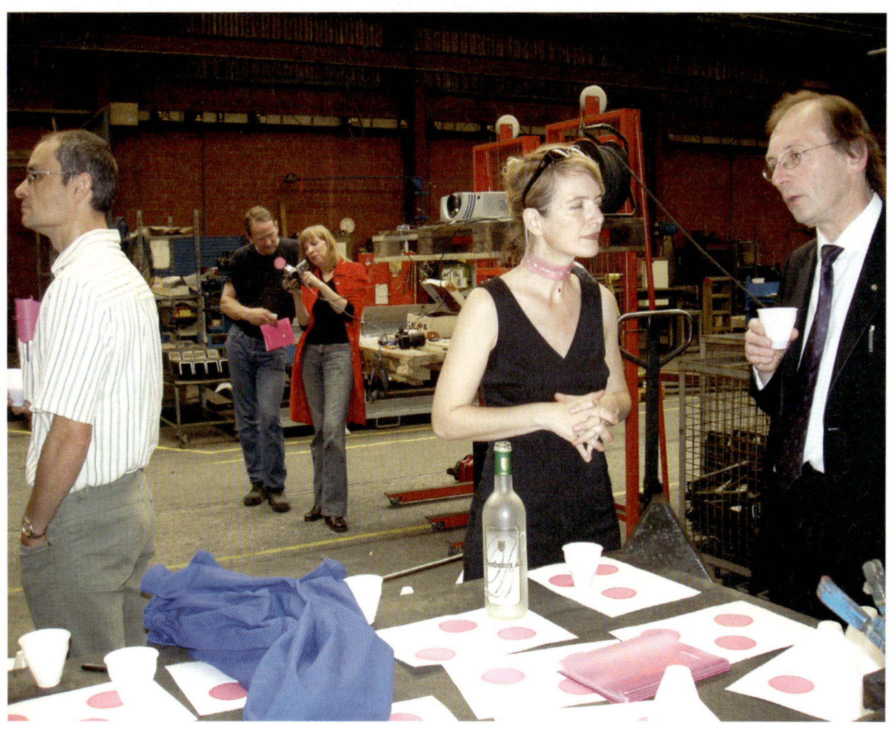

III

figs. 88, 89   Claire informs and thanks
the employees of Constructies Espeel for
their collaboration in the Bordeaux
event.

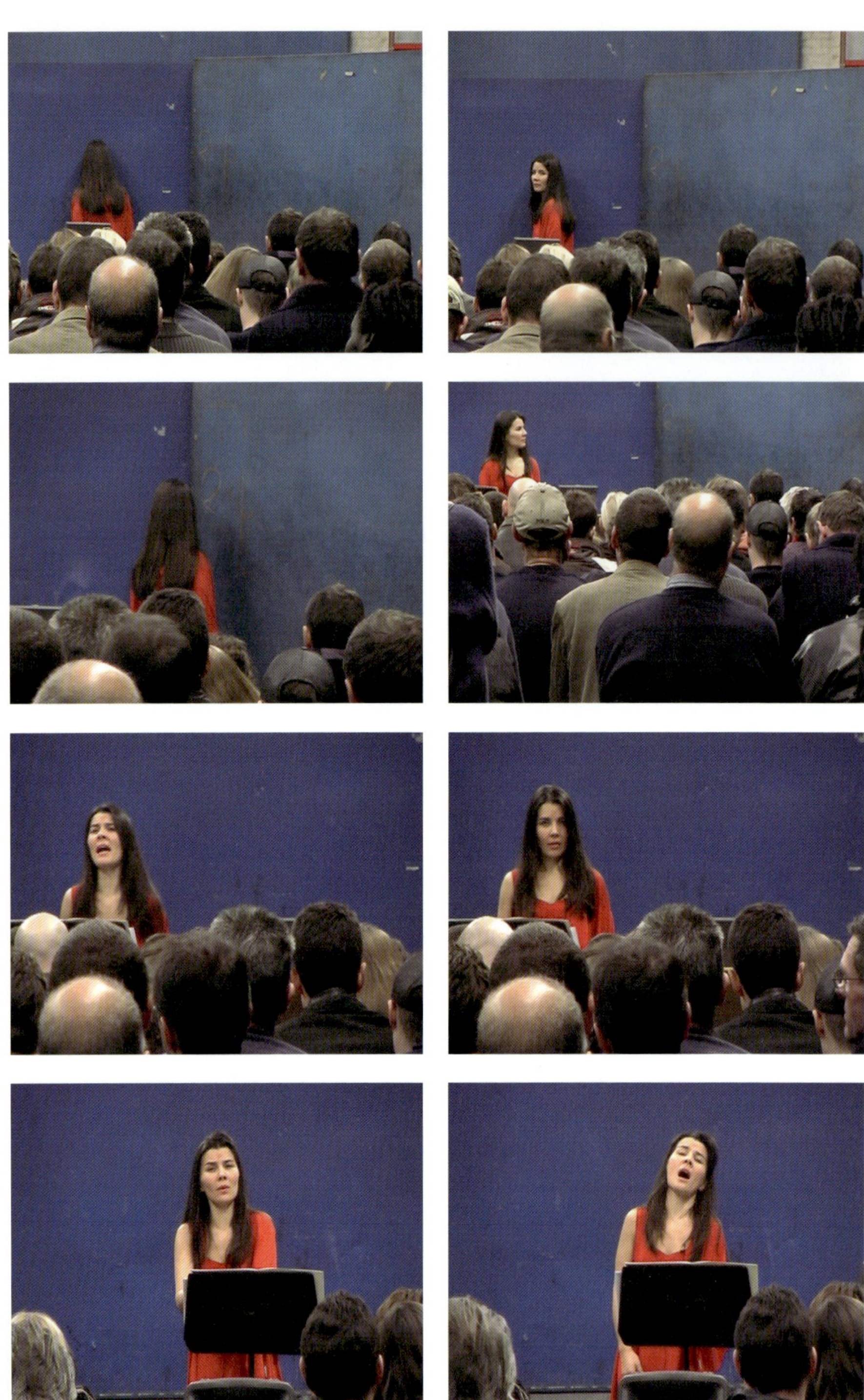

fig. 90

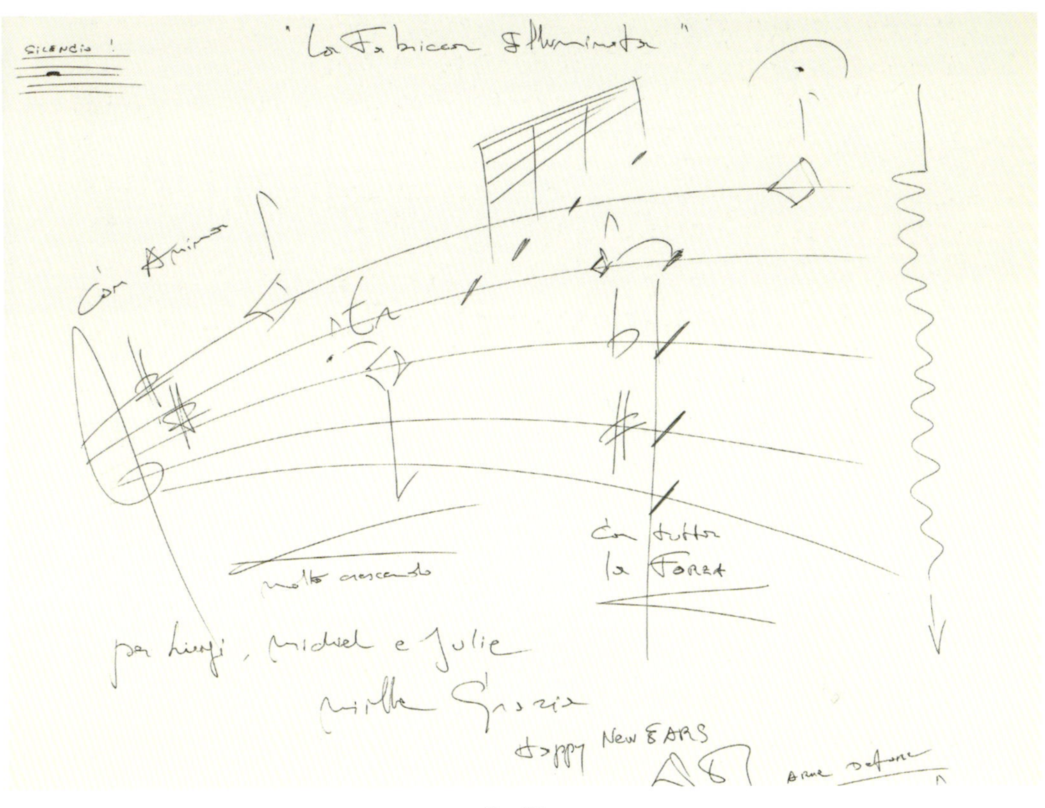

fig. 91

113

fig. 90   December 2005. Soprano Anne Hye-Mi Shin brings *La Fabbrica Illuminata* by Luigi Nono, directed by Arne Deforce, upon invitation by Claire Roudenko-Bertin. The composition consists of a four-track montage of sounds from a high-temperature furnace in Turin, known as 'the factory of death'. The raw sound was mixed with live singing by Anne Hye-Mi Shin, a Parisian soprano. The communist Nono wanted to protest in his own way against inhuman working conditions. The piece was first performed in Italy in 1965. The composer wanted it to be performed only in factories. No easy task. Only at Constructies Espeel was this explicit desire on the part of the composer honoured. Video stills: Yves Coussement.

fig. 91   Sketch by Arne Deforce, curator/director of *La Fabbrica* Illuminata in Julie and Michel's guestbook.

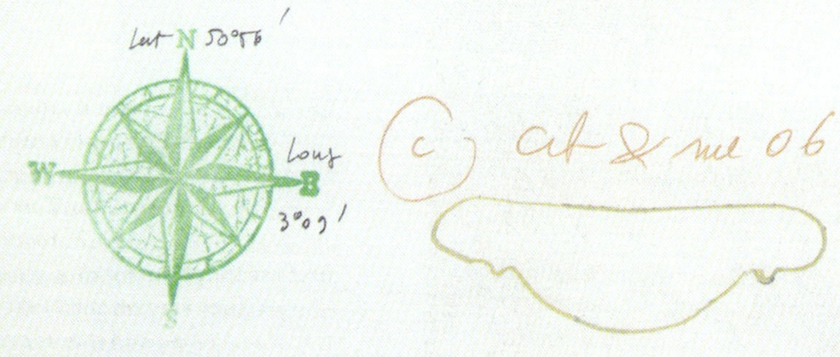

fig. 92

fig. 92 The 2006 New Year's reception at Constructies Espeel: each employee received a letter from Claire together with a small metal engraving, a stamp on which body and soul literally flowed into each other.

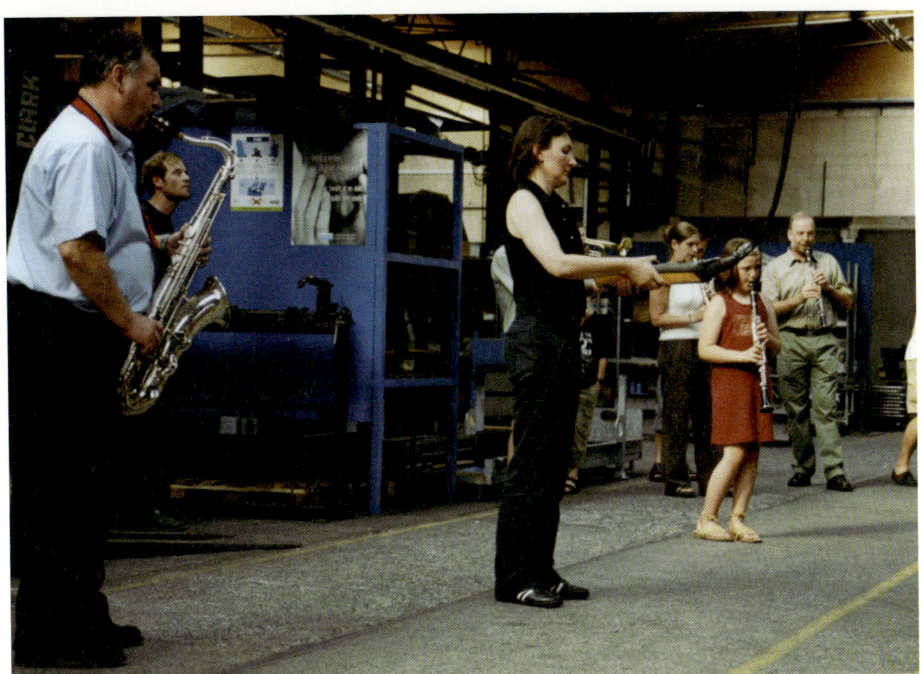

fig. 93

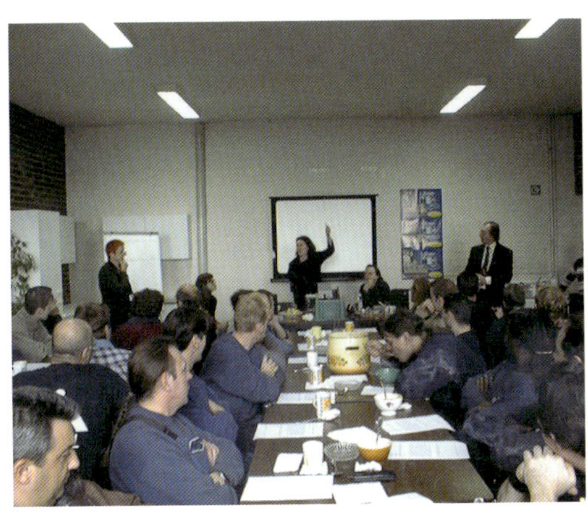

fig. 94

figs. 93, 95, 96   Joëlle Tuerlinckx sees in
the Constructies Espeel company a basis
for a longer-term collaboration. She is
present from time to time, as fleeting as
the breath on a cold window pane. The
first meetings are for discussions. Later
she concentrates on the auditory aspect
of the machines and the infrastructure.
A few brass bands from the area come
at her request to play in the factory hall,
while the factory serves as the percus-
sion section. At the time, Joëlle also
invited the poet Sila Blume. He brought
Three Long Poems. After some time,
further plans were no longer made.
The sound slowly disappeared. This, too,
is an example of collaboration, without
any fixed purpose.

fig. 94   Joëlle Tuerlinckx and her
husband Christoph Fink during a lunch
hour in 2004. She explains to the
employees what she intends to do.

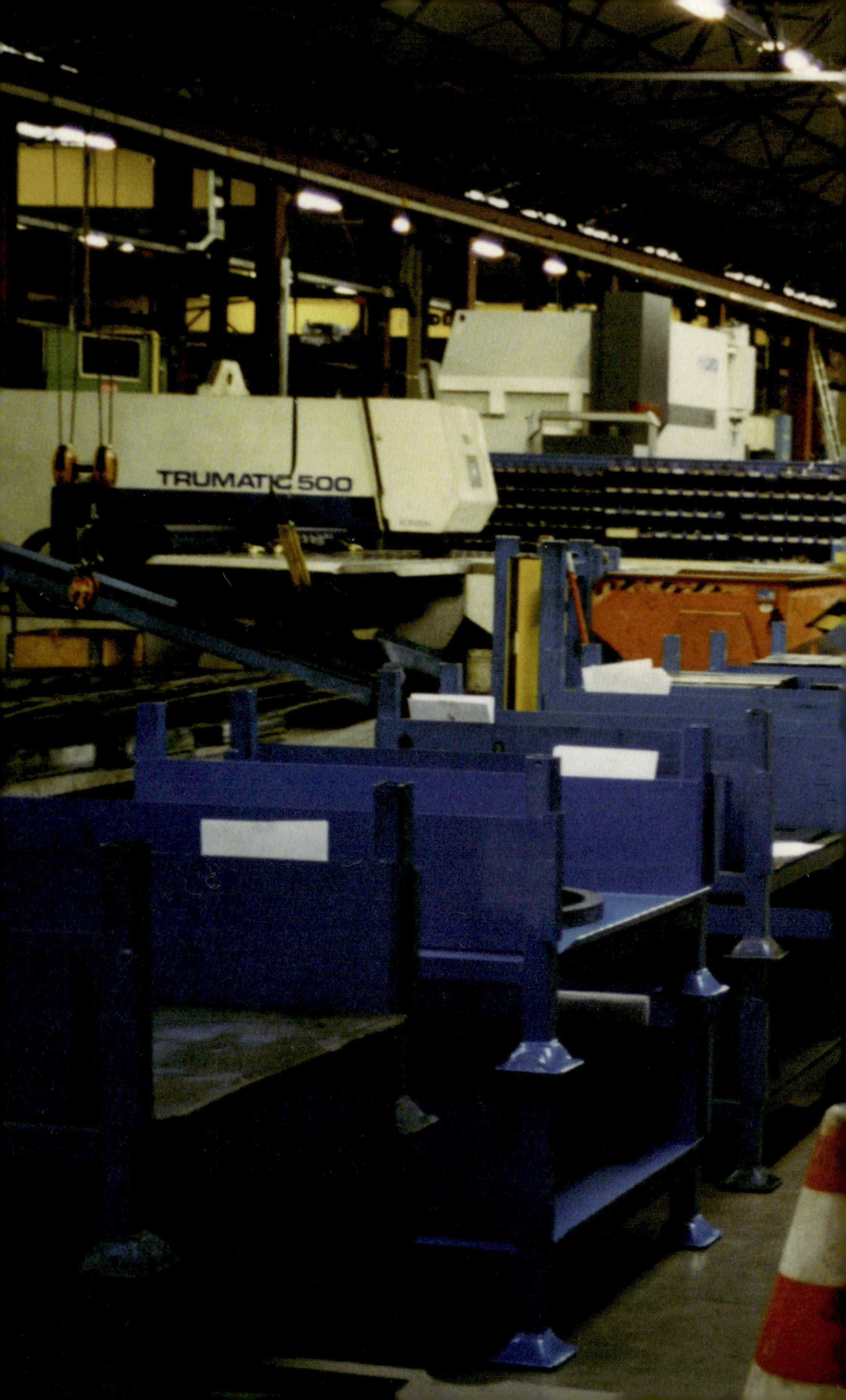

TRUMATIC 500

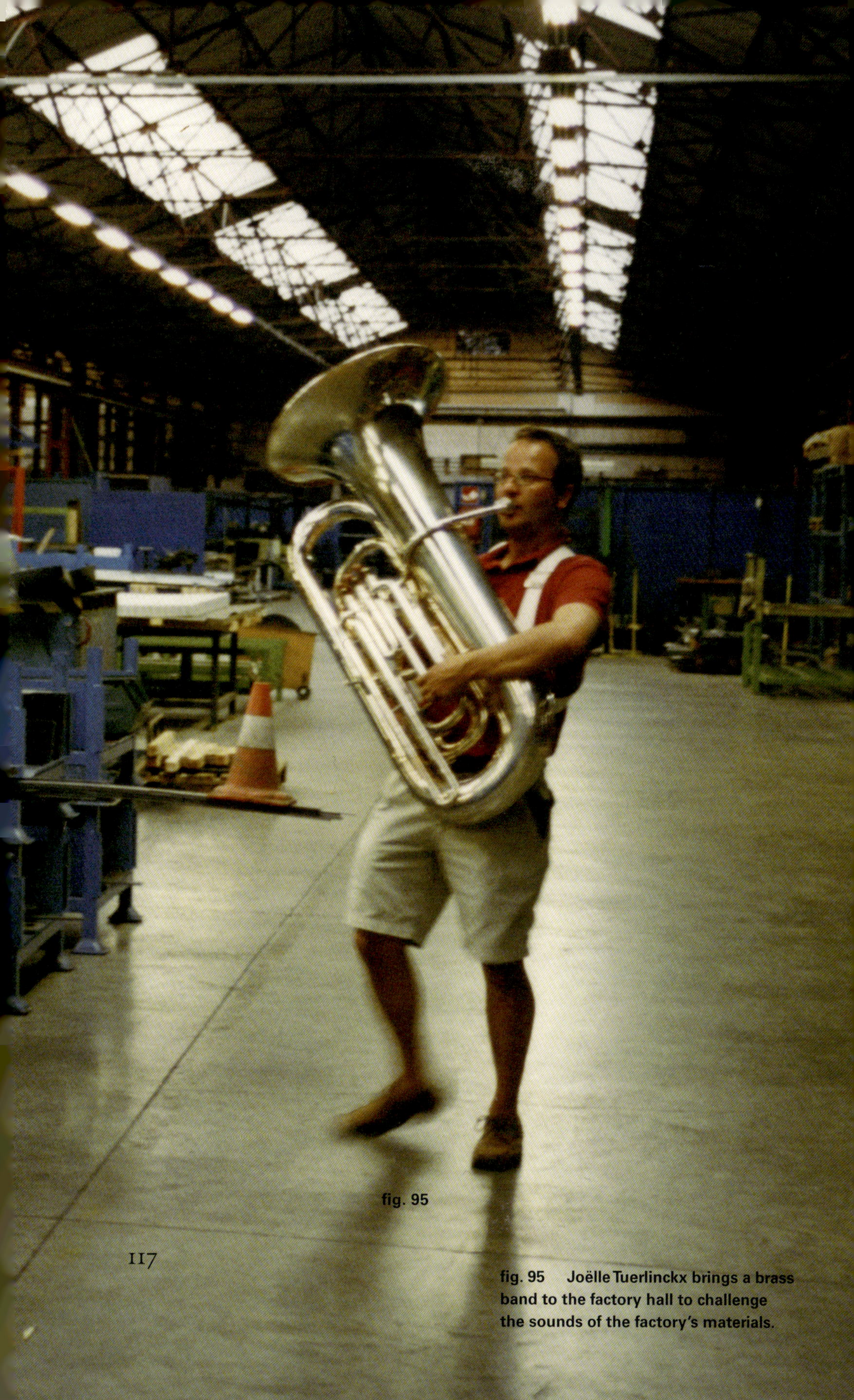

fig. 95

fig. 95   Joëlle Tuerlinckx brings a brass band to the factory hall to challenge the sounds of the factory's materials.

Constructies ESPEEL
Moorseelsesteenweg 22
8800 Rumbeke-Roeselare

'THREE LONG POEMS'

PERFORMANCE BY SILA BLUME

MONDAY 26 NOVEMBER 2001
20.00u

*

in the framework of /ACTION WITHOUT KNOWING ask!vzw workshop joëlle tuerlinckx
an evening of LA MATIÈRE DU VISIBLE SCALE 1:1 – EXPÉRIENCES D'ESPACE
anouk llaurens, joëlle tuerlinckx and ASK! invite Sila Blume

information and reservation ASK! tel. 0497/54 53 11 and 0477/28.66.13
info@askworkshops.be

organisation: ASK!
with the kind co-operation of Michel Espeel and Julie Vandenbroucke

*ASK! vzw (Architecture, City, Art) is pursuing the renewal of content and
teaching in art education. To this end it organizes workshops for graduates
from higher art education and the universities. These workshops are given by
artists, writers, philosophers… who invite a number of guests.*

fig. 96

**fig. 96   Sila Blume, *Three Long Poems*,
2001. The invitation.**

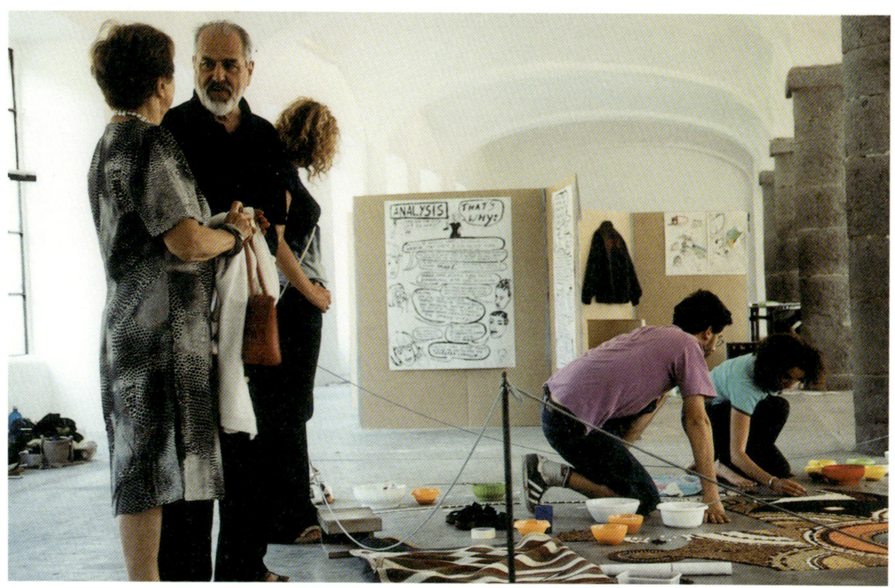

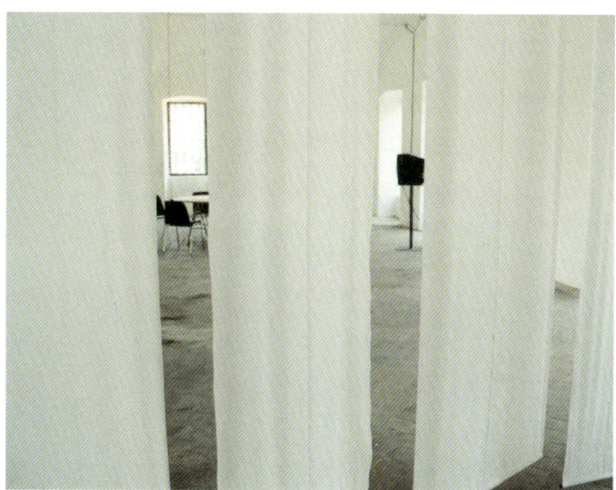

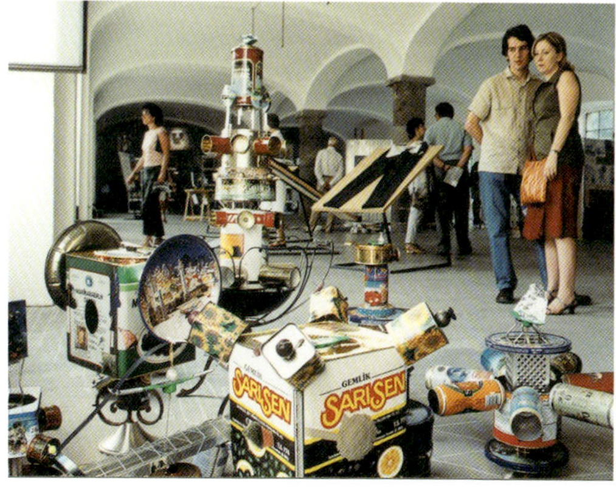

fig. 97

119

fig. 97   Cittadellarte (the city of art), spiritual child of Michelangelo Pistoletto, is a citadel for artists who work with politicians, philosophers, economists and industrialists. The city is revived when this artistic wind blows through it. Constructies Espeel, a meeting place for art and the economy, is a guest there in 1999. A dual delegation, consisting of Michel Espeel and Honoré δ'O, makes a contribution to the *Woolways* project by artist Fabrice Hyber that is also at home in several different worlds. Cittadellarte, Constructies Espeel and, later, Arteconomy as well, are ideologically closely linked. In 2001 the company was once again invited to present its collaborations with artists at *La 1° Fiera Internazionale di Arte e Produzione* (The 1st international art and production fair). In 2003 Michelangelo and his wife Maria pay a return visit to Constructies Espeel for a round table conversation about the relationship between art and the economy. Artists whom Constructies Espeel works with (including Joëlle Tuerlinckx and Christoph Fink), art critics and entrepreneurs are present. By way of a gift, the logo of Cittadellarte is carved in metal.

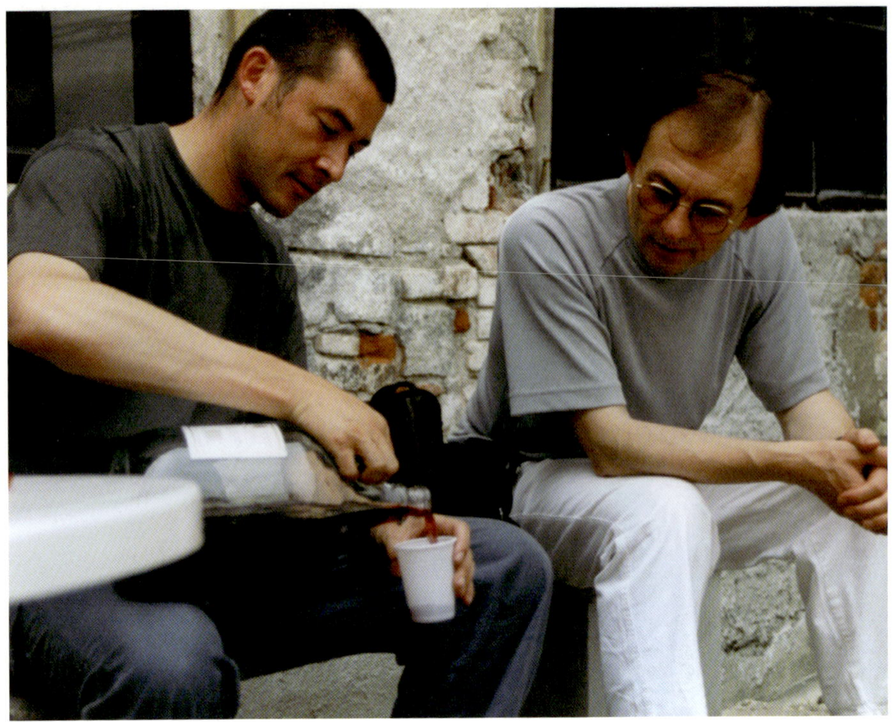

fig. 98

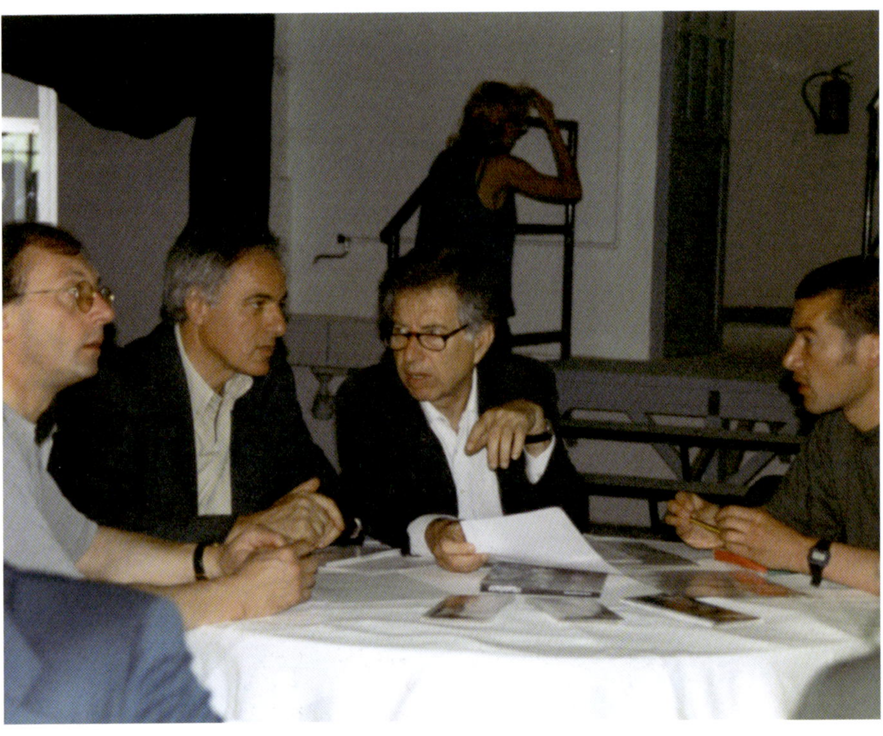

fig. 98   Participation by Michel Espeel
and Honoré δ'O in the debate on
Woolways at the Cittadellarte.

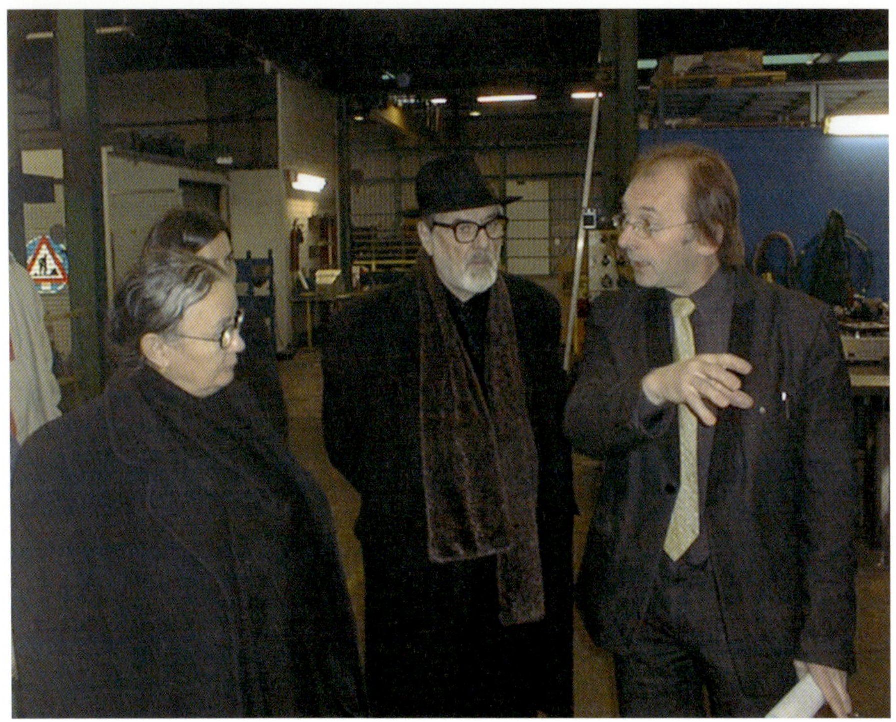

fig. 99

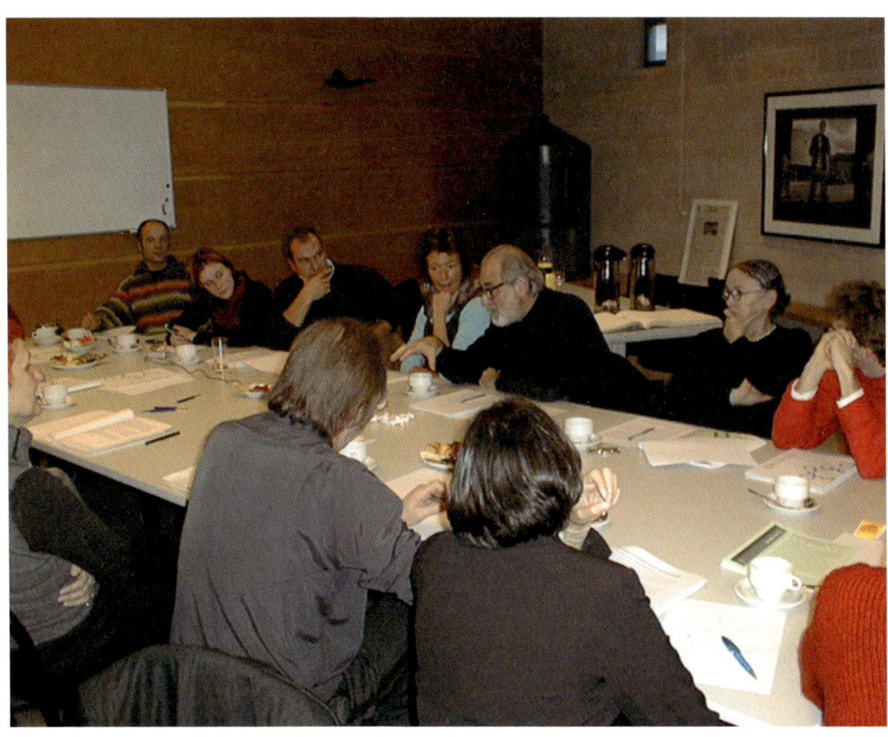

121

fig. 99   Michelangelo and Maria
Pistoletto in Rumbeke, on a visit to
Constructies Espeel.

Part V

Conclusion: Where the path becomes a landscape

Do you recognise this feeling? You are watching a movie that is reaching its denouement. Soon the screen fades to black and you begin to wonder: "Could it be over?" You yearn for more, hoping that the story will go on. Now that Michel Espeel has handed over his company, the images in this movie are also fading away. But there is more footage ahead – the projector continues to run. Soon a new stage in the travel story will emerge.

A love story

Remember that the journey was born out of love: Julie's passion for art, Michel's paternal care of the company and their attraction to each other. Despite all the intersections of their worlds, the difference still matters. Julie is drawn along to become one with art. But Michel remains who and where he is: the head of his company. He maintains a businesslike distance vis-à-vis the advances of art. The artists in turn respect that. After all, the company must continue to function. The marriage of art and economy does not promise a hybrid symbiosis. Each continues to be itself. The difficult times show this to be the case, and the good times transcend it.

By way of precaution

Remember the 'C for continuity' that is part of Michel's 'Entrepreneur's ABC'? Now is the time for it to play its role. Michel and his brother Luc have no successors from within their own families. In order to ensure the company's continued success, the umbilical cord that binds it to the Espeel family must be cut. Who will take over Constructies Espeel and its employees? At the beginning of 2008, Michel drew up his last balance sheet as an entrepreneur and passed the torch to Dacar Holding.

Moving apart: The body and soul of the factory

From an economic perspective, is seems logical. The firm continues to operate under its new owners. The contract with the Dacar team, David and Carolien Vanheede, means that Michel has cut his ties with the company. But there is one document that he could not leave behind – the contract between himself, Constructies Espeel and Claire Roudenko-Bertin.

Michel formulates the provisions of the contract anew. He refers to Claire and himself as the "*copropriétaires de l'âme de l'usine*": joint owners of the soul of the factory. Claire does not protest. Michel's interpretation is at least as important as hers. When Michel informed her of the sale, she asked: "Is the new owner also purchasing the soul of the factory?" "Of course not", Michel replied. "That is not for sale!"

If we are to follow the rationale of the contract, it means that once Michel left the company, the soul left the body. If that is the case, all we are left with is a sensational headline: "Espeel is left soulless". That would mean ending with a funeral procession. But that was not the intention. Otherwise it would mean that the whole thing was worthless, and even the beautiful song must come to an end. Or is it the contractual reasoning itself that is going to die?

Walk with me. An emergency exit beckons. Nothing is as versatile as the spirit of an artist. If a dead end looms ahead, it immediately sniffs around for a way out. Anyone who writes off the body and soul of Constructies Espeel after its sale is in desperate need of an artist. For this would mean you run the risk of getting mired in the logic of the contract. That is your loss. The absolute is not within the reach of human beings. Times change and agreements can be altered. Although the contract has not been broken, it is changing. Being open to new possibilities is called innovation. Economists are now discovering this, but artists have a centuries-old expertise in these sorts of manoeuvres. In the landscape of their dreams, nothing is immutable, there is no fixed longitude or latitude; rather, they have their own inner compass. The economist's landscape consists of efficient rail and waterways. Overrun by infrastructure, it is sometimes difficult for him to leave the well-trodden path. An artist can help uproot him, where necessary, and point him in the direction of an off-road trail.

According to Claire, the contract is unfolding like a butterfly bursting from its chrysalis. The soul is growing a new body. A body is never without a soul. A new articulation has yet to be found, but the enthusiasm remains. The new Constructies Espeel company has not yet made a statement about artistic commitment. But Claire does not mourn the company of which they are no longer the physical occupants.

"Everything is still there", she says. "Moreover, I am certain that the employees have no need for us, for they have surprised us." Already at the time of the Luigi Nono concert, they were able to get to the heart of one of the most difficult compositions in contemporary music. The employees spontaneously insisted on the artistically 'strongest' possible staging. "No one can ever take this away from them. The seriousness and yet lightness with which they approached this piece of music is proof that they do not need us."

The picture is now shrouded in darkness. Black. Although nothing can yet be seen in the confusion surrounding the sale of Constructies Espeel, we are struck by the sense that the story must go on. There are too many loose ends that still need to be tied up and resolved. So, once the picture brightens again, we see the Figure of Michel Espeel looming ahead. Year in and year out, he successfully ran his company, stood in the midst of his workers, taking the lead alongside them. The same was true when it came to the artists. He left behind his familiar surroundings to go in search of a new destination. That can take time. Our story of the collaboration with artists in an industrial environment is not over yet. Even if we have to watch a trailer first, the image suggests a sequel.

Walk with me, says Michel, for now that the home run towards Constructies Espeel is over, the journey can truly begin in earnest. The protagonist faces a greater challenge than ever along his quest. He is free of the bonds of former responsibilities, and now stands before a new beginning. *Walk with me*. For your feelings will not betray you. You yourself can pick up the loose ends and open-ended story lines and follow their lead. Here and there, new protagonists are already appearing on the scene. Perhaps that is the way of the future: expanding the circle of travelling companions. For something that grows bears good fruit.

We are going to new places, visiting other businesses, speaking
other artists and entrepreneurs, but the journey remains the same. The
greater the following the more radical the passage through the landscape of art and economy. Some day, policy-makers will issue an offi-
cial safe-conduct, for the journey of art towards the economy and back
again will have altered the landscape for ever.

Notes
1. Cited from the *Case Espeel* by Prof. Dr. J. Vincke, et al., *Kunstbedrijf / Bedrijfskunst?
   Een sociologische gevalstudie van het samenwerkingsverband tussen Constructies
   Espeel en kunstenaars*, 03-09-04. Commissioned by Arteconomy vzw.
2. In collaboration with the Cultureel Centrum De Spil in Roeselare.
3. In collaboration with the Villa Eksternest art gallery and the architecture
   firm Buro II.
4. Quoted from Julie Vandenbroucke from the invitation to *Heavy Metal*.
5. In collaboration with the cultural centres of Roeselare, Strombeek-Bever
   and Sint-Niklaas.
6. Cited from the mission statement of Arteconomy vzw.
7. Cited from Honoré δ'O.

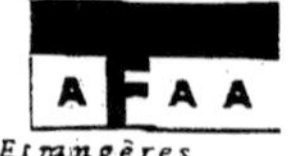

Date : 29 Mai 1997

ORGANISME :	
DESTINATAIRE : MICHEL ESPEEL	
N° TELECOPIE : 00 32 51 26 51 01	
NBRE DE PAGES : 1	
EXPÉDITEUR : MARIE-LAURE PERETTI	
N° TELECOPIE : +33 1 43 17 82 82 - N° TELEPHONE :+33 1 43 17 83 22	
OBJET : BIENNALE DE VENISE ART VISUEL 1997	

Cher Monsieur,

Suite à notre conversation téléphonique, je vous confirme que l'AFAA prend en charge votre déplacement à Venise à hauteur de 1800,00 FF.
Votre intervention sur le plateau du pavillon français est prévue le 13 Juin à 15h30.
L'AFAA vous a réservé une nuit d'hôtel le 13 au soir (Villa Tiziana Via Andréa Gritti, T 526 11 52 / F 526 21 45) que nous prenons en charge.

Si vous décidez de prendre votre billet par vous-même, nous vous rembourserons cette somme si vous nous faîtes parvenir la facture acquittée (avec la copie du billet) afin que nous puissions vous rembourser la différence.
Nous vous adresserons ultérieurement votre invitation .
Sincèrement,

Marie-Laure Peretti,

00.39.41 52 04 825   Pavillon

01 43178282

29/05 '97 11:03   ☎01 43178282   A F A A   ☑001

fig. 100

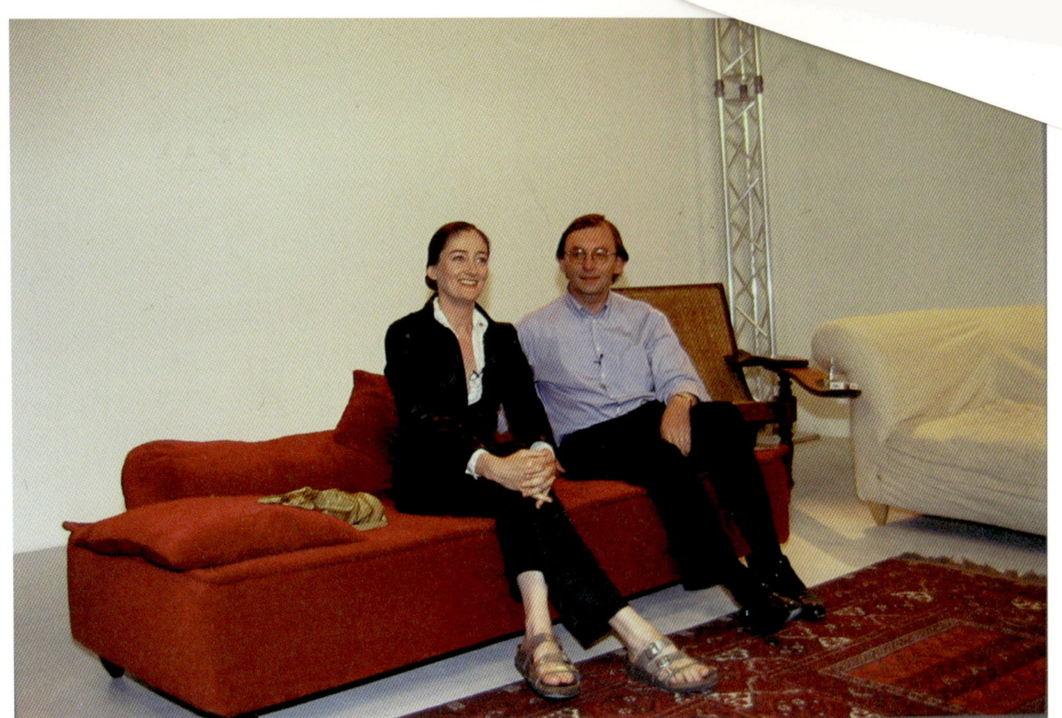

fig. 101

127

figs. 100, 101   In the context of *Wool-ways* by Fabrice Hyber, Michel was invited to the Venice Biennale, where he sat on the panel of a staged talkshow, 1997.

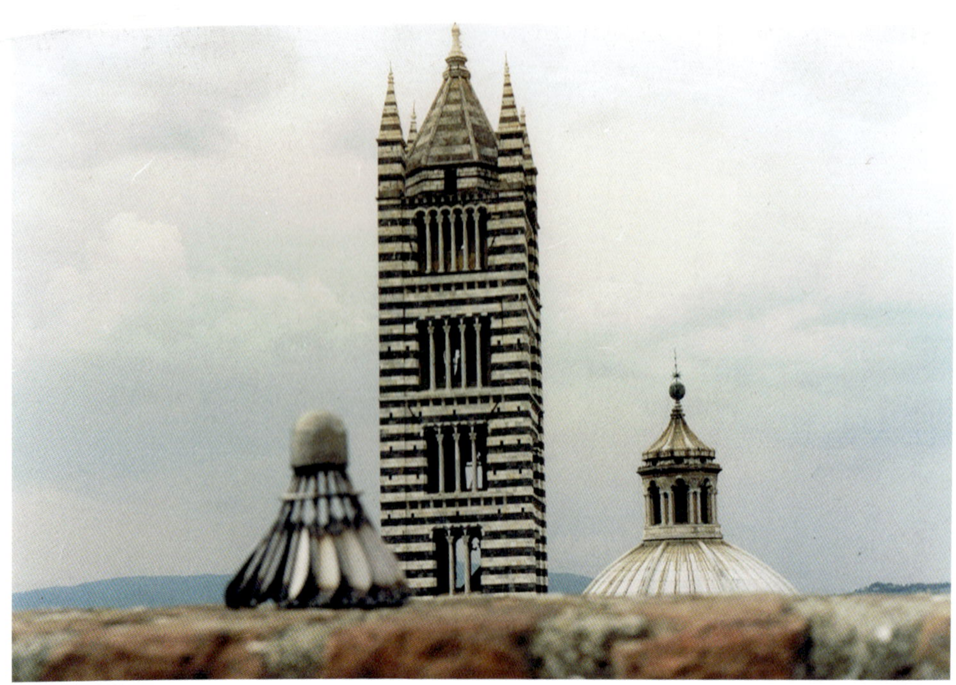

fig. 102

128

fig. 102   Honoré δ'O, *Idea Europa*
at the Palazzo Pubblico, Siena, 1988.

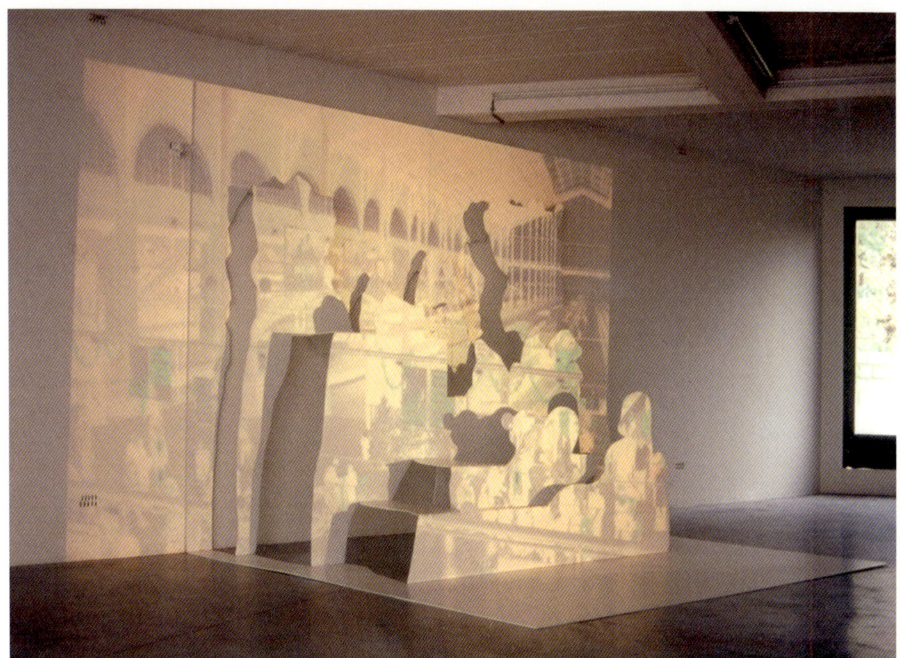

fig. 103

129

fig. 103   Ai Kitahara, *Pop Up*, exhibition
at the Galerie Foncke, Ghent, 2001.

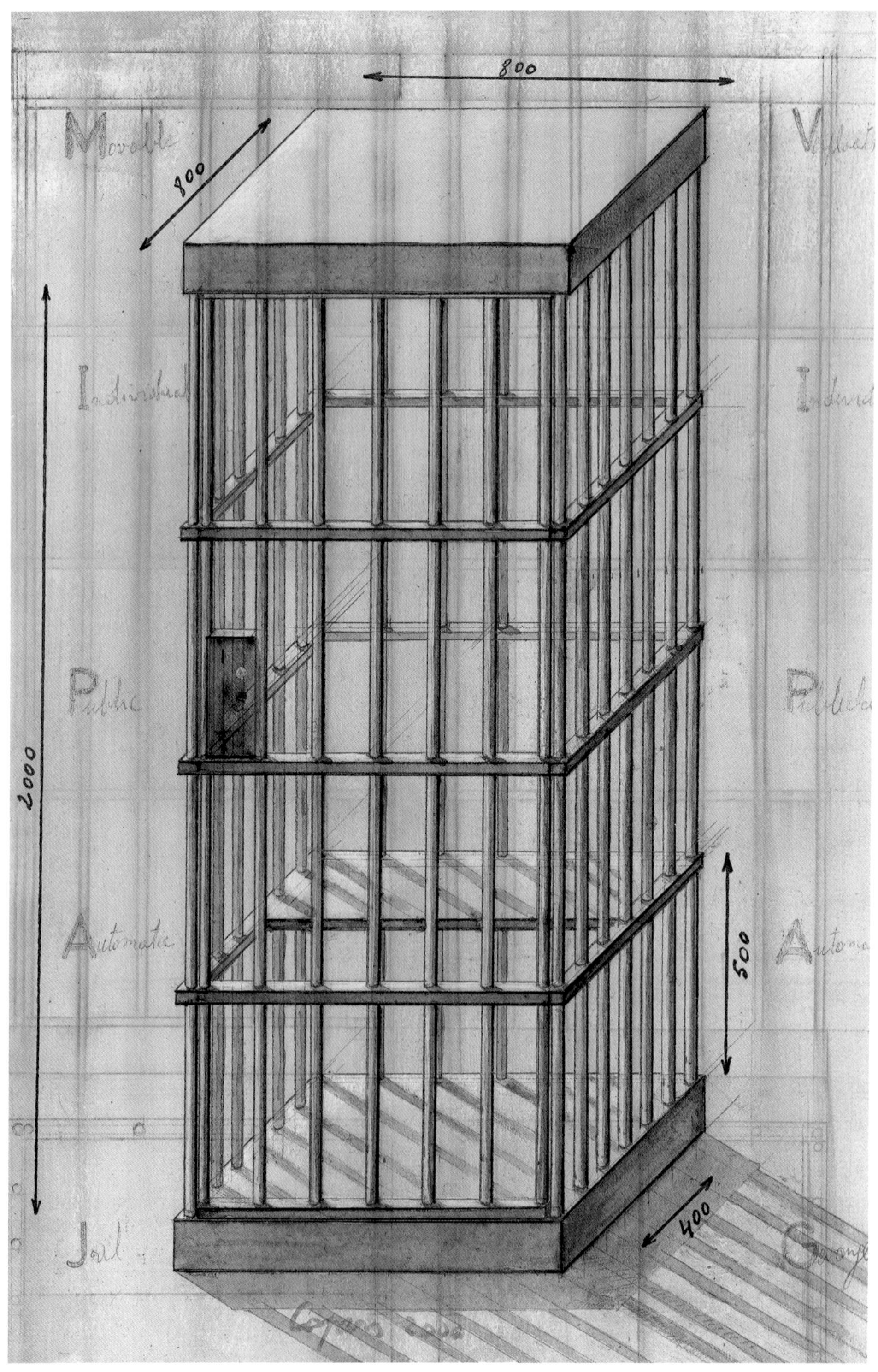

fig. 104

130

fig. 104 Leo Copers, VIPAG, 2002.
Preliminary study.

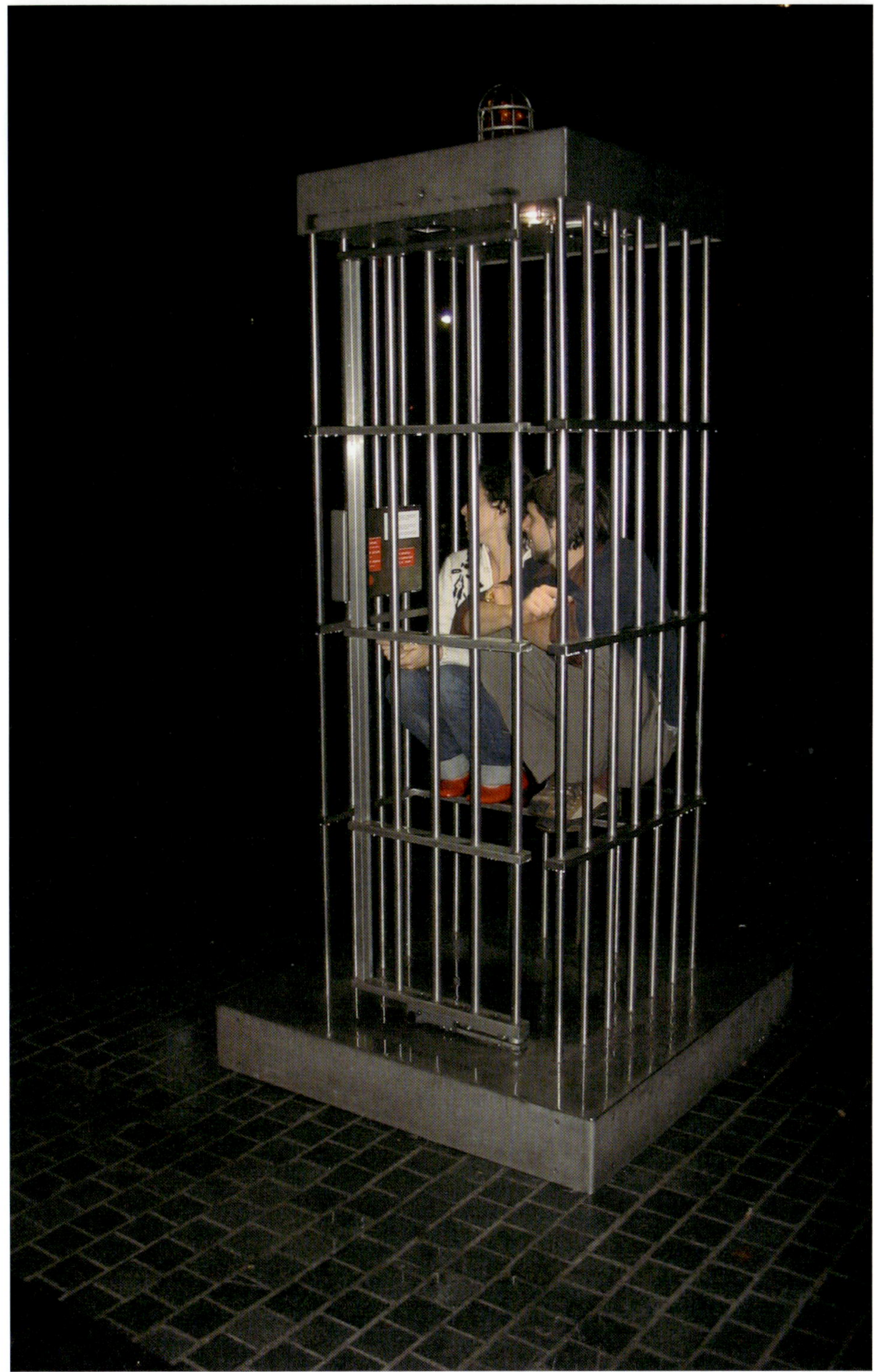

fig. 105

fig. 105   Leo Copers, VIPAG, 2002.

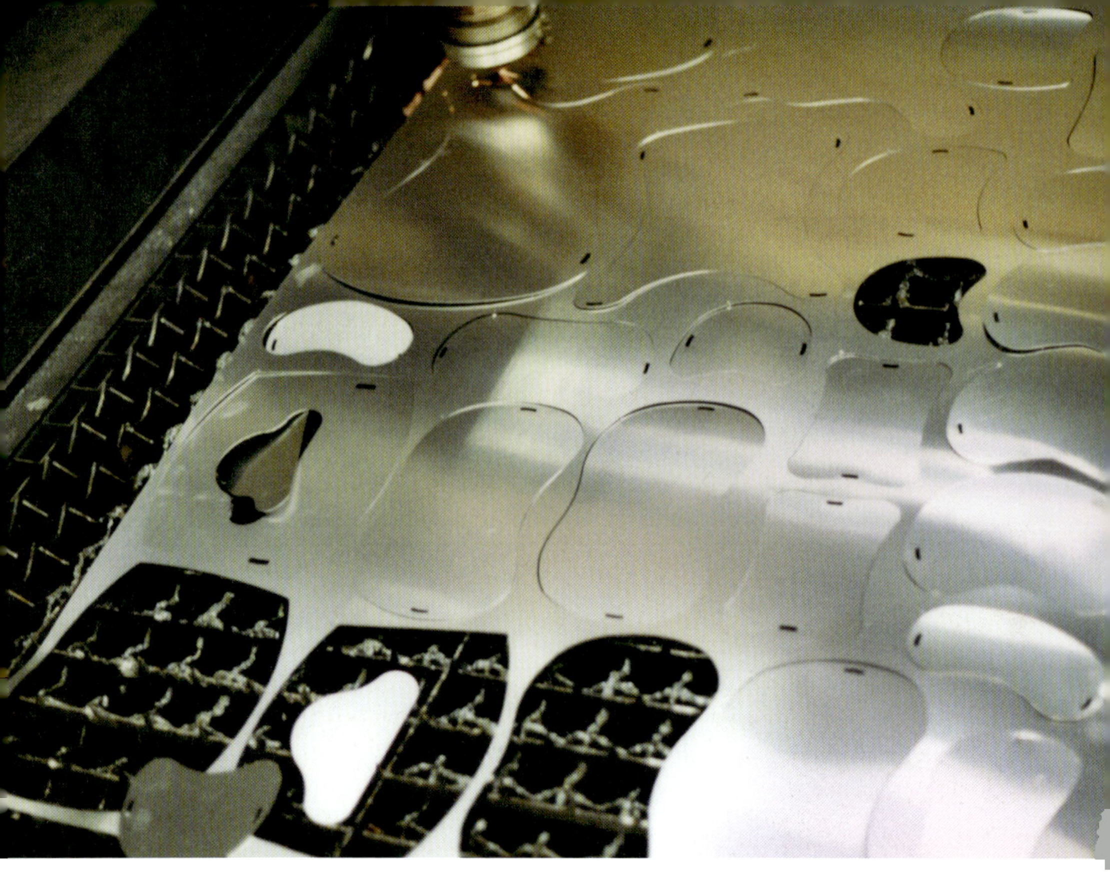

fig. 106

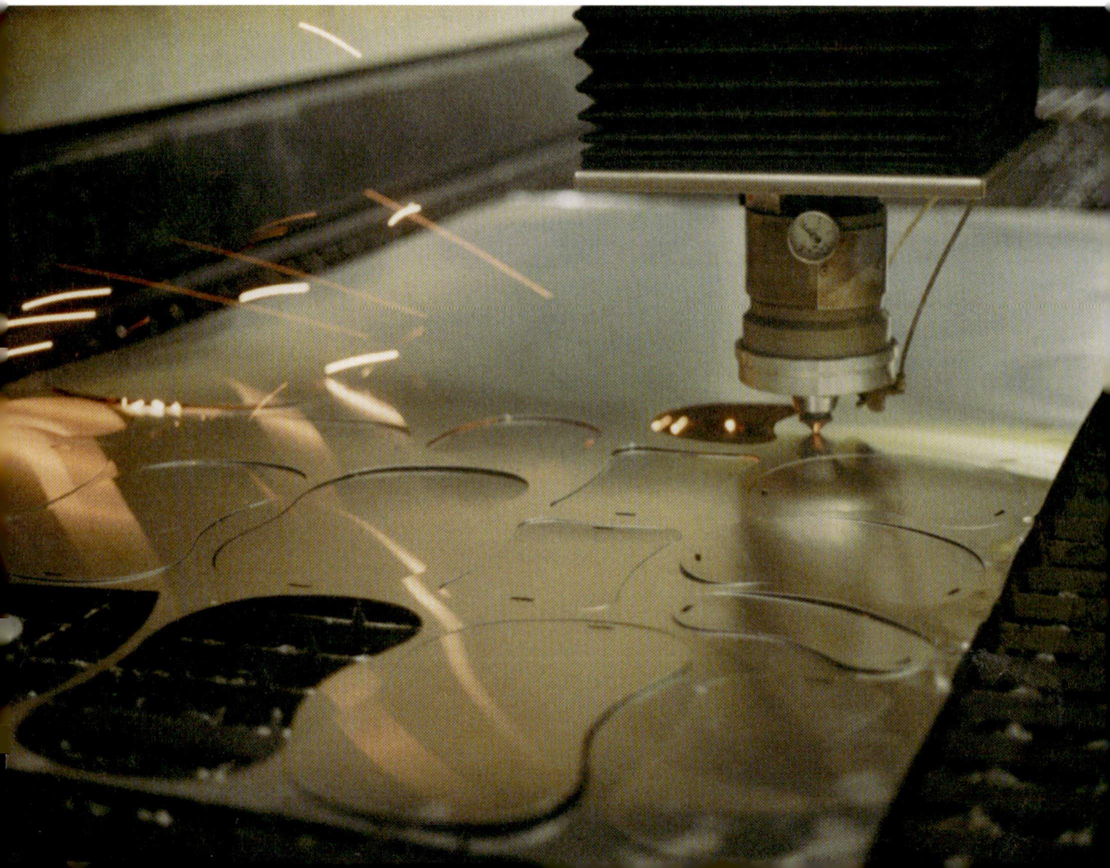

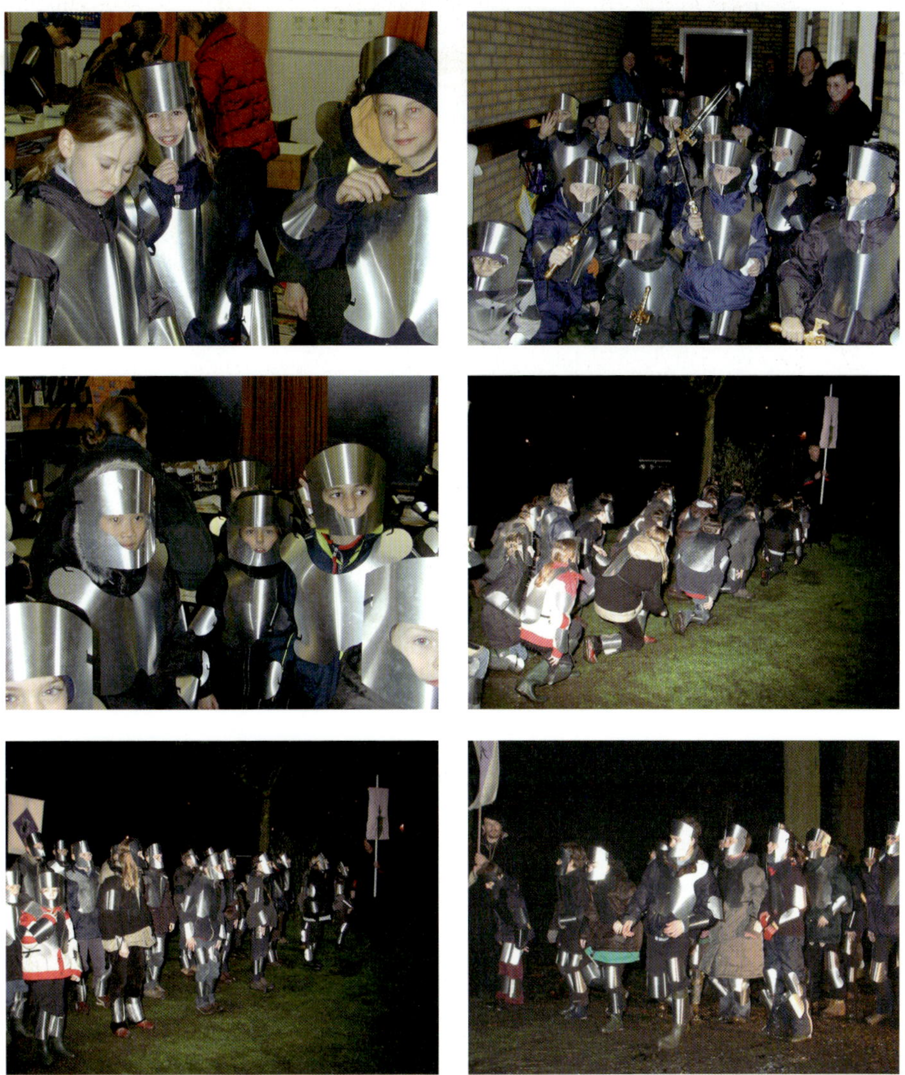

fig. 107

figs. 106, 107   Jan Fabre has Constructies
Espeel make armour for schoolchildren.
figs. 110, 111   For his performance *Je
suis sang*, Jan Fabre needed tables on
which one could dance. He came to
Constructies Espeel to test them out in
person. A few weeks later, the performance – with the tables – had its premiere
at the 2001 Avignon Festival.
figs. 112, 113   Jan Fabre, *Je suis sang*,
2001. Photo: Wonge Bergmann, ©
Troubleyn.

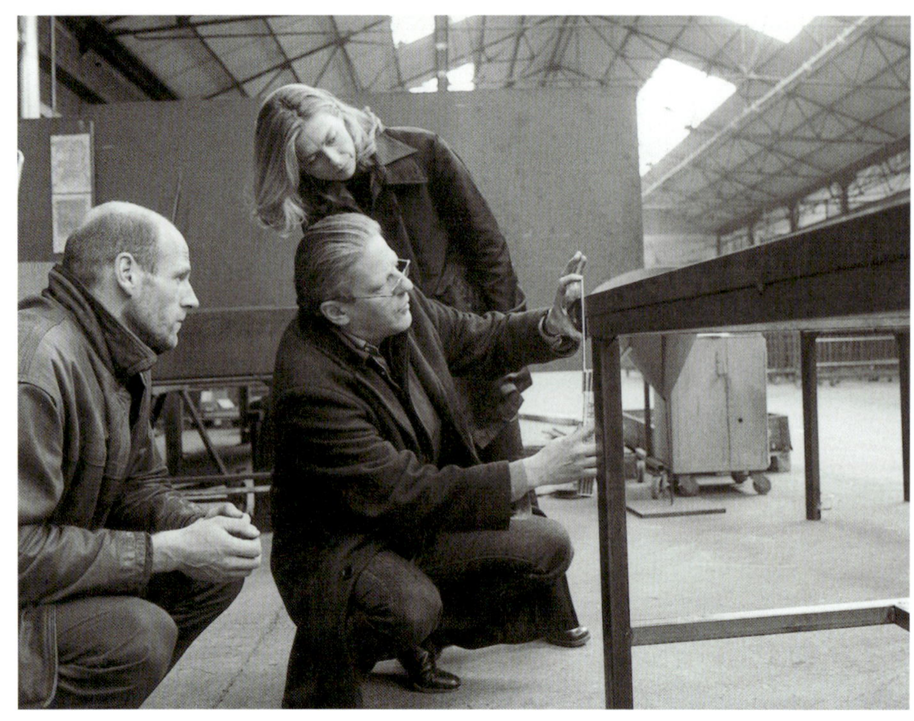

fig. 110

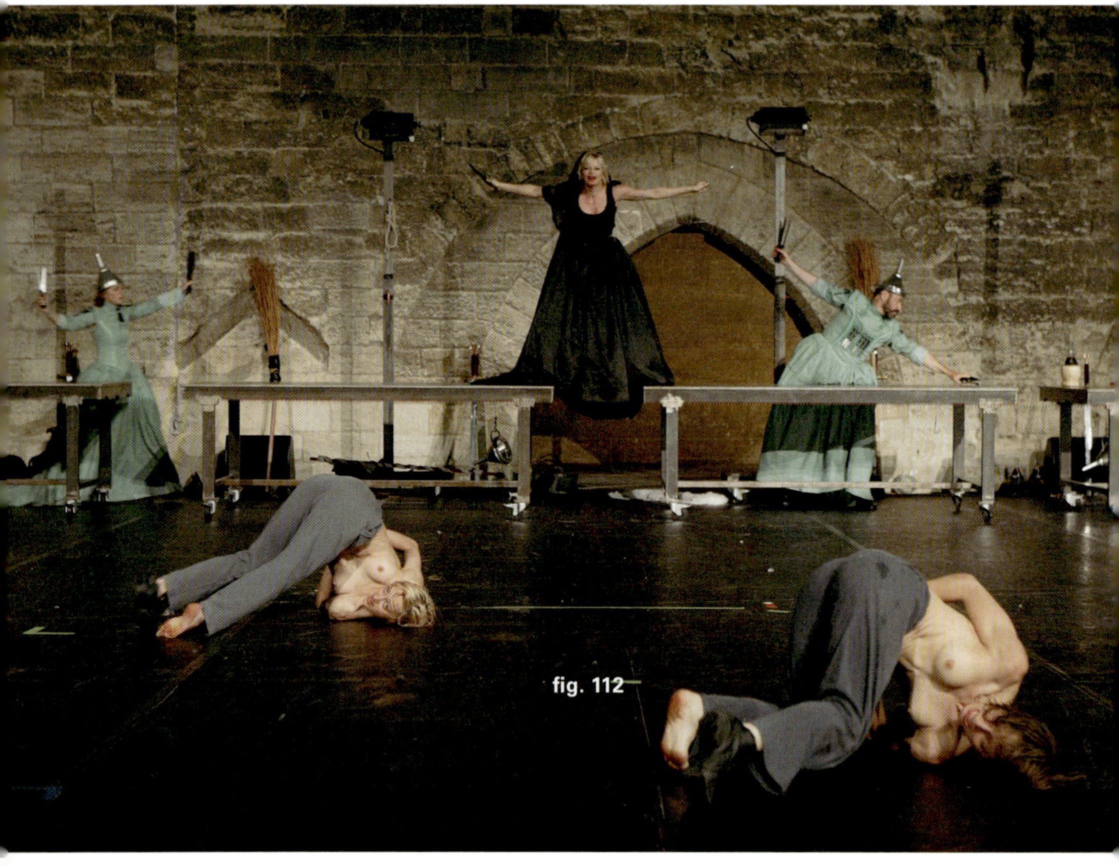

fig. 112

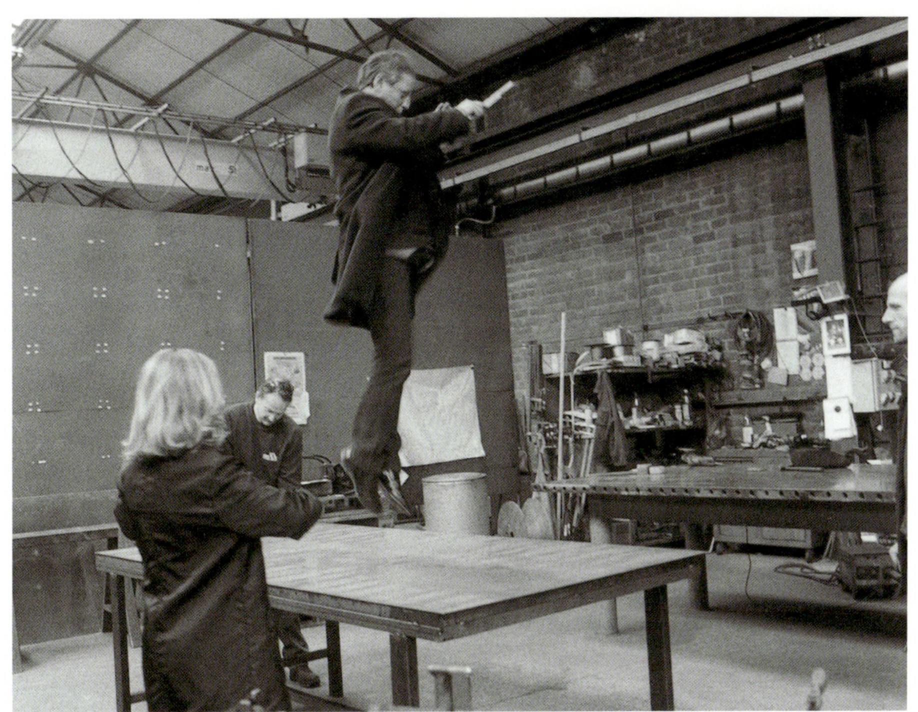

fig. 111

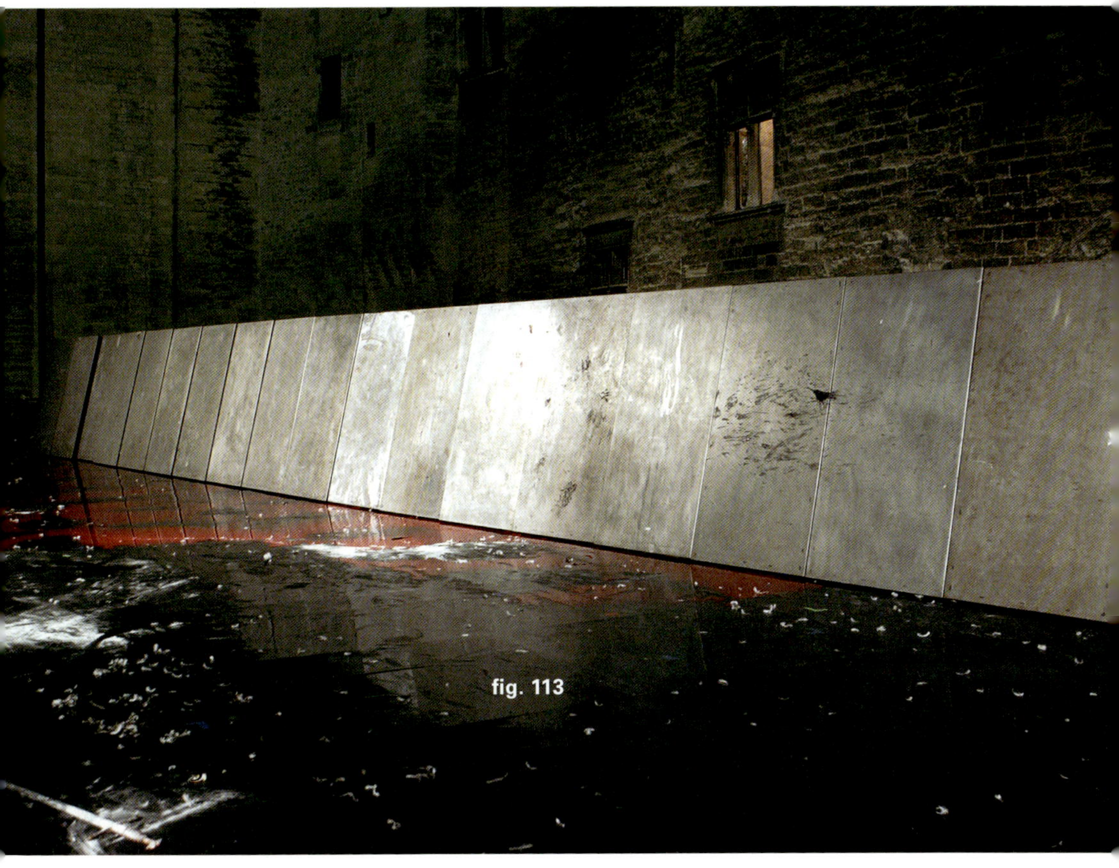

fig. 113

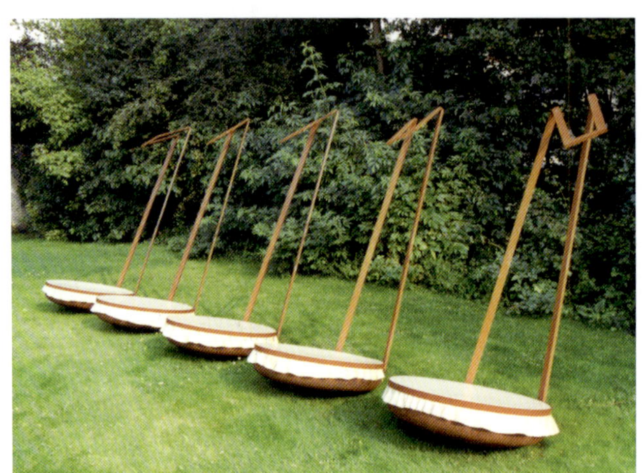

fig. 114

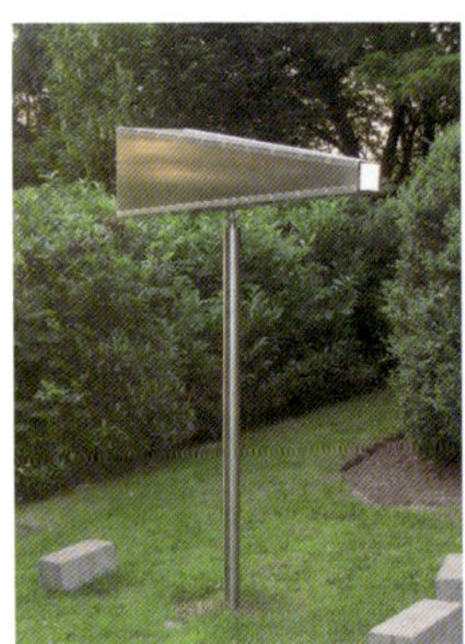

fig. 115

136

fig. 114   Martine Platteau, *Poème de terre*, 1996.
fig. 115   The viewer by Dimitri Vangrunderbeek, 2004.

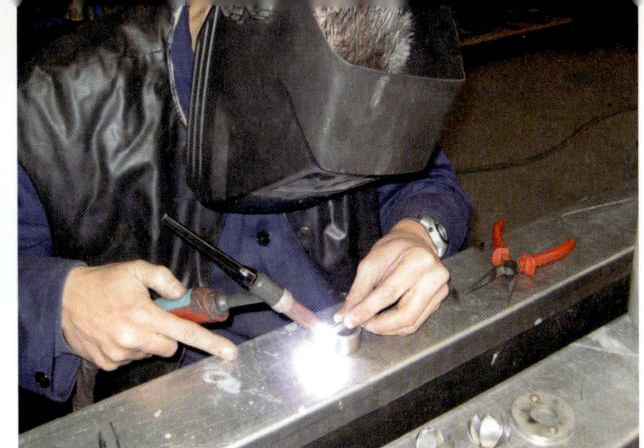

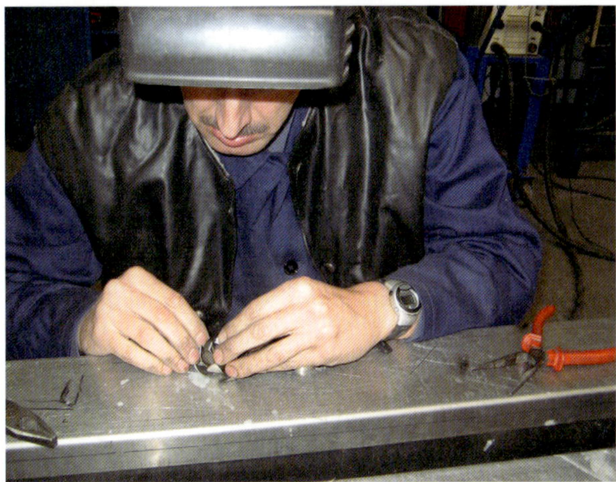

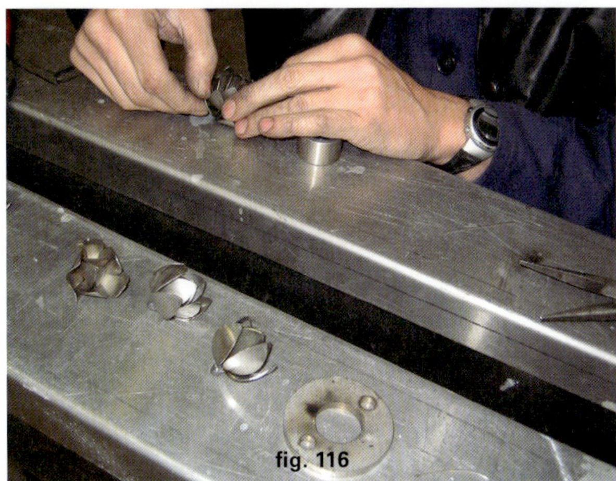

fig. 116

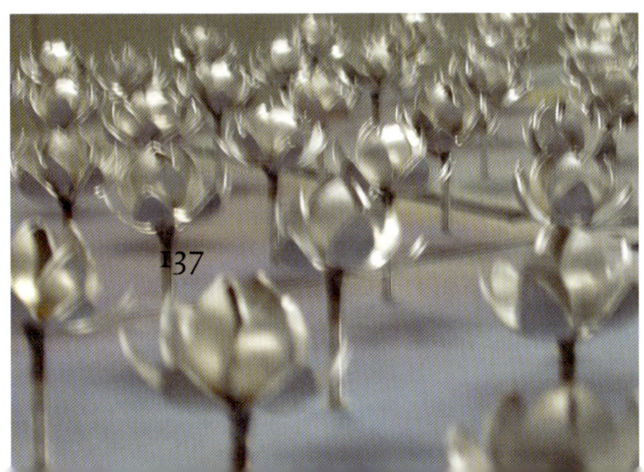

137

fig. 116   Hans Op de Beeck & Wim Maes,
Bloesems [Blossoms], 2006. Making the
slats.
fig. 117   Hans Op de Beeck & Wim Maes,
Bloesems [Blossoms], 2006. The
spraying.
fig. 118   Hans Op de Beeck & Wim Maes,
Bloesems [Blossoms], 2006.

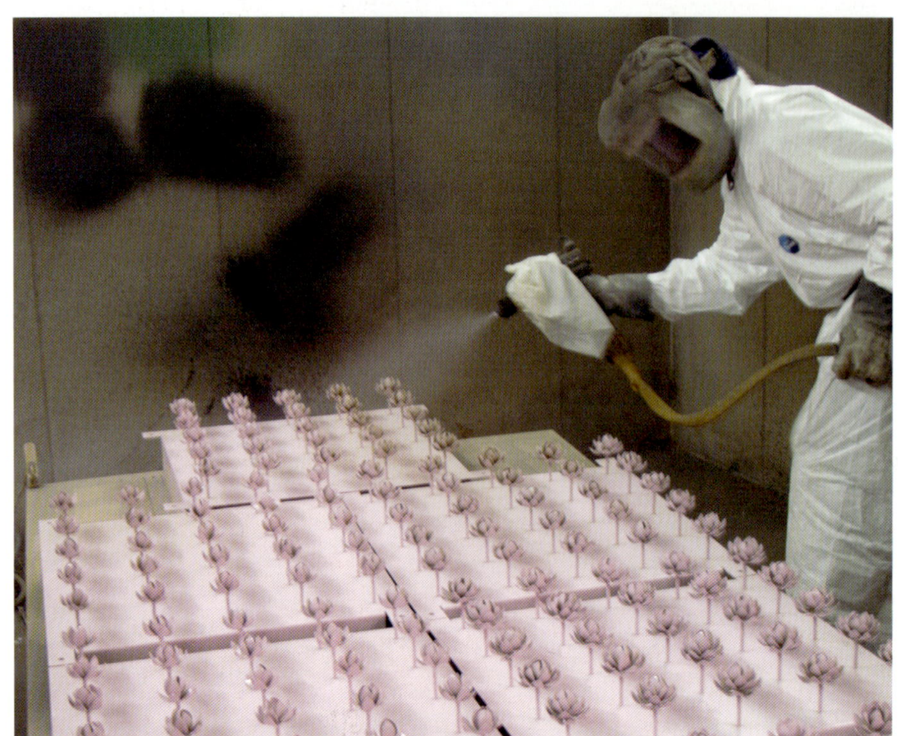

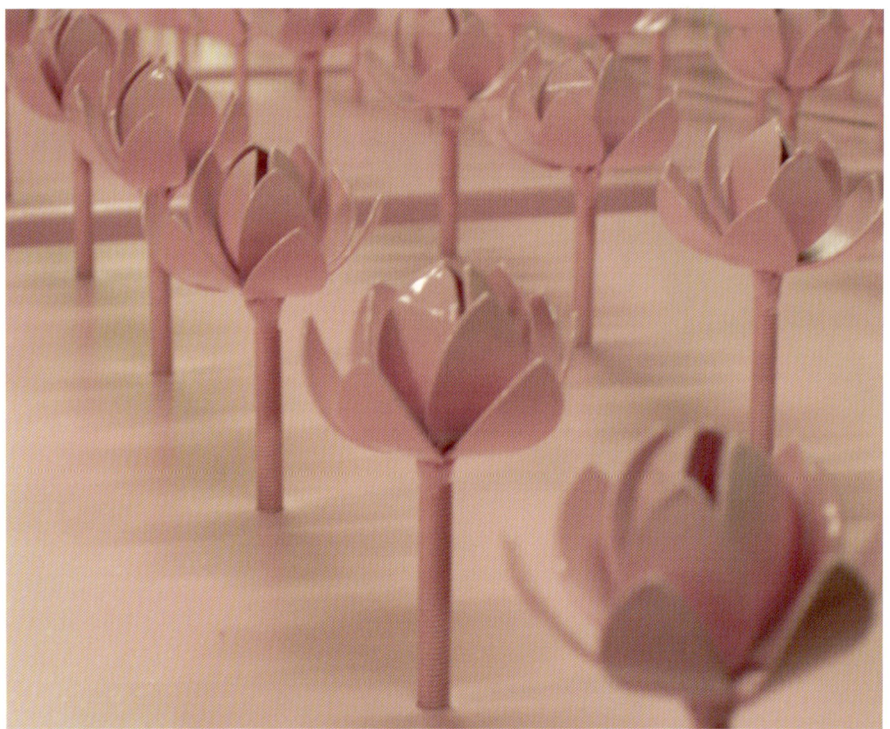

fig. 117

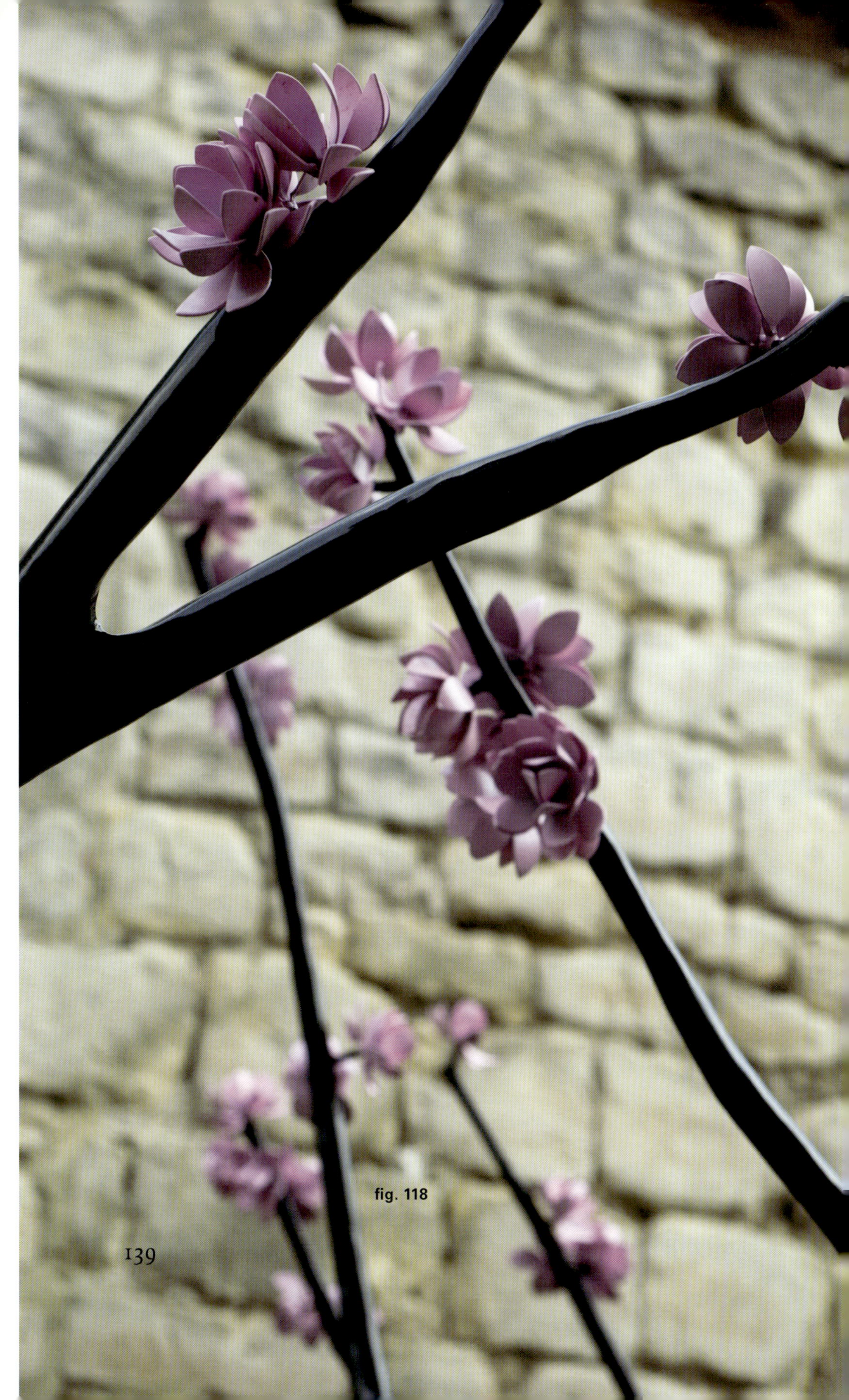

fig. 118

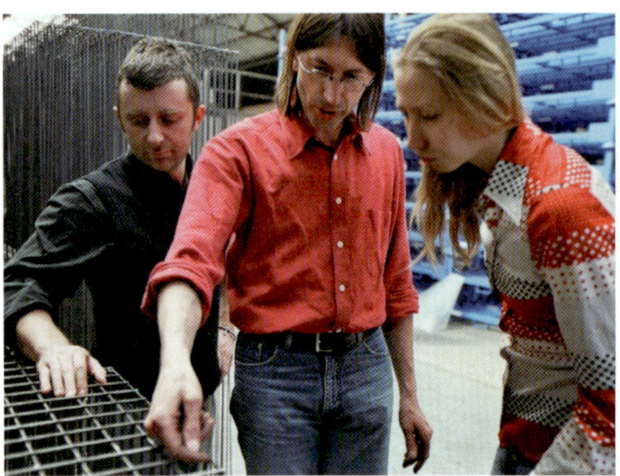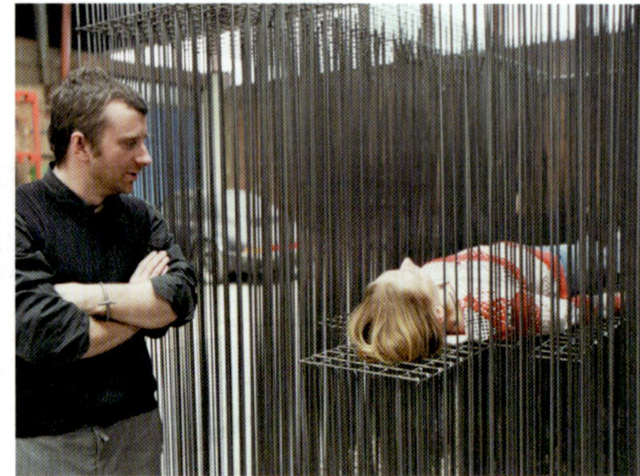

fig. 119

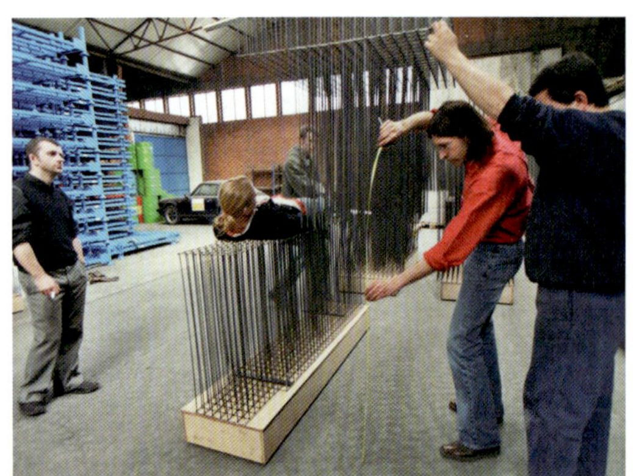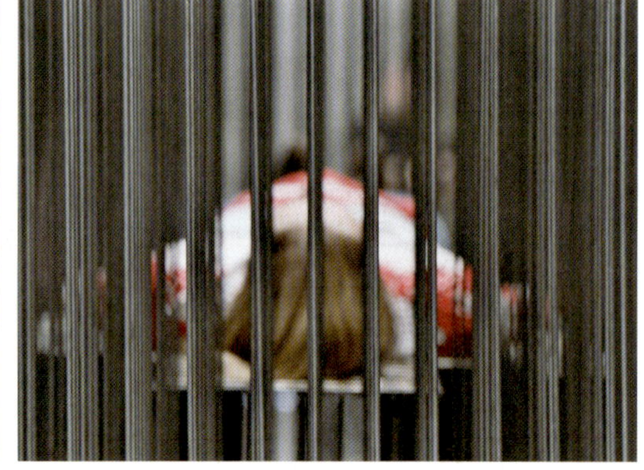

fig. 119   Kris Verdonck, *Patent Human Energy*, created in collaboration with Constructies Espeel, 2005.
fig. 120   Kris Verdonck, *Patent Human Energy*, 2005. Photo: Luc Schaltin.

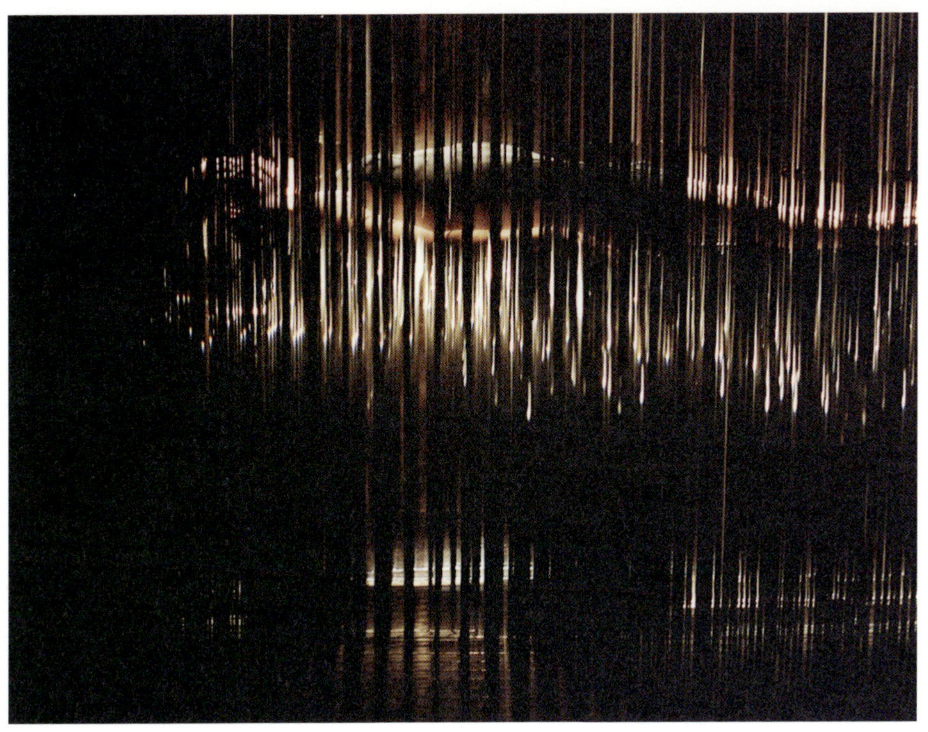

fig. 120

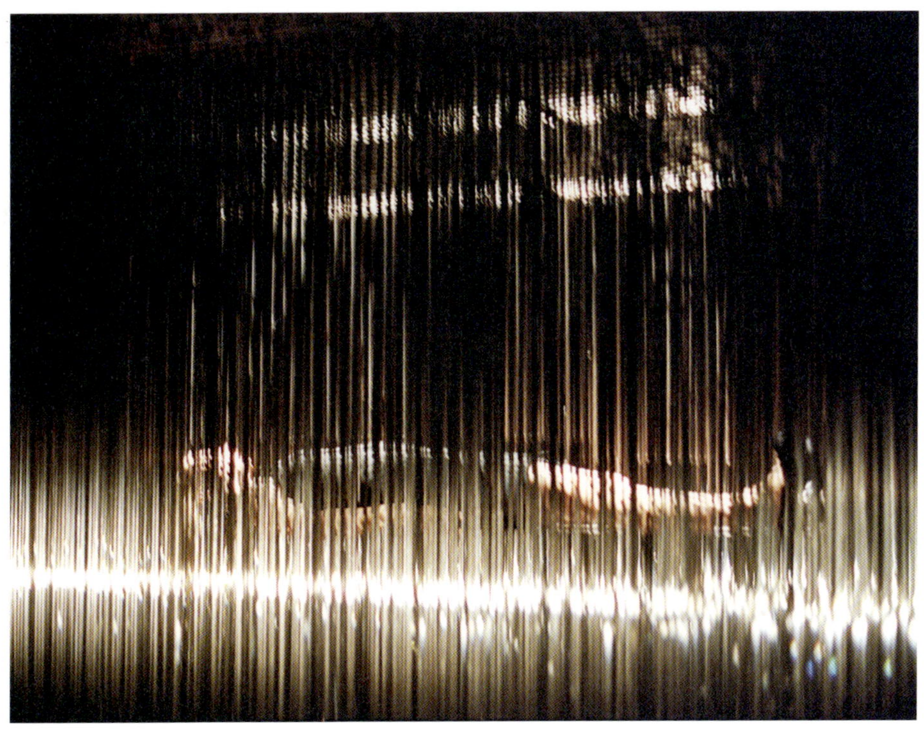

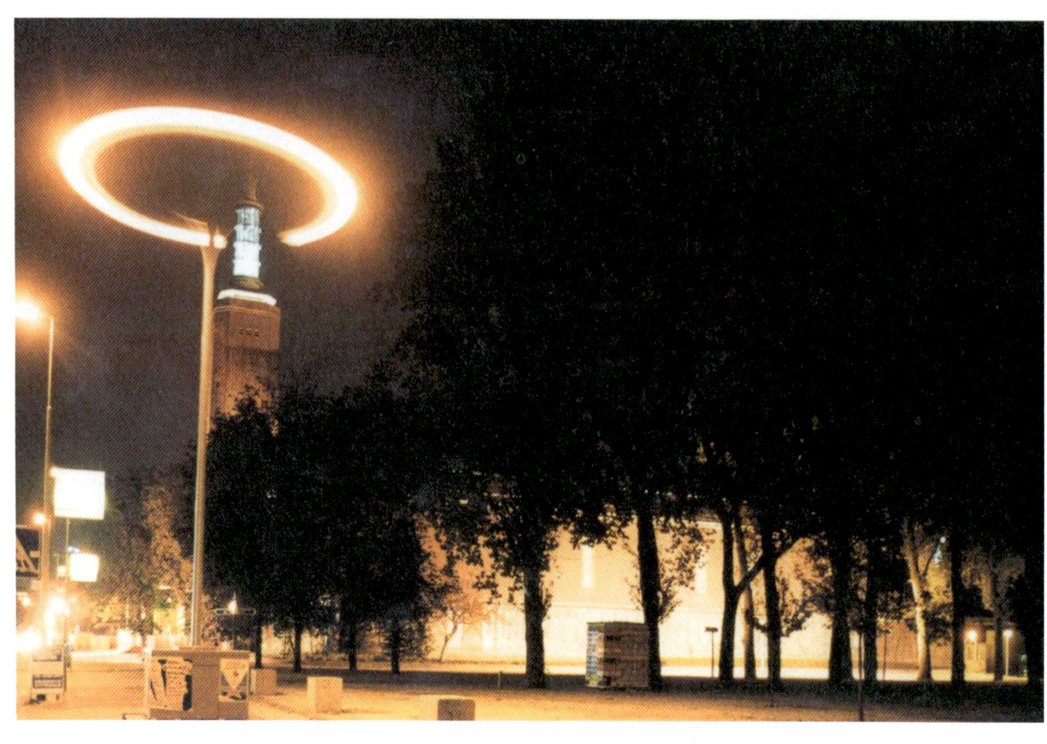

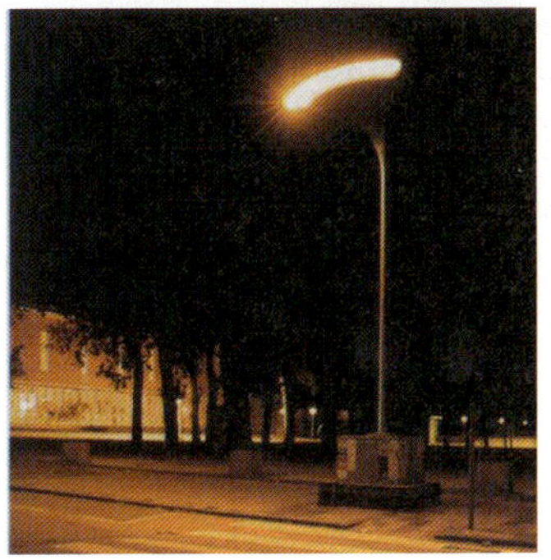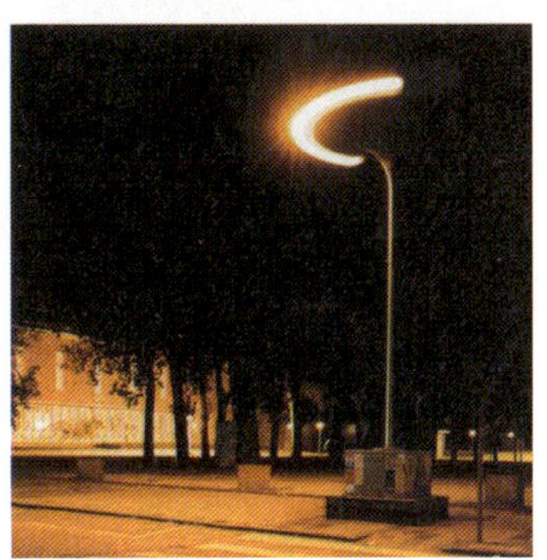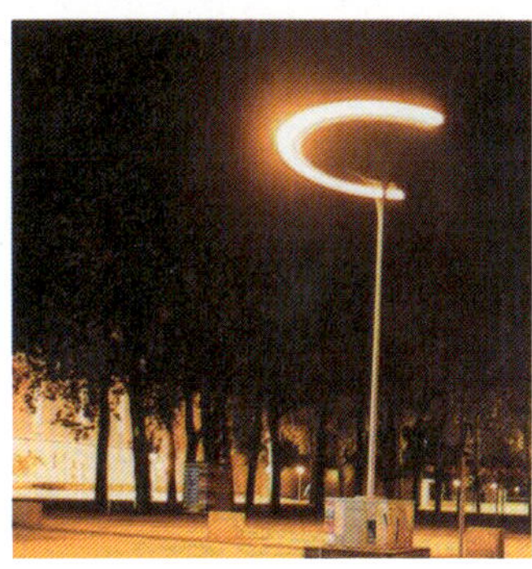

fig. 121

143

fig. 121 Honoré δ'O, *Waailicht* [Waving light], Rotterdam, 2006

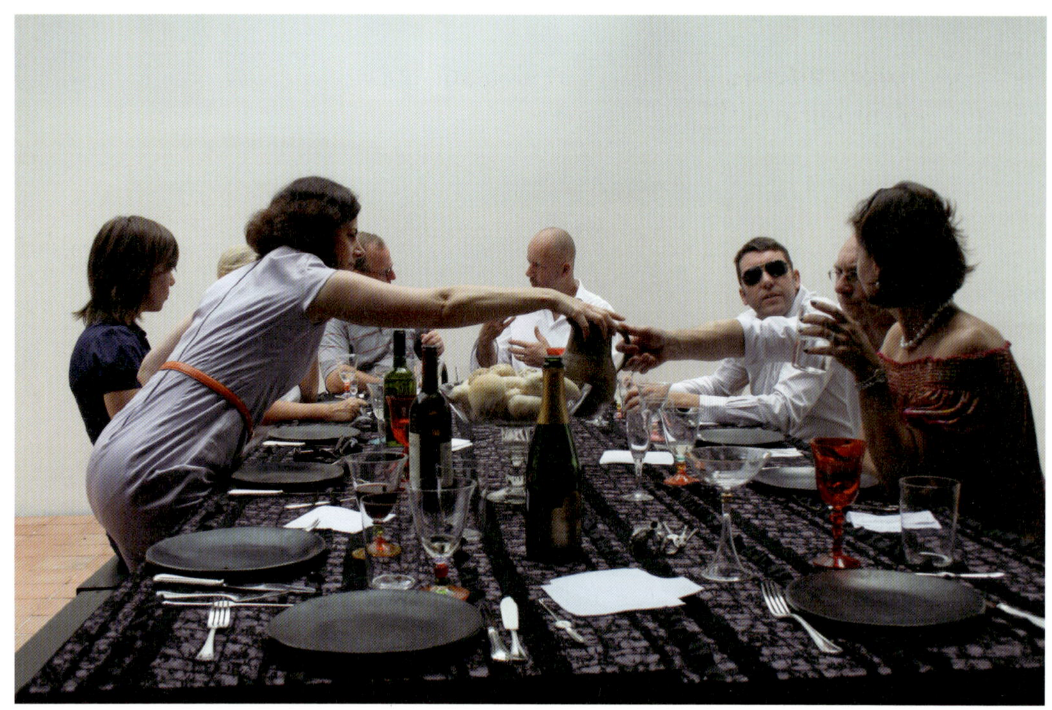

fig. 122

144

fig. 122   from left to right: Charlotte
Bonduel, Marianne Verkest, Daisy
Vyncke, Dirk Vyncke, Luc Derycke, David
Vanheede, Michel Espeel, Evelyne
Vanheede

Foreword or afterword (and acknowledgments)
A brief chronicle of the book's concept

The run-up to this book brought together a small group of people. On a spring weekend on the cusp of summer, first a group of artists and then one of entrepreneurs made their way to the state-of-the-art home of Michel and Julie Espeel-Vandenbroucke in Sint-Eloois-Winkel (West Flanders). Over the sound of the conversations both inside and out, the book came into existence to the accompaniment of the sound of birds chirping.

22-06-08

Allow me first to introduce the entrepreneurs. Dirk Vyncke is the head of the Vyncke Energietechniek company. Michel has known Dirk since 1974. What began as a business relationship has grown into a friendship, and every year the two men go on a walking trip. David Vanheede is the new owner who has taken over the Espeel company. Hans Crijns is a professor at the Vlerick Leuven Gent Management School. At Michel's request, Hans agreed to serve as a non-executive director of Espeel.

The first question the entrepreneurs asked themselves was: are we, as entrepreneurs – and by extension, economists – really all that different from artists?

First article of faith: Don't confuse an entrepreneur with a manager. They are complementary but not interchangeable. Nothing can get off the ground without entrepreneurship. Nothing can last without management. Starting a business, creating something out of nothing, calls for an entrepreneurial spirit. That is also true of an artist. First conclusion: an entrepreneur has a lot in common with an artist.

Second article of faith: both the artist and the entrepreneur are driven by a passion. It is something stronger than themselves. Second conclusion: this brings them even closer to each other.

145

Third article of faith: Given this passion, both the artist and the entrepreneur find themselves in an environment of uncertainty. They must be able to deal with this. What an entrepreneur does is simply to transpose this uncertainty into a risk that is measurable.

Thus, the entrepreneurs around the table follow their own logic: they go in search of a form of certainty – a definition of art. When they fail to reach a consensus, they acknowledge the difference. Art refuses to be defined. It does not let itself be circumscribed in one definition, but remains in perpetual motion.

21/06/08

The artists whom Julie and Michel have sought out are the pioneer Paul Gees, Claire Roudenko-Bertin, who is Michel's contractual alter ego – and who has brought along her partner John – and Honoré δ'O, who a few days later would record the agenda in a poetic email message:

> Hi cher MIchel
> en vrienden, amis et amies, MIchel en Julie!, chère Julie et cher MIchel!, dearest friends,
> (Claire, grand pardon de langue du moment!)
>
> many thanks as well!
>
> It was indeed a fantastic day, with a fantastic group, and last but not least experienced in a brand new enigmatic site specific architectural creation of the pointed mentality: iithe unique spot baptized Kuipebosstraat Seven *****!!. I suppose that the coordinates themselves are becoming part of the ambling walk.
>
> I also think that strong analytical lines are needed to give more backbone to the highly narrative aspect of our meeting, to the agreeable, chattering bundle of memories, for the book is meant ultimately to contribute constructively with ideas to Flemish society and far beyond, including the distant yet-to-be-discovered planets!
> It is my nature to choose art over history (therein lies the art). Paul and I, for instance, cannot put the poetic force of our work directly into words. Claire, on the other hand, has the philosophy of her combative alchemy dans la bouche. The fact that it was not the tongue but the theme chosen by Claire that set the overarching tone of our meeting says enough, says it all, expresses the heart of the matter.
> I will try to grab hold of a few of the main lines as I felt them in actual fact or as I see them in an ambitious product.

'Walk With Me' is a suggestion. It refers to my sense of the future more than of the past. It sounds like an invitation. An invitation catches one's attention.

What is distinctive about the whole thing is that the book wants to be written at the moment when the rug has been pulled from under the trusty feet, at the moment of uncertainty that everyone in the field must come to terms with the changing identity of ESPEEL. The rules of the game of 'moving together' on route towards 'walk with me' require diagrams and legends.

The split between the 'Espeel company' and 'Espeel Michel' must be made once and for all! New definitions temporarily cloud both our view of the past and our vision of the future. If we succeed in defining the fine particles, we can avoid falling into a suspicious 'flou artistique' (artistic vagueness).

As yet there is no explicitly new functionality for the concept 'Michel Espeel': the person in his new status is an unfamiliar revelation, one to which the title of the book seeks precisely to offer a response. The new 'Espeel company' for its part has not made any statement regarding an artistic commitment. The less the product to be made sounds 'creative' and the more pragmatic it becomes, the more the new Espeel NV is keen on producing it.

'Walk with me', as an interpretation of the past, moves the sale of the company into the background, one that, once the dust has been swept away or settled, will undoubtedly show what the future brings, but the emotionally loaded nature of our beautiful day together blossomed primarily around the most fascinating many-headed dragon of a question!!!!!: who is espeel, who was he, who will he become? This question, and the associated one of whether we are talking about the person or the company, yielded six different answers!!!! In terms of its substance, the question, along with the issue of whether the split was a matter of the soul or of the body of the firm, ultimately yielded twelve chestnuts to be snatched from a roaring fire. The more readily the fruit popped out and the more the puzzle was unveiled, the longer the secret was preserved (hidden more deeply than the eternal paradox between art and the capitalist economy).

On the other hand there stood the entire œuvre of all the art works that were made at/ by Espeel. The more in-depth this inquiry went, the more lovely the florilegium, the more colourful the petals, the sweeter the scent of the pollen. That made it all the easier to trace the path of a surprising promenade.

This initiative involves first and foremost an exceptional opportunity to emphasise the schematic build-up of events, and to see current events as the fulfilment of an episode that has now been firmly set down as the foundation of the belief in the fulfilment of a dream…

1. Julie fascinates Michel with her passion for art.

2. Michel, who as a human being feels the need to step outside the habitual routine (reinforced by his own birth in the midst of the toponymy of the subject at hand), Michel, who not only qualitatively recognises the sensitivity of a person but who wishes to give it tangible form, introduces art into his company.

3. Julie, spurred on in no small measure by the results, establishes Arteconomy, in order that, through the development of a collaborative practice and an overarching concept, ultimately a new 'draft law' might be formulated. In this approach, art will be anchored in the solid relationship between art and the economy. The advantage of such a collaboration for both parties can be measured in hard Figures, art is given freer rein in which to find refreshment and inspiration – and workspace!, for as painting is transformed, so the easel changes its shape, the 'status' of creativity (in the body and mind of the entrepreneur) slips into the steel cage of the economic land-scape, which, fortunately, becomes acquainted, not a moment too soon, with tender-ness. The economic world is all the better for it, on an ever more beautiful planet; and if society cannot hope to attain paradise, it can at least reach a garden of creative delights, in which capital fulfils its social obligations, makes money more ethically, and as a by-product, makes room for the highest good, namely art....

.... from art to julie, from julie to michel, from michel to julie, from julie to society ...
full of intervening steps:
jumping diving swimming getting up falling walking climbing, cherishing, conjugated in groups or in the singular;
a verb on its own private path:

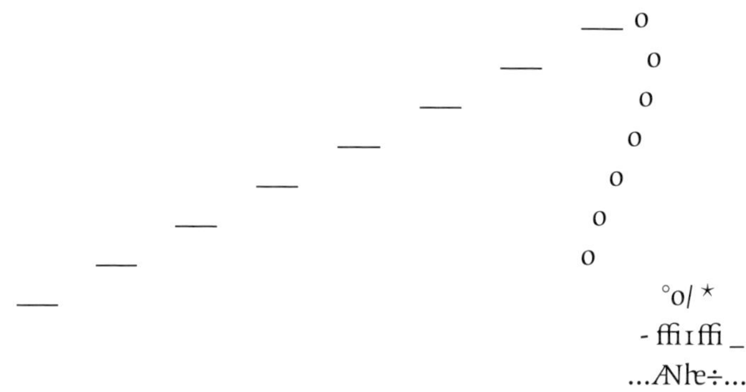

°o/ ⋆
- ffi ı ffi _
...Ælʜ÷...

Simply put, I think that the gap signified by the end of our familiar Espeel can be resolved/filled by the ambition of Arteconomy itself to become a company, to develop from a purely non-profit idea into a socially committed for-profit enterprise. Looked at from this vantage point, the soul moves readily, without any signs of rejection, in the wake of this closing narrative, under the rightful guise of a necessary alibi.
On the reverse side there remains, of course, the soul of Claire nestled in the new 'shares' in Michel.
Our curiosity was aroused to know how their artistic expression would look like under a new light, and on which side of the world?

148

For the echo of NoNo is YeS.
If this book succeeds in giving the reader who holds it in his/her hands the sense that
he or she holds art and economy in a perfect balance, and that nothing else can destroy
that, then this is the most beautiful and living book cover possible, one that opens up
further, from mouth to mouth by the very act or drawing breath.

The wealth represented by the works produced at Espeel is as deep as a treasure chest.
All the other artists who were not included nevertheless carry these riches around the
world, by means of their functioning product, or as travelling artists, itinerant
salesmen, human and touristic animals, filled somehow with an outward pleasure
and an inward delight, to towns and cities where the seeds are once again bound up
with inspiration, aspirin and growth hormones, where new generations of 'people
and products', stimulated by our admissions, make decisions, bring in new har-
vests, far from the forgotten places and times of initiation. Instinctive life processes
are unleashed as if by their own impetus, and pass through the officials of satisfac-
tion. Yesterday it was exactly 150 years ago that Darwin first set out his theory of
evolution, 'unnoticed', before specialists and the general public at an academic sit-
ting in London.

And – seeing is believing:
The process brings with it an unstated constant rejuvenation cure for those who take
the initiative!

The struggle in this strategy deserves a good deal of space in the book, for if art is to
think in a capitalistic way and the economy in an artistic one, then we end up creating
a user's guide for a roulette of accidents that one may rightly compare to a dangerous
casino.
In a shorter term, I see a book in which
1. pure art is addressed
2. the company presents its artistic products
3. this ideology finds a platform
and the readers dance while rooted in the ground and branches in the butterflies of the
holy but polluted light (only so warmed up and squeezed as to stick a good signpost
into the sentence)

the artist is often under the influence of powers of attraction that start out from the
opposite, from the underside of the senses, from the zones next to the site of understand-
ing in the mind, of empty and pent-up existence, the lightest way of being, in the
importance of weight and yet far beyond it, the most unexpected, the funniest or the
most malicious anxiety, or the calm that has fled in the tension between presence and
absence, always flipping the inside and the outside of the mask back and forth in order

149

to complete the truth of reality without removing the key from the mirror – the main
verb on tour

the first signs are always:
if someone jokes I speak seriously
if something is beautiful to others I see ugly spots
if everyone is disgusted I find it terribly nice
what has no value seems precious to me
what others hold dear I find cheap
if everyone calls out in excitement I mumble drearily etc.
the second signs are not bound up with the first,
they arrive on another flight,
royal and military, those go together, that is what I read, and copied down, this
week

so many warm greetings, as big as a loaf of organic country bread!
I spread it with a layer of the finest kisses,
For, in search of causal interventions,
I am going on holiday, something I see as an effort,
apart from the excess kilo's I'll be back,
as a tale told in fruit and vegetables, eco-skillfully removed from the maternal body,
the tree of a lying transport, sport as sculpture,
full of undivided land, the third signs of the apple on the wall,
votre honoré, toujours,
en guerre de lutte ou en paix de bénédiction, well said badly pronounced,
whoever thinks of barbed wire is shot down with a kiss
XXXXXXXXXXXXXXXXXXXXXXXXXXXXXXXXXXXXXXXXXXXXXXXXXXXXXXXXXX
XXXXXXXXXXXXXXXX

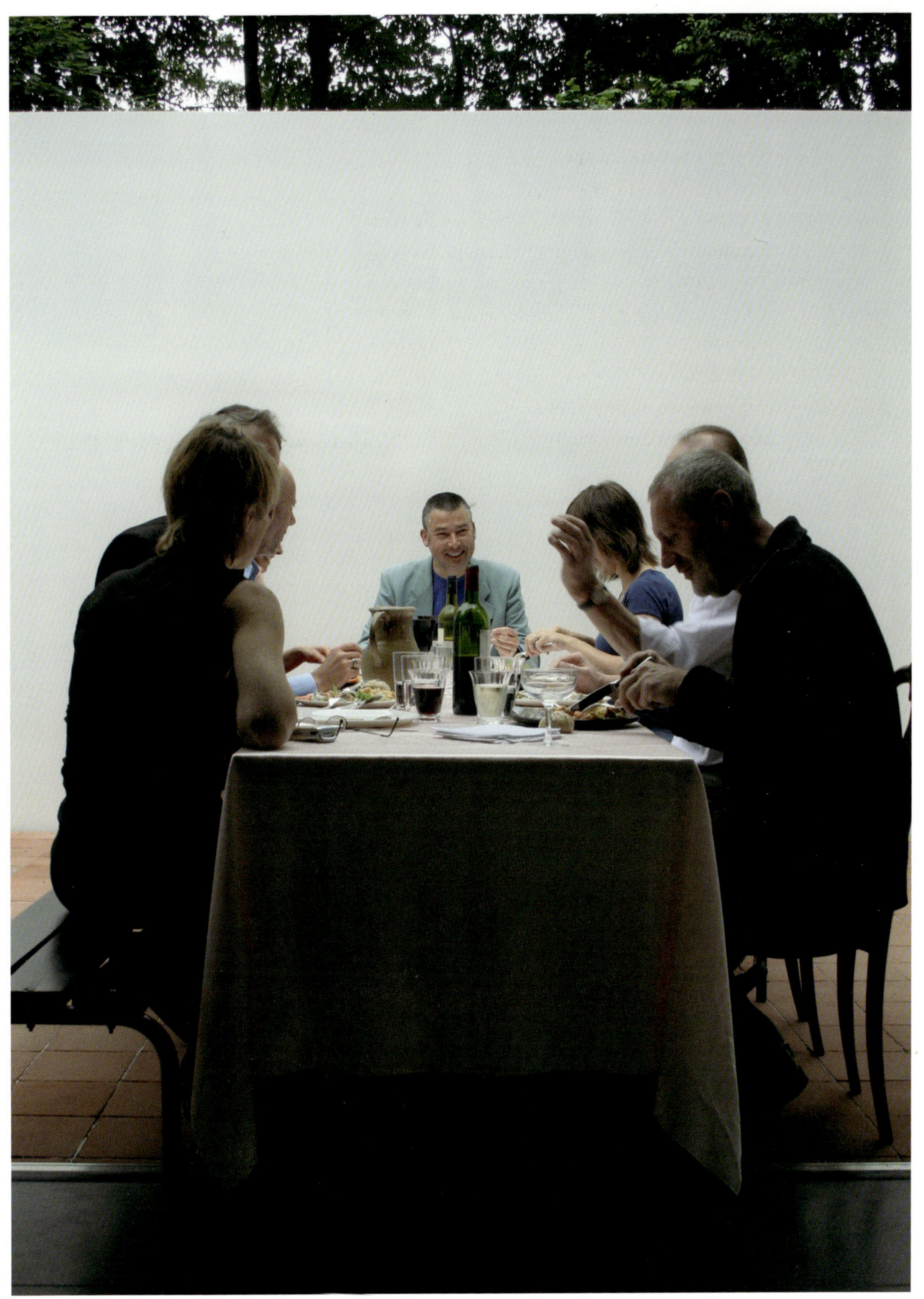

fig. 123

fig. 123   From left to right: Claire
Roudenko-Bertin, her husband John, Luc
Derycke, Honoré δ'O, Charlotte Bonduel,
Michel Espeel, Paul Gees

Artists who have played a role
in the creation of artworks
in metal at Constructies Espeel
(the following is not an exhaustive list)

Nicole Baert
Mo Becha
Benoît
Frederic Bryon
Betty Callewaert
Willy Cauwelier
Leo Copers
Yves Coussement
Wim Decauter
Anne De Cock
Koen De Decker
Jan Dekeyser
Jo Dilo
Hans De Pelsmacker
Tjok Dessauvage
Peter Downsbrough
Eaves Dropper & Christoph
  De Boeck
Jan Fabre
Christoph Fink
Paul Gees
Isa Genzken
Pascal Ghyssaert
Marc Goethals
Ronny Heireman
David Hernadez
Honoré δ'O
Aiko Kitahara
Ann Veronica Janssens
Brice Leroux
Trees Leroy
Emilio López-Menchero
Anne Maes
Kris Martin
Herman Maier Neustadt
Hans Op de Beeck

Martine Platteau
Stefaan Roelstraete
Claire Roudenko-Bertin
Albert Rubens
Boy & Erik Stappaerts
Patrick Steen
Joëlle Tuerlinckx
Dimitri Vangrunderbeek
Hannes Van Severen
Peter Verhelst
Tim M.C. Volckaert
Richard Venlet
Kris Verdonck
Angel Vergara
Tine Vindevogel
Kris Vleeschouwer
Peter Weidenbaum
Sisley Xhafa
Dirk Zoete